Dig Deep

Tales from the Depths

David Bereson

Franklin Street Press

Copyright

Copyright © David Bereson

First published 2023 Franklin Street Press. All rights reserved. No part of this publication may be reproduced, distributed, or transmitted in any form or by any means, including photocopying, recording, or other electronic or mechanical methods, without the prior written permission of the publisher, except in the case of brief quotations embodied in critical reviews and certain other non-commercial uses permitted by copyright law.

ISBN 978-0-6488998-4-6 (paperback)

A catalogue record for this book is available from the National Library of Australia

Book Cover Design by Lara White
Book Cover Portrait by Miriam Bereson

Contents

Introduction   XI
   Phillip Adams

1. Family   1
   Pizza
   Rabbi Google
   Unconditional Love
   The Angel of Odessa
   My Peter Pan
   The Dame
   Four Generations, One Uni
   Uncle Croissant
   Lost and Found
   The Piano Stool
   Nessun Dormitory
   Chupa Chup
   Colon Before a Full Stop
   Heart Attack

2. Childhood   31
   Grand Age

    Paper Round
    Acland Street
    Camp
    Best Birthday
    Hotel Sorrento
    TV

3. Growing Up   48
    School
    The Teacher
    The Drug Addict
    Firsts
    Camellia Day
    Anzac Day
    Theatre of Life
    Competition
    Uni
    The Train Trip
    Dear Comrade

4. Bang—The Accident   79
    After
    The Day
    Brave New World
    Elephantosis
    Lonely
    If We Truly Care
    Hospitality

5. Health 99
  Each to Their Own
  Near Life Experience
  The Doctor Won't See You Now
  Fitness Testing
  Health Care
  Taking A Break
  Overriding My Instincts
  The Drink of Life
  Body Image
  The Longest Journey
  The Cone of Silence
  Isolation

6. disABILITY 133
  All Is Not Lost
  Just Because
  Therapies
  Let Me Ask
  DISabling
  Disability Never Leaves You
  DISempowerment
  G & D
  The Voice
  The Trick
  Care Worker
  Thanks NDIS

7. Being Me 157
    Songlines
    First Nations
    The Dreamtime
    Book Shops
    My Word
    My Brain
    Smoking
    Chatterbox
    I Like to Spiel
    The Good Walk
    Life's Perpetual Challenge
    Dig Deeper
    I Am Valuable
    Complain —Why bother?
    Giving It A Crack
    Patience

8. Friendship 199
    Our Friends
    The Tram Girl
    The Gnome
    The Sunset
    Modern Man
    The Road Not Taken
    The Schnitz
    The Reindeer

    My Mates
    Shared Journeys
    The Coeliac
    A Sad Story
    Discord In The Workplace
    Skyhooks
    Neighbours
    Taxi Driver
    Closeness
    The Undead

9. Food   251
    "The Nappy"
    Covid Coffee
    Breakfast
    Cake Shops
    The Doughnut

10. Home Grown   265
    The Garden
    The Gardener
    The Guru
    Enjoy the Market
    Ice Cream
    Self-Entitlement
    Climate-Change Warrior

11. Humour   285
    Parent Teacher Night

      Hebrew
      A Footy Tale
      The Jab
      Hanging in There
      The Singer

12. Guiding Lights   295
      The Sage Plants
      You Can Be a Life Coach
      Secular Rabbi

13. Reflections   305
      Gazing Back
      Resilience
      Partner Ship
      Point of View
      Choice
      Help
      Responsibility
      If Only ...
      Faith
      Enough
      Child's Play
      Covid Not All Bad
      Chit Chat Email
      Home Maintenance
      Clean Heels
      The Freezer

The Author — Why I Write	339
Acknowledgments	345

Introduction

Phillip Adams

I have never met David. We have never spoken. I haven't even seen a photograph of him. And yet we are friends. And I know him very well because of his remarkable writings.

David has been sending me fragment of his prose for years. Sometimes one or two emails a day, sometimes weeks apart. And sometimes, when David is back in hospital, an extended silence.

David, fighting his personal Goliath of disability, writes with such raw passion that it overwhelms grammar and spelling — and his punctuation is wildly erratic. To which I respond with tidy-up suggestions. But in my efforts at editing I have never touched the content, his 'tales from the depths'.

I 'met' David via my daughter — Dr. Rebecca Adams, a psychiatrist. He is her friend, not her patient. Rebecca marvelled at his writings, seeing them not merely as therapeutic for David but potentially for anyone fortunate enough to read them. I agree. We are all privileged to share David's utter honesty in his thoughts and observation.

While David truly speaks to 'the human condition' his writings are not bleak. Despite David's profound problems he is undaunted, forever hopeful and frequently very funny.

I commend his book to you — and thank David for living it and writing it.

One

Family

Pizza

They say if you know where you are coming from you will have an idea where you're headed. In essence, this is the story of a pizza. I am a pizza this and a pizza that, like most people in this immigrant nation.

My great-grandfather came from Russia to Melbourne and established a good life for himself. There is now a decent-sized family as a result of him. No one knows for sure why he came but the story goes something like this: to avoid the army in Tsarist Russia, he took someone's identity and left the country. On the way here he asked, 'What's an Australian Jewish name?' Someone told him 'Rabinov' so he took this as his own. He arrived in Port Melbourne but didn't go far from there. He established a pawnbroking business and did very well. Over time he built enough wealth to live comfortably. He married and had a couple of children, one of whom was my grandfather. A bright boy, he was encouraged to develop. In time he studied medicine and became a doctor. One result is I that am a third-generation graduate of Melbourne University. My great-grandfather funded him to go to Trinity College, Dublin, so he could specialise. While living there he met my grandmother, a Jewish girl, and married. Returning here eventually, they ended up living in Footscray where he became a partner in the first joint medical practice in Melbourne: hard work, but he was up to it.

Once, at a family gathering, I met an American cousin who had visited the original family home. This cousin said it was just a little place, like the one in *Fiddler on the Roof*. During the war the Nazis took all the townsfolk to the cliff overlooking the place and threw them all off it. No one left, all dead: that community was just one of many that vanished. The Holocaust looms large in my personal history so it is not an easy thing to escape from. The sins *inflicted on* one generation always seem to be visited on subsequent generations, you need only look at the stolen generation here.

Mum's family went to Ireland to escape persecution in Lithuania, a sensible thing to do. They lived there happily over the years but they have all died or left the place — no one in Ireland anymore, that chapter is finished. Mum also had relatives who went to Cyprus and from there to establish themselves in Israel, in a town called Rishon LeZion. With six generations there I would say they have become real residents of the place. I think this is from her father's family: on Mum's side there is an extensive network of relatives dotted around the globe. They have a large website that keeps track of everybody, with close to 20,000 people listed there, a large enough population to make any Mormon proud. Dad's family comes from Bialystok, Poland. It was a large family. My great-grandfather was an important rabbi there. From him the family spread far and wide. Sadly, they all died in a concentration camp. Being a Zionist family, a number went to Israel to live, including my grandfather. His life there was happy but at one point he took the opportunity to run a Jewish orphanage in Cape Town. There, totally unexpectedly, my father was born and he grew up there. When the war was over, my grandfather decided South Africa was no longer a place for a decent person to be, so he cast around for where to go. All his Bialystok kin had been killed by the Nazis but there turned out to be two other relatives in the wild outback of Australia – or there was Israel. This time Australia was chosen, so here it was that my family ended up. It was later discovered there was actually a family connection in Cuba who ultimately moved to America.

So my uncles lived in the rough and ready mining town of Broken Hill. There they lived as religious Jews and became part of the community, accepted and never persecuted: a synagogue was even built. Australia, they found, was the true land of the free. The most famous person to come from this community was a girl called Marie Wein who later became Mary Fairfax so, in a removed way, I am related to that publishing empire (but I have no real connection). From South Africa they came by ocean liner, a different sort of boat to the one that had brought my Russian great-grandfather to these shores. They arrived in what turned out to be the real Promised Land. In Melbourne they encountered none of the anti-Semitism they had been used to, and found the freedom to practise Judaism as they wished. My parents met at university and that was the start of a sixty-year loving marriage. So this is where I come from and now you know the baggage I carry into my life. Not that it feels such a heavy load, and every day I rejoice at having ended up here in a spot that looks after and cares for me so well.

Rabbi Google

Rabbis have been around for thousands of years. Through the generations the title has become revered, carrying great weight and importance. In the modern world Rabbi Google possess something of this authority — a storehouse of knowledge and wisdom assisting us with the conduct of our lives. This has been the task of rabbis since before the days of Jesus.

I've had many interactions with rabbis over the years and, despite my confirmed atheism, who I am is the result of rabbinical influence. My great-grandfather was a highly respected rabbi in Poland until the Nazis killed him. His keen intellect was inherited by my grandfather who had many rabbinical talents. He administered places of learning in Israel where he taught Hebrew to many students, perhaps the most famous being a leader of the Stern Gang. From there my grandfather went to South Africa where he ran a Jewish orphanage, raising and looking after many children. Without adopting the title of rabbi, he practised a nurturing role similar to theirs. This sense of human responsibility for the younger generation was passed on to my father whose vocation in life was to teach — a rabbinical function if ever there was one.

And so we come to me, the product of these upright generations. I have no formal rabbinic training yet I hope it doesn't sound too conceited to say that I do try and play my part as a secular rabbi. Rabbis as a recognised source of knowledge could be described as human search engines. In the modern world, of course, the community is a lot less tightly bound than those of, say, nineteenth-century Europe. In our century, no rabbi today can serve as the sole source of knowledge since there is so much more to know, and in many fields — some of them of comparatively recent origin. But even in this day and age a rabbi is useful, interpreting and deciphering the puzzles that beset us in everyday life. This critical role is why secular rabbis and what are known as life coaches are needed. Books and encyclopedias — both printed and online — exist to help us navigate and investigate the world around us.

Which brings us back to Rav Google, the ultimate search engine. This mighty rabbi possesses a vast array of knowledge, from the essential to the trivial, and all of it is there at our fingertips. Great as this rabbi is, the electronic Rav has just one critical defect. It cannot help us navigate the deeper reaches of our existence. With Google, as with the human rabbi or any teacher — a satisfying outcome to your search depends on the quality of the question you pose in the first place. To get the right answer, you need to frame the question properly. Provided we keep that point in mind, in my view this mighty rabbi merits our unstinting praise, for delivering good answers unfiltered by the prejudice of a religious outlook. This appeals fundamentally to the atheist in me.

Unconditional Love

Over the course of my life I have received many things that I have learnt to value and cherish. The two most valuable are genuine friendship and unconditional love. When these rare commodities are visited on you together you strike pay dirt, the proverbial El Dorado.

Unconditional love is a total act of giving, there are no borders, no boundaries. You are loved for yourself — or despite yourself. To receive this builds good, strong, self-assured people. There is no greater act of human giving and I have been blessed that throughout my life I have had this love handed to me in large doses. It begins with wonderful parents who are supported by equally loving grandparents. I had all this, a bedrock on which to construct my life. Among my life path various people have extended this gift with no request from me. It is best when it comes this way as I can feel it is a heartfelt thing, emanating from the soul.

I see many others who were not the beneficiaries of unconditional love and that is obvious in the way these people behave. Something significant has been lacking in their lives. I find this so sad to witness. In this book you will encounter the special uncle who delivered me floods of love and affection, which developed into an email correspondence full of mirth and wit. When he died a significant part of me was taken away.

I had a similar relationship with an aunty in Israel. Through the hard work of nursing and rehabilitating me after my accident, we built the closest of bonds. No matter what I did or said, her love for me was always overflowing. She had a daughter who used to collect me from school when I was a little boy. We have boundless love for each other. It does not matter that our beliefs are diametric opposites. This is put aside due to our love for each other.

I had a friend who was both teacher and mentor to me. I maintained contact with him after my accident. One day, when I was lying in hospital after my heart attack, in he walked with his wife, their faces wreathed in smiles. Instantly I could feel and touch the unconditional love they had for me. This gave me a warm glow and made me feel strong. Their presence was the loveliest present they brought me that day and I do my best to return that love. His dear wife is now in care. I keep up contact and do what I can to give her a connection with the world. Unconditional love is a two-way street. When received it must be returned or its value is diminished.

Those with whom over time I have developed unconditional love accept me for all my flaws and we rejoice in each other's company. But my vision is broader. When people give me their time, I regard it as a gift of great value. I feel I am worthy of people's time but not everyone feels that way. Some are generous with theirs; others never bother. But even that precious gift must cede priority to the most treasured of them all: the magnificent upbringing bestowed by my more than wonderful parents. How lucky am I.

The Angel of Odessa

Well, the angel we are talking of lives in Odessa Street, so this is about how she earned her title. It's a story about values and decency, aspiring to treat people as they deserve and handing them a brief moment of decency, a very precious gift. Our angel doesn't talk about the many kind acts she does, she just goes out and does them, knowing this is how life should be conducted, that you should aid people in need whenever possible — with no expectations in return.

Her desire is simple: let's help people lead better lives with a moment's grace if we can. Yes, this is a values approach to life where action coincides with belief. What it requires is an accumulation of many small touches of decency, no grandiose feats of exertion. Angels are known for their light touch, after all — and her ability to drive assists her in fulfilling this angelic role. It may be the simple act of picking up a friend after they have had dialysis and giving them a lift home, or perhaps collecting someone after they have been to the doctor. On her numerous hospital visits she always brings with her some kind and simply inspired touch of joy. Then, after the object of her kindness has come out of hospital, just when people are most likely to feel lonely at home, she pays them more visits as they are convalescing.

The list of her deeds goes on, it is never-ending. One fine lady resides in a poky room at a rather dour aged care home. The Angel of Odessa makes her feel she is never alone by leaving presents at the desk for her, although in Covid times she resists going inside as this is dangerous given her age. Every act she undertakes with loving thought: she cares for people, her only reward the joy and delight in their faces, reflected in hers. Whether today's gift is a book that might be of assistance to them, or tomorrow's a newspaper she knows will be of interest to them, hers are not occasional acts but everyday feats of altruism. When bad things happen in the lives of those she cares for, the Angel feels for them and extends both warmth and sympathy.

The biggest problem we have with the Angel is finding ways of stopping her doing too much. The Covid crisis has restrained her activities but it has no chance of stopping her. I happen to know that she recently drove across town to leave a packet of Tim Tams and strawberries for a lady in care. It gave her great delight and was the highlight of her week. Covid has met its match in her: she zaps around leaving papers in people's letterboxes. But it is when you witness the Angel interact with people that you see her special qualities at their finest. In her world all people are equals and all are treated well. No wonder she is much loved and adored by all. To observe her with grandchildren is an unforgettable experience. She does not treat them the way adults are wont to treat children but recognises them as people in their own right. She raises them to the special level reserved for friends, and spends vast amounts of time considering how to make their lives better. To borrow a biblical phrase she is a light unto the nations. If we all took a leaf out of her book, the world would be a better place. One angel is goodness brought to earth, but we need so many more.

My Peter Pan

Peter Pan, the story of a boy who never grew up, is classified as fiction. But I know it is true to life: my father, who lived a charmed existence till his dying day, was that boy. A lifelong childhood innocence and wonderment about everything was his charm. It captivated people, endeared them to him. As we love children for what they are, everybody loved my father for being like this.

My father was born in an orphanage run by my grandfather. He was the only non-orphan there so from birth he was always in the society of children. This was his natural environment. His whole life he treated the world as such: everyone around him was a kid to play with. As I said, he led a charmed existence.

Well, my father reached the age of eight and there he got stuck. For eighty more years he regarded the world with the wide-eyed wonderment and enthusiasm of an eight-year-old boy. It was lovely to see.

An orphanage life is, by definition, a sheltered existence. His was made even more so because this was in Cape Town, where outside the orphanage walls many children were faced with the harsh realities of life. Inside the walls was a society of abundance, which would continue to be his lot right through to adulthood. The one experience that jolted him out of this comfort zone was a trip he made to Bialystok, Poland, to meet the family. He saw this place in all its glory before the Nazis laid it waste. As you would expect, he greeted this alien northern city through the eyes of a child. Even its destruction by the Nazis never managed to deprive him of this image, this ideal. The way he spoke of the place never changed.

Before leaving for Australia, Dad's family moved to Johannesburg. There he went to university for a year, which by putting off his exposure to the real world enabled him to sustain his youthful innocence even longer. His youthful idealism drew him to become involved in social justice issues. This was in the heyday of apartheid and, although he had done nothing rash like joining the ANC, the authorities told him — when he was leaving the country with his parents — that he had been seen joining demonstrations, and they curtly warned him not to come back. If anything, this reinforced his hunger for social justice so when he arrived in Australia and went to university here he threw himself into new causes with the same drive as of old. He was a member of the Labor Club and even joined the Communist Party.

University doesn't force you to grow up — not being in the workforce, with all that entails, can slow the journey to maturity to a crawl. Still living under his parents' roof, he didn't need to worry about accommodation or food. In time he found a vocation that would allow him to keep on this trajectory and remain in the company of equals — others who saw the world as he did. He became a teacher, a role to which he took like a duck to water. His boyishness made him much loved among his students, who could feel that he understood them like few if any adults they had encountered.

He had the good fortune to find a lovely companion whom he married. She loved him for who he was and did not try to change him. She gave him space and latitude to express himself, to exert his childlike charm and exuberance. So, with neither work nor home life impinging on him, he greeted every fresh day with delight and anticipation. Next came the experience of fatherhood, and this allowed him to explore being a kid at first *and* second hand. He was a great dad, a natural. Only one problem: as they grew, his children had to bring Dad up. All too soon, they were more worldly — wiser than their not so old 'old man'.

None of this upset his equilibrium, though. Parenting responsibilities did not interfere with his core self. When finally he retired, his life entered what became like a never-ending summer holiday. He tasted all the joys of life that his childlike nature allowed. Soon a couple of grandchildren came along, and they brought great joy to him as he could meet them eye to eye. Like his own children, they saw him as a fun child to be with. In their advanced years, many people degenerate into senility, their 'second childhood'. With my father a conundrum developed: how could we tell if he was 'losing his marbles'? He could hardly enter a second childhood when he had never left his first. I remember one afternoon at palliative care sitting in the sun with him, my mother and older sister. He sat there totally lucid but behaving like the child he had always been. We all enjoyed the moment very much. Right until his dying breath, in his mind's eye and in our sight, my father never grew up, never grew old. His life was charmed as long as it lasted, and he was our charm too. May his soul rest in peace.

The Dame

My grandmother was a large and colourful person from Dublin. My great-grandparents couldn't believe that my grandfather was able to find himself a Jewish woman in Catholic Ireland. They were even married by a rabbi who went on to become Chief Rabbi of Israel. Till her dying day my grandmother's voice carried a lovely Irish lilt that was a pleasure to hear.

My grandfather only got permission to marry if he would allow my grandmother frequent trips home. This did occur, even with the cost involved in those days. My grandmother took great advantage of these trips: a mere Great Depression wasn't going to deter her from travelling the world in style, and hang the expense.

When I was born, my parents lived in a house near my grandparents. This meant we visited them daily. It was a grand house in a lovely part of the world. They had moved there after living in Footscray for many years. As the first grandson you can bet I was spoilt rotten, and so children should be.

When my grandfather died, the family home was sold. It was then my grandmother became a Gypsy, as she called it, moving from place to place. First stop was the Southern Cross Hotel in the centre of Melbourne where a friend gave her an entire floor to herself. My older sister and I spent many hours playing downstairs as Mum visited her. Our pay-off was dinner at Pellegrini's, which was just around the corner. We didn't think that such a bad deal. To this day, Pellegrini's is part of my life.

The Gypsy's temporary homes were not confined to Melbourne. Being the dame she was, one of them was in Monte Carlo. Coming from an Irish family, she was smitten by the gambling bug. I have heard various takes about her exploits on the roulette wheel. She worked it with the precision of a machine. Once I asked if she would teach me how to play the wheel. She replied, with a wave of her hand, 'Darling, you don't want to know.' I had no comeback to that. It was in Monaco that she found her second husband, a well-heeled doctor, and while she went happily to live with him that did not stop her pursuing life with her customary flair. One little anecdote: once her husband sent her out to buy a nice dress, so she popped across to London to get it but, once she was there, decided she had enough nice dresses and bought herself a David Hockney lithograph instead. This, you will understand, is not the act of an ordinary person but of a genuine dame.

One year this true woman of style arrived back in Australia by plane just before Cup Day so I went out to the airport to collect her. Out she came wearing the most magnificent hat, ready for the races. A fascinator for a fascinator: why look anything but her best?

Although she was living comfortably in Melbourne by the time I came along, she never lost her taste for travel. In later years my uncles were left to care for my grandfather. All the children were put in boarding schools so that she could enjoy this lifestyle. The art of travelling is something she understood. I remember once being in Paris at the same time as her. She raced me round to special haunts she insisted I must see — from ancient restaurants to fashionable cafés. To be with her was to be caught up in a whirlwind; shopping with her was always fun. She dispensed wisdom as if it were home-made jam. 'David, paying a lot for something is always cheapest in the end,' she would exclaim, 'because it lasts.' And 'David, live well, because the alternative is for the dogs.'

Nana used to entertain a lot so to provide for her guests she had to be a good cook. Every day when I visited she had a different cake for me.

Now style was not like a coat my grandmother only put on overseas: she wore it at home as well. In fact it could be said that she was a bit of a party animal. It was nothing for her to hop into a cab at ten at night, go to the famous parties that were held at the Rippon Lea mansion and not return till the next day. I can see her still, standing around the pool in a slinky dress, cigarette in one hand, whisky in the other, immersed in light conversation and breathing a bubbly atmosphere, as if the Gatsby era were still in full swing. She always carried mints in her bag and one day I asked her why. In all seriousness she turned to me and confided: 'They are there to hide the smell of the whisky.' Until her dying day my grandmother was still queen of the kitchen, and created ribbon sandwiches that were nothing short of spectacular. Sadly, no more cakes for me, but there is one consolation. If her soul is resting in peace, as I devoutly trust it is, she must be spending eternity in a well-equipped kitchen somewhere.

Four Generations, One Uni

After my great-grandfather arrived in Melbourne on a ship all the way from Russia he didn't move far from where it docked, setting up a business and his family in Port Melbourne. His son, my maternal grandfather, was a talented child. He walked all the way to the city — to Melbourne High –— to get his education (there were no trams to the city in those days and it was quite common for children to trudge long distances to school and home again). But the effort was worth it: he did well and went on to study medicine at Melbourne University. His was the first generation of my family to attend university and this would have been seen as a great privilege and source of pride. Immigrant families lay great emphasis on education. His musically talented sister also attended a branch of the university, the Conservatorium. What had been a precedent now became something of a family tradition.

My mother was a bright and gifted student and remains so today in her advanced years. She even won a scholarship there. The university connection strengthened further when one of her brothers followed their father into medicine. My mother met Dad at university, during her studies there, and in due course – no pun intended – the time came for my sisters and me to begin our tertiary educations. Naturally, we went there. I walked in and was totally at home, as if the place had been built for my personal development and enrichment. Nothing there felt alien to me. We did our degrees there. My elder sister did her PhD at the University of London but her initial degree was at Melbourne. Now my niece becomes the fourth generation of my family to finish school and head off to Parkville. Nothing could be more natural. I eagerly await the opportunity to take her there and show her over her birthright. Over time this family of mine has been blended into the fabric of Melbourne by the pursuit of tertiary study to supplement generations of rabbinical learning on my dad's side. I think by now we are pretty well as educated as it's wise for anyone to be.

Uncle Croissant

One thing I do well, in my opinion, is go out with friends and their children and have a good time. I believe I am a positive role model on how to live well. So spending a few hours with adults and kids makes for a nice occasion. Then I hand back the kids. I don't take them home. My worries are over: I have done my job.

I take my uncle job seriously, and do my best to engage with children and teach them the joy of life. I do hope Uncle David is considered a good influence. Through me children do get to learn that people are varied and different. As the children grow, where possible I like to keep up conversation with them. Sadly that doesn't always happen and I understand and accept that. Many years ago I had a couple of friends who used to enjoy doing breakfast with me. This contributed to my quality of life. I am always delighted by anyone who is able to do that. My friends had a young girl, a lovely little thing. Her great thrill in life was to eat croissants. She thought it the best joy there could be. So each time we went out I made sure we went to a place that had croissants for her. In fact, to make the occasion extra special, I would buy croissants that I gave her.

I do believe children should be spoilt but in a positive way. This was a loved and indulged child. I would laugh when I saw her father take the pips out of her orange juice or she would cry from the back of the car for the air-conditioning. As a result I would jokingly call her the JAP in training – which isn't nearly as racist as it sounds because in my mind the acronym stood for Jewish Australian Princess. But she did then, and does until this day, call me Uncle Croissant. A memory and an event both stuck. Sadly, as she has grown up and created her own life, I have lost touch with her.

Children are accepting; they are happy to have anyone as their friend. Here I as a person contribute to their education. It is good for them to learn that people are not all the same. They can learn through me it is OK — a very valid thing — to be different. Over the years I have fulfilled this role in the lives of various children — an alternative role model to what they experience at home. I have enjoyed this contribution I make to their lives. I don't do the hard yards that parents do but I feel good adding something to the growth and development of the young. This feels good to me as the course of life has deprived me of children of my own. I do have my real niece and nephew with whom I have a close and involved relationship. Over the years they have learnt to accept me for who I am. So we have built something special between us. Happily, we give to each other.

I realise that at times I may not have much to offer. But I also feel there are some jewels in what I do that enhance the lives of children and adults alike. Over the years I have had many wonderful outings with various families. I like to think these have contributed to their well being as well as mine, and I do love the idea of being considered tasty so the title of Uncle Croissant is one I cherish.

Lost and Found

Sometimes in life things are lost and we have no idea that they have been lost. When eventually they are found we accord them great value. This is the story of one such loss and rediscovery which happened to me.

One day, while I was recovering from my accident, a friend came over to pick me up so that we could go out. He brought a mate along and when they entered my parents' house my mate introduced him. Mum immediately turned to the guy and asked, 'Who's your mother?' When he uttered her name, Mum then said: 'Do you realise you are a cousin?' The poor bloke was dumbfounded. My grandmother, who was there at the time, turned to the bloke and said, 'You look like your grandfather.' This pleased him very much as he had no recollection of his grandfather, who had passed on.

Well, I have a large extended family — thousands of relatives if you add up both sides of the family — but I fall into something of a black hole. You see, there are relatives a bit older than me and then there are those a little younger but none that I know of who are my age. I have always found this a pity: no one to share things with. But, lo and behold, here I am looking at this boy my age — and now I learn we're cousins! Great, I thought. Wonderful. Remarkably, he had also recently had a head injury (happily not as severe as mine). As you can imagine, I was keen to find out more about this bloke, see what he was like and where had he been. I soon discovered that he had grown up in parallel to me. Yet for some amazing reason our paths had never crossed, so the connection had never been made. This was even stranger when I found that many people whom I considered to be good friends of mine turned out to be intimate friends of his.

Until this point our lives had not meshed, so I chose to stand back, observe and as I learnt more of who this bloke was I hoped to learn a bit more about myself. In contrast to many of my contemporaries he was not a loud and raucous type. For many years now I have been witness to how he has maintained a gentle approach to life. I don't think this is something that can be learned: you are either born with it or without it. But it does have an uplifting effect on everyone he comes into contact with.

Before long I discovered his life passion, something he has immersed himself in over time: this is the simple art of playing the guitar. I must admit to being a bit jealous. I would love to have learnt the guitar myself but what is required to achieve competence in that field has always been a bit beyond me. One day this led to a light-hearted discussion between us. We were talking about hand physio and comparing notes. He told me that his hand had suffered damage from many hours spent strumming the guitar but I came to it from a totally different tangent. I was intent on regaining the use of my hand after several injuries done to it, but in the end we both used the services of a hand physiotherapist, and our goal was identical — to improve our quality of life. My cousin and I both realised our lives needed to be enhanced so how I saw it was that we needed the same therapy. Two people can share the same destination arrived at by different paths.

My cousin has elderly parents. When ill health strikes our parents it is a test of who we are as people. Alas, the ill health of my cousin's parents has been of long duration. During this time I have sat back and watched how he has conducted himself, in the most exemplary of ways. He has put his own life on hold, devoting himself to their care. There are many who wouldn't bother doing that. He has bought homes so that he could be close to where they live, enabling him to tend to their needs. Never once in all their declining years have I heard him whine or complain about it. I feel silent self-sacrifice signals strength of character. As he is particularly close to his father, I fear for him when his father eventually dies. I hope he continues plodding along life's path in his quiet, subdued manner.

Without being overly sociable, he has a healthy sense of play and likes to throw the occasional party. When he does, he never forgets to give me a ring inviting me to come along. These parties are real events. As the musician he is, he will have bands playing all night long, and the party guests are an eclectic bunch, always including plenty of people I haven't seen for a long time. (I'm not always glad to see these people, mind you, but that's my problem, not his.) The catering is always first-class, right down to cocktail bars and food in lavish quantities. He knows how to live and always rises to the occasion.

I may not see this cousin of mine very often but that doesn't matter. My interactions with him, now spanning most of our lifetimes, have always been worthwhile and I feel I cannot ask for more than that, only that he live long and — as he has always managed to do — well.

The Piano Stool

I have a sister four years younger than me. Perhaps foolishly she was often put in my care. I was very tough on her. This is the tale of just one of the many ordeals I have inflicted on the poor child. Actually, the result has not been so bad. I feel I contributed significantly to shaping the tenacious and capable businesswoman and clothes designer she has become. Since her life has turned out well I cannot really feel any guilt.

One Saturday night my sister was left in my care as my parents went out — not something I desired but something I must deal with. To help me cope, I had a friend over to keep me company. Well, a couple of hours passed and we got hungry. Being 'grown-up' teenage boys we decided to walk down the lane to the pizza shop, which wasn't far. We didn't think it would take long and told my little sister what we were going to do. Suddenly she got very upset and began crying. She didn't want to be alone in the house: something might happen to her. We pleaded and tried to pacify her but with no success. This tried our patience sorely — we weren't pleased, we really wanted that pizza. So we came up with a solution that has become legendary in the family. We found some string and tied her up to the piano stool so that she couldn't escape. This, we figured, would occupy her so that she would have no thoughts of anything bad happening to her while we were out. It was a caring act as we saw it — all for her own good. Well, our visit to the pizza shop took longer than we expected and during our absence my parents returned to find my sister looking like a hostage. You can imagine the hell there was to pay when we walked back in the door with our pizza. It turned out extra well in the end — for one thing (surprise, surprise) she was not put in my care as often. The price I had to pay was that when I got my driver's licence I had to drive her everywhere. My comeback to that has been that now I am unable to drive she has to give me lifts. Yes, what goes around comes around. Her son is not fed pizza dinners so every few weeks I take him out for one.

Waiting for the pizza still often takes longer than you expect, so it's a good deal for him and we always have a nice time.

Nessun Dormitory

Like many children, my nephew and niece share a part of their house where they have their bedrooms and bathroom. Sounds well and good, doesn't it? Well, read on. My niece is studying opera: she is well on her way to becoming a diva. The greatest feature of her voice is its volume. She is loud, very loud in fact and, being an active young lady, her life is very full: she is always doing something. Often she has to get up early to go places. As you would expect, she likes to sing in the shower at full volume. My nephew, being a normal teenage boy, likes and needs his sleep but far too often the poor lad is startled into consciousness by his sister. As a consequence he is dazed and sleepy all day long. There is no escape for him but he doesn't complain. It is a heavy load to bear. The point to all this is that when we live with people we need to accommodate ourselves to who they are. For the record, may I extend my sympathy to my lovely nephew.

Chupa Chup

When my niece was of primary-school age, like any young girl she had a love of lollipops as if she weren't already sweet enough. So as an indulgent uncle — despite being in fear of her mother — I chose to feed this love of hers. Her mother was concerned about her teeth but I was concerned about her mental wellbeing. Let children be loved, indulged and feel secure: that was my belief.

So into her life came Chupa Chups, which according to Dr Google is Australia's best-selling lollipop. She relished this treat and should I forget to get her one I would get a curt reminder and a brutally brief interrogation: 'Where is it, David?' This was the beginning of the foundation of my building a good sound relationship with the child who soon would become a young lady. Funnily enough, once on a holiday I bought her brother a lollipop and he just dropped it: he wasn't into sweet things. Well, his sister thought this was OK, she got an extra one and implored me to keep buying them for her brother. Eventually I worked out a different thing with the boy: each holiday I would take him out for a pizza. The challenge for him was to eat the whole pizza all by himself. I would watch as he'd do it — incredulous. His stomach was like a bottomless pit or, as my grandmother would have said in her Irish lilt, he had hollow legs.

These acts were about bringing joy and self-worth to the children's lives. I felt that was a part of my task as their uncle. But the kids did not get off scot-free. In return for their indulgence I would quiz them about every aspect of their lives, inquiring about everything, leaving no stone unturned. I just wanted to be assured they were travelling through the world as problem-free as possible. I am glad I did this. It established a relationship with them where they could talk to me free of all inhibition. No need to hide things from Uncle David, they could be frank and honest with him. Yes, I had to tread very carefully if the topic strayed onto the parents. I didn't want to cause trouble for myself or conflict at home for them. Sometimes it is wiser to refrain from full frontal honesty. As the saying goes, discretion is the better part of valour.

As tends to happen, over time my niece has grown up. The good relationship I created with her through Chupa Chups has developed and matured with her. No longer is she a sweet little girl; now she has become a talented and formidable creature. I have done my best to contribute to that. As she progressed through school I discovered I had talents that could assist her on the way. She was eager for my help and I offered it. This really turned out to be a great joy for me. In English, history and economics I had the knowledge she needed. I would sit and discuss with her the essays she needed to write for school and would read the books she had to write about. Importantly, we would sit and discuss ideas. She was a good student, so it was a real pleasure to help in her intellectual development. If she had a problem of some sort she felt free to ring or email me to get some clarification.

It turns out the young lady possessed real talent. This she has pursued with a focus and maturity well beyond her years. I have had no great need to ground her or put her in her place. I feel she has a good measure of things. I think the role model I have provided, very different to her parents, gives balance to her life. My older sister, very different again, has also provided a balance in her own way.

Our niece says she has not been spoilt, just *indulged*. I would reply, well and good. But you have been spoilt with the most valuable thing of all: unconditional love. That she has received in abundance from a variety of people. So all the diligence has paid off and we have ended up with a strong, self-confident and assured young lady possessed of multiple talents. Now her life will be what she makes of it. I feel I have played my part and, yes, it all began with something as simple as Chupa Chups.

Colon Before a Full Stop

Many years ago my mother contracted colon cancer. She had a rough time of it until, happily, she found a gifted doctor who saved her life. In time I was taken to see him. He explained that given my mother's medical history there was a very high likelihood my colon would cause me problems sooner or later so I must have it checked out. Now I don't know what a colon does but I do know it can kill you. One thing I have learnt is that undergoing a colonoscopy can bring on a fit for me. But that doesn't detract from the prudence of having the procedure. Lo and behold, when mine was done, polyps were found.

These had to be lasered out and as a result I need to do a colonoscopy every couple of years. Yes, a *real* pain in the butt. But there is no denying the repercussions of failing to have these rather frequent checks. A family friend about my age battled with colonic cancer for ten years before, sadly, dying. During this time she brought up two girls. It was unspeakably tragic. Two weeks after her death I heard that a mate of mine had died, also from cancer of the colon. Picked up too late, its progress couldn't be arrested. So I learnt in the most graphic fashion what a powerful and real danger looms for the negligent. It's a simple but hard lesson: I must do as doctors direct. Genetics is a lottery that grants us occasional jackpots along with unkind bequests. There is no choice in the matter: we have to take what we end up with. Still, I have much to thank my parents for, along with gifts I wish I'd never received. Once we accept this is our lot in life, the point is to get on with the living of it.

Heart Attack

As long as I live I will never forget the day when as a boy I came home from school to have Mum greet me with the words, 'Hop in the car, we're going to hospital. Dad has had a heart attack.' I started to argue with her: I didn't believe her. If Dad had really had a heart attack, I insisted, she would have taken me home from school immediately. It was simply an impossibility. Dad was still fairly young and not ready for such an emergency to strike. My certainty soon crumbled.

With a cup of coffee in one hand and a smoke in another Dad had indeed suffered a coronary at work. We were at our wits' end, what could be done? Eventually a then experimental kind of surgery called a bypass was decided on. The outcome was a remarkable success: he lived for over forty years more.

I have since learnt that weak hearts run in the family so, as time progressed, it was extremely foolish of me to become a heavy smoker. Upon reaching the same age as Dad was when he had his heart attack, I had mine. Fortunately, I was smart enough to use this as an opportunity to give up smoking — and also survived to carry out my good intention. Amazingly, the surgeon who had operated on Dad also operated on me, a rarity in medical circles. Our survival gave me great respect for the genetic factor, so I watch out for other family maladies I might inherit, such as prostate cancer but apparently not, in our case, Alzheimer's. My heart scare taught me to respect my body more and, who knows, I might live to the grand old age my dear dad eventually reached.

Two

Childhood

Grand Age

I was brought up in close proximity to both sets of grandparents — and often had the good fortune to visit my great-grandmother. Besides these anchors, our family also offered an array of elderly relatives — people of diverse kinds — plus we had elderly ladies for our neighbours, on either side of our house. So, growing up, I was in contact and learned to live with older — far older — people than me. Being in close contact with grandparents you learn that elderly people can be your friends, a very good starting point. I was taught to treat them all well, no matter how they behaved — which wasn't always easy. There were a few crazies among them, some much more so because what they saw and heard in the Holocaust had loosened their hold on sanity.

Old people, I was taught, were like all other people, except that they had aged a bit so you must ensure you treat them with the respect all people deserved anyway. I was also taught that old people should be cared for, as they cannot always care for themselves. I remember very clearly Mum sending me next door with dinner on a plate for one of our elderly neighbours. I was also instructed not to bother her as she was entitled to her peace and quiet. Old people weren't strangers to me, they were part of everyday life. As I myself have aged and developed, my attitude, relations and understanding of old people have evolved and what I consider old has changed. I now value and appreciate old people and try to understand why they do the things they do. For example, the endless repetition of certain questions that annoyed me a lot as a child, I can now deal with. I now understand that this is often due to hearing issues and, when they don't hear the answer, they repeat the question. Yes, there are factors that account for this behaviour and with maturity comes comprehension.

Over time I have come to the conclusion that people don't change with age, they are what they always were. Somebody who has always been on edge doesn't suddenly become a mellow person. But some people do age better than others, and you can observe this for yourself through the sustained practice of people-watching — a favourite hobby of mine. Through interacting with elderly people, I have come to regard them as an invaluable resource that we should make the most of: pardon my language but in many cases they are living history. They have lived through successive eras of history and can give us eyewitness accounts of what has gone before. I call this not oral history but lived history. Great insight into the past has been afforded to me by my elders: I remember my grandmother telling me of how she would take bags of clothing down to the docks to meet 'the reffos' as they arrived here with nothing at all. This is the sort of thing history books don't tell us about. Or how my aunty told me about how she escaped being killed in the Hebron massacre of 1929. She also told how the leader of the Stern gang was her babysitter. This way she learnt that he wasn't just a terrorist but an actual human being. Lesson learnt.

I had a friend who was a very wise and learned man before he grew old. But as he aged and became even wiser, I drank at the source of that wisdom. I consulted him on most things, from holidays to crickets to speeches. I freely admit, his death was a great loss to me and I wish I were able to consult him still. We must listen to the old. They can teach us how to combat our demons — such a hard thing to do — because they have fought that battle themselves and emerged victorious. My wise old friend was a master of the art of reflective action — a cherished gift. His rest has been well earned.

Paper Round

One of the delights of childhood is getting your first bike. Mine was a green Dragstar. Having a bike gave me freedom, mobility and, well, independence — something I craved and grabbed.

When I was growing up, parents didn't have the kinds of worries with kids that they have today. It was safe for me to go out of the room. I was allowed to roam as long as I returned on time. I visited (and returned from) friends as I wished, no more hanging around and waiting for lifts. It was a dramatic step up in my quality of life so I sought to take this further.

In my youth people still commonly read newspapers. They were delivered door to door. This was called a paper round. They barely exist now. In those days we in Melbourne had an afternoon paper called *The Herald*. For independence and self-respect, I wanted to do a round. I knew my parents would not allow me a morning round, plus I didn't want to get up so early. So I found a happy compromise and landed an afternoon round delivering *The Herald*. There weren't too many papers to deliver so it wasn't a burden in any way but there were a few hills to climb with all the papers on my bike. I used to do it after school; it fitted in perfectly and I felt great about it. For doing this I received a couple of dollars a week, the first time I had got my own money. To me this was something big.

I would not say that my father was an adept financial manager. That was not his focus, not his thing, but it was at this point that he taught me a very important financial lesson that has accompanied me my whole life — the importance of saving. He set up for me at the bank what was called a Christmas Club account. So each week I went to the bank and put in my paper round money, then when the end of the year came round I had saved a tidy sum with interest added.

Then came the conundrum: what do I spend it on? I thought like a young boy and, seeing that I had enough to purchase something big and good, it was with total joy and delight I bought myself a pool table. We only had just enough space to fit it in the rumpus room. It dominated the house but I had bought it from my own money. It was all mine; it wasn't a present, an indulgence, it was something that I had earned. I was in seventh heaven, so to speak.

Good habits endure. Even on my small pension I have made sure to save. I would hate to live from cheque to cheque. But this mindset does have a downside: I am very unwilling to spend money. In fact I have to force myself to do so and enjoy life a bit. My lifestyle is far too frugal. Trying to force myself to break out of this attitude was one of the reasons that spurred me to install solar a few years ago even though it didn't make financial sense. The system will never pay for itself with the amount of electricity I use. But I decided that, in an obscure way, I was giving myself the holiday I refused to take.

Acland Street

Let's take a walk into my own private Dreamtime, the cherished days of childhood. When I was young my grandparents lived in Elwood. My grandfather, a religious man, kept Shabbat. This made it a bit useless going over there on Saturday. So each Sunday I was taken over to visit him and my grandmother with my elder sister in tow. We would go for walks together in what today is called Acland Street but was then known as the Village Belle. We never tired of this neighbourhood, which was always a place of wonder and amazement. On a Sunday it was full of old men talking and drinking coffee. I was told they were the Holocaust survivors. What you couldn't mistake was their zest for enjoying life. As we walked up to the Village Belle Hotel, my grandfather greeted and chatted with friends as we went. The place was alive like no other.

I was not allowed to sample the delights of the cake shops. For one thing, they weren't kosher. But no one could stop me looking. Further up Acland Street we would walk to Luna Park and, if we were lucky, we were allowed to go on one of the rides. From there we would be taken down to the beach to play. There they had ponies and riding them was always great fun. Later, if we were even luckier, my parents would take us to Leo's Spaghetti Bar, still in existence today. Such is the Dreamtime of cherished childhood days when I was indulged with love and affection.

St Kilda offered plenty to see beyond the Village Belle. Further on, you would come to Saint Moritz ice-skating rink, a wonderful place. A cousin of mine who visited when I was young fell in love with the rink and would take me there often. Not being very co-ordinated and unable to skate well, I spent much of the time sitting on the wet ice. Seeing me there, she would never fail to get me back on my feet. On the way to Australia, this cousin had stopped over in Singapore and bought me a number of presents. This created great excitement — and, as most of the presents didn't work and still don't, great disappointment. But to this day we are still close.

We were often left with my grandparents. My grandfather had years of experience being in charge of an orphanage and was good with children. Informed by his brand of Judaism, life was a party to be enjoyed; and as his only grandson I was spoilt. We were often taken to the local Botanic Gardens where I could play with the birds. To this day, I still go there.

Sadly my other grandfather died when I was very young so I have few and dim memories of him. At one point, my other grandmother lived in a flat in Punt Road, South Yarra. From time to time she would take us to a Sixties café called *The Flight Deck* in Toorak Road, not far from her home. The interior décor was all set up as if you were in an aeroplane. Unlike today's children, few of those in my generation would have flown, so entering this café was like going on holiday. When the place closed many years later, I was most upset.

When I go to Acland Street today I am very sad. That thriving village atmosphere I recall from my young days has vanished. All that remain are a few cake shops: as the people who used the space died off or moved away there was no longer a need for the treats they stocked. The Jewish cafés, the hives of activity and discussion, are all gone, replaced by urban commercialism and a restaurant or two. What once pulsated with life is now dead. On a Sunday, instead of friends communicating and cavorting to the sounds of loud music, the crowds have turned the Acland Street I knew into a theme park. The past is lost; modernity reigns. But I, and others like me, will retain our memories.

Camp

My parents decided they wanted me to meet and interact with other Jewish kids and have fun doing it — a reasonable enough desire. The solution they found, on the advice of some good friends, was to have me join one of the Jewish youth movements. Now there are a number of these, representing all persuasions of thought and ethos: in the end they chose a group with a progressive stance whose meeting place was not far from us. Odd though it may sound to outsiders, it was a Marxist-Leninist movement with a strong Scouting bent that owes its history to the Wandervogel 'free wanderers' groups that could be found all across Germany in the first third of the twentieth century. Not people who did things by halves, my folks threw me into this full throttle, so not long after joining I was sent off to summer camp for ten whole days — a big adventure at the age I was (my eighth birthday was spent in camp). I was not the only one to benefit: my parents being teachers, this allowed them the chance to have a bit of a holiday themselves.

The Scouting aspect of the movement was manifested in our daily schedule: there was lots of hiking and building of things. Of course there was fun stuff, too, like playing games and sports. Our education was not neglected, information being imparted to us in the rustic setting just as it had been back in town, with the stimulus of ideas and the discipline of thinking for oneself emphasised. It really was something to be away for this more than a week, given I had never been away from my parents for anywhere near as long before. The camp was sited on the oval in Marysville. Many years later, when one of the Black Saturday fires tore through that spot, killing, injuring and devastating so many people, I felt part of my childhood had been ripped out of me. It is notable how people can view the same events through different prisms.

Every summer a similar camp was held somewhere in Victoria. Through my annual attendance I developed a good group of friends with whom I hung out as a teenager, and that grew — courtesy of this youth movement — into a large social group, responsible for the opportunity to spend the most wonderful gap year in Israel and Europe.

In a way, the camp never broke up. I grew up in this youth movement and it exercised a significant influence on me. Given its political inclination, it brought me up to be a thinking person fully engaged with life and it served as a springboard to university. Discard the 'Marxist-Leninist' label if you will, there is a lot to be said for the philosophy of materialism.

Best Birthday

My birthday falls at a very bad time of year — January 5. This is when everyone is away on holidays or recovering from Christmas. When I was young it meant there was no point in having birthday parties like other kids. There was no one around to invite if I did, and I swallowed that. My family always tried to do something special to make up for it — but it never did.

Later on I learnt that the source of my grievance was not just a case of poor timing but of unlucky placement. Had I been born in France, things would have been different. January 5 is the eve of their holiday for the Epiphany, when they bake a special cake called a *galette* (*galette des rois*) in honour of the three wise men. As a child I always thought how things would be better when I grew up. Not the case, I'm afraid. As those who haven't left for the beaches tend to return to work at this time, I have learnt to treat birthdays as no big deal and, even though I've had a few special ones over the course of my life, I tend to look on them now as a mere chronological milestone in the ageing process.

At the very least, however, I do try to mark my birthday as something a bit special by going out to a nice restaurant. I have even given myself a supplementary birthday — the date of my accident and a rebirth, so to speak.

Some of my birthdays have been special, although the most special is hard to pick, so I will describe a few of them.

The first would be when I turned thirteen and had my bar mitzvah. As the occasion was all about me, I revelled in it. To avoid my birthday-date problem, we delayed it till later in January so more people could attend. My parents threw a large party: hundreds of people swarmed the family property, including the entire Bereson clan. Members of my youth movement attended en masse. It was stinking hot on both days — the bar mitzvah on Saturday and the party on Sunday. My poor parents watched on helpless as all the food they had bought went off in the sweltering heat. There wasn't much you could do but laugh at the farce to which all their planning had been reduced. Fortunately, the big present I received from friends of my parents was not so perishable: a set of golf clubs, what a delight! They had selected wisely: I was very much into golf at the time.

On another of my anniversaries my elder sister organised a mystery flight for the day. We ended up in Sydney, which turned out well as she had a number of friends there. We did a few touristy things that were fun, like a boat cruise of the harbour. We then caught the RiverCat to Parramatta and back, which was worth it to give us less familiar perspectives from another Sydney waterway. In the evening, before heading to the airport for our flight home, we had a very enjoyable meal at Darling Harbour. In my view, no birthday is complete without a satisfying meal to cap it off.

Another memorable birthday occurred while I was on holiday in Israel. A friend tracked me down and asked straight out, 'Would you like to go to Egypt? I've done the research.' 'Sure thing,' I replied. When they heard about it, my parents back in Melbourne threw a fit, so concerned were they with what might go wrong. They needn't have worried.

Early on the morning of my birthday we took a taxi to the central bus station in Tel Aviv where we boarded a coach bound for Cairo. What a trip! In no time at all we found ourselves at the famed Rafah Crossing on the edge of Gaza and were waved through, no hassles. Australian passports are good. We continued on across the desert, passing through a couple of exotic-looking oases which left enduring impressions of palm-tree groves and placid camels. We arrived unexpectedly quickly at the Suez Canal — I recall it looked a lot smaller than I'd expected. Our bus then rolled onto a punt and, on reaching the African side, we just rattled our way to Cairo with all its mystery and spicy aromas. This was the great first day of my most wonderful holiday — and with a birthday to celebrate it was very hard to surpass.

On turning fifty I felt a twinge of pride, telling myself, 'You've done rather well to make it this far, given all you've been through.' Nothing less would do than to greet it with joy and aplomb, to get out and embrace middle age. So I decided, 'What the heck! Let's throw a party.' Having invited a good number of people, I was in a state of shock when all but one turned up. A good lively crowd we were. The only no-show was a woman who was having chemotherapy just then. I couldn't argue with an excuse like that. Her condition served to remind me how lucky I was to be around to celebrate my good fortune. Things could so easily have been very different.

My elder sister likes organising special celebrations on my special day even though my birth came as a huge shock, robbing her of her centrality in our parents' eyes. One year we went to Hobart and sussed out a wonderful vegetarian restaurant. The beauty of Hobart is that you can see it on foot, no need for a car. Another year we went to Launceston, also a great car-free destination. So you see why when someone asks what was the best birthday I've ever had I'm forced to pause and ponder. There have been so many good ones that my mind goes blank and I'm about to declare it impossible to say. Then I catch myself just in time, and realise the right answer. Best birthday of my life? That honour must go to the actual day I was born.

Hotel Sorrento

Our lives are marked by milestones and rites of passage. I have had all the normal stuff but since my accident all these milestones have been coloured and distorted by my disability. I do try to accommodate that and rise above it. I am told that on my first birthday I celebrated by putting my fist through a chocolate cake, so I do feel I started in style. And as I hope to go on.

On turning thirteen, of course, there was the bar mitzvah. My parents threw a massive party: it was a very big deal. Not something I could share with the kids at school as they weren't Jewish. So I had to handle and deal with it on my own. Doing this set me up for life. Being able to swallow and digest the big things that came my way all by myself has been an important tool to have in my kit-bag. The perishing-food fiasco on that burning hot day didn't faze me. As the centre of attention, soaking it all up, I didn't really notice. If this is what life is going to be like, so be it, I thought. The event was overwhelming: my focus was *not* going to be distracted by a 'catering malfunction'.

The next big thing was turning eighteen. I cheered when the day finally arrived that gave me all my rights in one go: to drink, to vote, to drive. I was now an adult with reason to celebrate. Well, when I reached twenty-one I ignored the event. My contemporaries would hold large parties to celebrate their twenty-firsts but that age gave me nothing: I couldn't see the purpose in it. What got me was that I had spent a small fortune on twenty-first presents for others but because I didn't make a big deal of it I received nothing in return. To some degree I felt cheated and foolish to have ignored a milestone. I have carried that baggage with me ever since. The turn of a decade is considered significant by many folk but I am not sure of the big deal. On reaching thirty I didn't want to do anything. There was definitely no reason to celebrate one milestone — my accident — that had cheated me of the life I wanted, and I marked my thirtieth in a modest way. A number of the guests who turned up then I have not seen since. I am not happy about that or with them. I treat these people as they deserve and am happy to be abrasive if I see them in public. No free rides from me.

Over the years fewer and fewer people remember my birthday so I have decided not to bother with theirs. Forty was no great celebration. Not long afterwards I had my heart attack, then got all the way to fifty and concluded 'Well done', given all the health scares I had survived. Even though the arrival of middle age was hardly cause for celebration, I decided to have a party and invited everybody I regularly saw or was in contact with. There was a real crowd: my parents' house rocked. The updraft of time blew stronger through my life and soon I was approaching sixty. Covid came as the strangest act of mercy from my perspective. Since it was not possible to have a party I could ignore the event, but my sister decided a vacation break was in order as I never go on holiday. So she booked us into the Hotel Sorrento, a good place to mark the move into my mature years. As children we used to go with our parents to Sorrento on holiday. But our accommodation then was nothing like what we found in 2020. We rolled up at the hotel, which was approaching its own milestone birthday —150 years —a wonderful place with charm, character and delightful gardens. We had luxurious rooms with wonderful vistas out over the bay. My sister knows how to party so we enjoyed some very fine dining and spent relaxing hours overlooking the water. My sister deserves, and gets, full credit for knowing exactly how to usher me into the next phase of my life. Now it is up to me to sustain this level of pleasure whenever possible, without waiting for another age marker to loom into view. It won't be easy but the good life is worth aspiring to — whatever you consider the good life to be.

TV

Over my lifetime the way people watch and relate to TV has evolved a great deal, something worth considering. I also watch and use TV in a way that is peculiar to me. I was born not long after television came to Australia: it was not yet a common item in almost everyone's home. Those were the days of black-and-white transmission. As I grew up, colour came along — a real revelation — then came the VCR (videocassette recorder) and DVD (digital video disc). Cable TV also arrived, offering lots of choice, and later ABC iView and similar services.

So TV has developed and, as it has done so, my relationship to it and the amount of control I can have over what I see on it has changed. In the early days the 'telly' supplanted radio as the central focus of life in the lounge rooms of Australians. Families would congregate around the set: viewing was not something you did on your own. Favourite shows were discussed afterwards: viewing became a shared social experience of the type familiar to radio listeners just years before. Even though this was new technology, people related to it just as they had to the old technology.

Our elders said of us, the first TV generation where this new device dominated and had a great influence on our lives, that the new medium was destroying our brains and was bad for us. Children were warned they must not be allowed to watch unlimited amounts of programming. I had very liberal parents and their attitude was a lot more relaxed. Few if any controls were placed on me and this was a fortunate thing. TV gave me, and still gives me, a lot; and this brings me to an examination of the purposes and patterns reflected in my viewing habits.

Like most other people, I watch it for entertainment and this can be a very valuable thing. But I also use it so expand and develop my imagination, much as books do. To me, TV is a visual book and, after all, both are in the business of storytelling. So I rely on television as an information resource through which I gain knowledge and a greater understanding of the world.

Lastly, I go back to the viewing template of those early years, watching — and discussing — the news, and other shows, with my family. This habit goes a long way back with us. An older sister had some friends with no TV in their houses, so they would come over and watch ours with us. Every afternoon after school I would have to look after my little sister so we spent many hours together in front of the box. We had great fights about what to watch: while I would mount good arguments about the social worth of the shows I wanted us to watch, big fights would erupt over *The Brady Bunch*, which I despised for its unedifying representation of middle-class America. As I grew up, the social aspect of viewing now embraced a large group of friends. We would watch *Countdown* with rapt attention, and embark on lively discussions about our musical preferences. This quickly became a good bonding experience for all those involved.

In recent years, watching TV has become a far more individual thing but the ways I have learnt to interact with it continue to evolve. Till this day it remains for me a learning device, an electronic educator. I don't have cable but the one cable network I would like to have is the Discovery Channel. While people have come to see viewing as an individual pursuit, I have not fully adapted to that change of perception. People in the same room get very upset with me because I still regard it as a very social medium and am prone to talk and comment all the way through a show. So, if I could speak to that generation long gone that feared it would rot our brains, I would say: on the contrary, a lifetime of telecasts has given me a rich set of experiences and I am proud to say that I am part of the original TV generation.

Three

Growing Up

School

Education can be formal or informal, social or non-social. My first foray into the education system was harmless enough: kindergarten. Mum was happy to have found a place without too much fuss. She delivered me there and drove off just before realising it was a Catholic pre-school, came right back and plucked me out of it. I took it all calmly enough. Eventually she found a place nearby which is still going, I hear. Mum always says little boys at the back of that room were so quiet compared to the girls. By the time I was of primary-school age I could already read, thanks to my parents teaching me. They chose to send me to the local primary school. As it was just a kilometre or so up the road, I walked there at first and later rode. It was 'old school': every morning the flag was raised and we sang God Save the Queen. Also in those days each child was given a small bottle of milk to drink at morning recess. This has been stopped now; maybe it should have continued.

A big advantage of going to the local primary school is that my first friends lived not far away, making it easy for us to visit each other's homes. We played, we made up adventures: the usual stuff. But the teachers were not equipped to extend the more curious among us beyond the contents of the grade book in our various subjects. There was one teacher who on learning I'd finished the maths book asked me to go through it again. No wonder, when boredom set in, my friends and I developed an independent streak. I remember one Moomba festival we caught a train in to town together. We wandered around looking at things, then eventually sat on the banks of the Yarra, ate the lunches we had brought with us and watched the water-skiing. Those were golden times. I think today with stranger danger kids would not be allowed such freedom. For this loss they miss out greatly.

My parents did their best to include things that broadened my education. I was sent to both Cubs and Scouts but neither really interested me. I was taken to Little Ath's and joined a cricket club but I don't think sporting prowess is in my gene pool. I was also taken to things like drama and art classes. The one thing that tickled my fancy was a Jewish youth movement where I made friends and joined a social group. This youth group, as I mentioned in an earlier story, had a Marxist-Leninist orientation so there was a strong emphasis on developing the mind and introducing you to social issues. Of course it was also about the broader Jewish ethos and was pro-Zionist, linked to one of the kibbutz movements.

When I finished primary school my parents wanted me to go to a private secondary school. I point-blank refused. Even then I believed in public education, not private and elitist education.

I also didn't want to be restricted and made to conform (seeing conformity as a hallmark of private schools more than it was of their state counterparts). In the end I won the argument and went to another local campus, Camberwell High. Actually I saved my parents a fortune doing this, especially given that Dad's wage as a teacher was a long way off stratospheric. My parents having no clue as to what Camberwell High was really like, I didn't let on. I was very happy with the leeway I got to be lazy and get on without too much effort. The school was a bit like the proverbial blackboard jungle and I was happy to hide in it, taking the view that wherever I went to school I would still end up going to university. To me it was just a matter of getting past these years.

I made friends with various teens — a couple of girls in particular, I recall — but formed no intense relationships. To expand my education my parents wisely bought season tickets to the Melbourne Theatre Company and with these girls we went to see all the plays. Sadly, the girl with whom I was particularly close died in a car accident during my gap year. This was a terrible loss to me. With a group of friends from the Jewish youth movement I attended, among other entertainments, the original *Rocky Horror Show* starring Reg Livermore. I also developed a keen interest in footy and ended up going to most of my team's games. I loved the theatrics of the event as much as anything else. You wouldn't say I was very sporty: I played a bit of squash and tennis, and pursued an interest in golf that my parents couldn't understand.

You could say I had an easy time of it till the end of Year 11 when my parents abruptly changed schools for me because where I was I couldn't get the subject combination that I wanted. Fortunately, the pre-VCE qualification known as the HSC (Higher School Certificate) proved no hassle for my hard-playing study-averse self. The Saturday night before my English exam I attended a David Bowie concert while everybody else was cramming. I couldn't see the point in doing that: you either knew it or you didn't. In the end I did reasonably well — not brilliantly but well enough to get into most courses except science. I had no idea what I wanted to study. On a. whim and at my mother's suggestion I enrolled in town and regional planning, far from the correct course for me. Before I started I took a gap year, deciding my enrolment in the university of life must take precedence.

I spent the first half of the year in Israel, doing a special course in Jerusalem called Machon (for leaders from overseas Zionist youth movements) and after that went to live on a kibbutz. Finally I did a lightning-fast tour around Europe before returning home primed to confront life. Arriving in Jerusalem for the first time was a bit of a shock. Although I had to look after myself, I was doing so in the company of a bunch of people my age from all around Australia and New Zealand and, oh yes, some South Americans, so you can imagine it was a bit wild. Everyone was out to make the most of life and live it to the fullest. You learnt about people in ways you never had before. On the course you learnt Hebrew and were taken around the country to see it in great detail — a most wonderful thing.

So that was my year — six months of full-on rage and learning followed by six months immersed in rural life and practising agriculture together with contemporaries from many nations. When in Jerusalem the group of us from my youth movement created a co-op. This is where we pooled all our money and lived off it collectively. This taught me a lot, firstly about managing money and secondly about how other people use it. As you can imagine, a co-operative based on the principle of one in, all in can create some very tense moments. There was one big benefit from the experience: I ended up living a year on next to nothing.

On returning to Melbourne it was crunch time to discover that the town and regional planning course was a bad choice for me. I found the curriculum very conservative and regimented. The history of town planning I found rather interesting, especially as I had visited some of the European cities we studied. The course did require some drawing, which was not my forte. I also did first-year economics, which I sort of liked and wasn't too bad at; and statistics, which I found beyond me, probably because I didn't apply myself. So I passed Year 1 of the course but during the second year I decided this was a useless waste of my time and dropped out. I decided to transfer to arts, which would be possible if I picked up a subject. I chose politics, which agreed with my natural inclination and interest. I found myself a good job and would attend lectures after work. The only problem was that after a day of hard physical labour I would take my seat in the lecture hall and then fall asleep.

Arts suited me to a tee. I accumulated knowledge that has served me well. What pulled all this together was a subject I did in my final year called social and reflective history. It brought all the social theory I had learnt into a coherent whole that has equipped me to ride the ups and downs of my life. My professor taught me wisdom in the form of several gaudy clichés that I use to navigate my way through the turbulent tides of life. Reflectivity has given me a perspective on life and a means to dissect its mysteries.

Well, I enjoyed my studies but I dislike the pressures of sitting exams and having to hand in essays on time. Arts being what it is, though, I was free to do as I wished most of the time and I enjoyed that liberty. My social life was very active and joining in various groups on campus taught me a few lessons outside the classroom setting: for instance, that you really oughtn't to talk religion or politics unless you know people very well. Being guarded with my opinions in the many houses I entered involved a cultural leap after I had been used to express my thoughts freely, and having them listened to willingly, wherever I had gone previously.

Upon finishing my degree, I had no desire to go on and do a Master's or a PhD: I have a sort of contempt for those things. I wanted to go out into the world, to live and learn from the act of life, to engage in what I would call praxis. I wanted to travel, see and discover how people react to things. To me the wider world is the high temple of learning, so it was only on leaving uni that I finally felt that the environment I found myself in was where I truly belonged.

The Teacher

During our lives, we have many teachers. Their impact on us is both good and bad. It all starts with our parents. I am fortunate to have been blessed with fine parents. They taught me well over the years, not only all kinds of knowledge but, as importantly, good values and ethics. I clearly remember being taught to read by my parents sitting in the front room of our house, me slowly working my way through *The Herald* newspaper with them. By the time I reached school, *Fun with Dick and Jane* was no problem at all.

We must recognise that not all teachers do their job well. I attribute my poor spelling to a bad English teacher in second grade. I also had a maths teacher in primary school who didn't know what to do with me. I finished the maths book and she just said, 'Do it again.' This was a failed opportunity to develop my skills and interest in maths. Skipping to my high-school years: they were a blur and had little impact on me. I was always headed to university. I guess the only teacher who had real impact on me was my dad. When he taught me eighteenth-century history it was not the content that had an influence on me but the theatrics in the way he delivered the lesson. During these years I did have other teachers of sorts, they were the leaders in my youth movement who at times had a great influence on me.

When I reached university, I found some great lecturers and teachers awaiting me. I was eager to drink all that they poured out. To have such quality people impart knowledge and understanding to me was a great joy. Amazingly, I even had one great lecturer who had taught my father. He had been a member of Dad's cadre in the Communist Party. Though almost totally blind, he would deliver lectures without notes and timed to the minute — a wonderful performance. But it wasn't just the lecturers: from some tutors I learnt a lot as they helped me understand

and master the theory of their subject. In contrast, some others were pathetic, indeed a hindrance to my learning.

Eventually I reached my final year of study. I had heard of a subject (social and reflective history) that could bind together all my learning so far and turn it into a coherent whole. But there was an obstacle. It was an honours subject and I was not doing honours. I had to plead for special permission to enrol in the subject. Happily, my request was granted as there I met not just a supreme teacher but a person who delivered me the skills to deal with the life I have led. I have an everlasting debt to this man which I can only repay by writing stories that deliver insight into my being, into the way I confront the world.

Every seminar found me in attendance; I skipped nothing, gained and learnt so much. This master was a relaxed man. His face bore a permanent wide smile and he showed an interest in everyone. He looked forward to seeing us and through him we would see the world. An ex-priest, he exuded the warmth and joy carried over from his previous life. One great gift he endowed all of us with — by example — was the art of storytelling. After I had my accident I visited him to tell him what had happened to me. When he responded with genuine heartfelt compassion and concern, I could feel he was one person who didn't just mouth platitudes but seriously meant what he was saying. As time passed, we became great friends. With his wife he would come and see me and they would take me out to lunch. I looked forward to these occasions, considering them a highlight of my life. Later, through email, we engaged in a vibrant conversation that covered all aspects of life. Whenever I had to give a speech I would consult him to fine-tune it.

The funniest thing was that upon retirement he became a huge fan of the TV soapie *The Bold and the Beautiful*. To him this was the stuff of life. Being hooked on this show also, it became my job to report to him each day what had transpired in the latest episode as he often missed it. This daily synopsis was a difficult challenge of composition, nothing like writing to an Oxford don each day!

When he died my life was robbed of a lot. I often think of him. His writing guides me at every turn. As I sit here working on my iPad, a framed photo of him looks down on me. To this teacher I am greatly indebted. Many more stories that I could tell you of him still sit in my memory and soul, along with all the other things he gave me. If any of us can find a great teacher we are privileged beyond price, and should cherish their memory as well as what we have learnt from them. So I say, Greg Denning, rest in peace. You have done your job well. I could not have asked for more.

The Drug Addict

A change of course at one point in my university years suddenly meant I had plenty of time available to me. Instead of wasting it I decided I should go out and get myself a job.

Fortune smiled and I found myself a great one — storeman at Myer's furniture warehouse.

It was from here that furniture bought at one of Myer's department stores was delivered to homes all over Melbourne. It was a large and busy place with lots of workers going to and fro all day long. The work was seriously hard and physical — moving about sofas, beds, heavy cabinets and couches: you needed to watch your step or you could easily get hurt if you were careless — but I adapted. The bosses were good to me, paying an adult wage even though I was not yet twenty-one. So each week I took home a good wage packet that was supplemented by plenty of overtime (there was always more furniture to be delivered than we could keep pace with). Evenings and Saturday mornings would find me hard at work. Another kind of bonus that came with working evenings was that you got dinner money. I would bank my wage and use the dinner money to meet daily expenses. This way I soon accumulated a tidy sum of money but I was permanently exhausted.

As a workplace it was ideal in other ways too. This was a fully unionised work 'shop' and the union helped any member who had a problem related to the shopfloor conditions. I even got a couple of mates summer jobs there during this period. Twice a week after work I would hop into my car and drive to lectures at uni.

One of my fellow workers at the warehouse was a quiet Australian bloke. He wasn't into chit-chat much, it was all about getting on and doing the job. He had a good, relaxed Australian attitude and I eventually learnt a considerable amount from him.

One day he said to me, 'I have to piss off this afternoon and I'll have to do the same twice a week from now on. Naïvely I said, 'No worries' and wouldn't have thought any more about it but then he began to explain to me what was going on. I had worked with him for months and knew nothing of his inner life — or what he did away from work. He said, 'Well, David, I have to go to a methadone program but it's in St Kilda as there's nothing around here.' My jaw dropped. He smiled at me and said, 'Yes, David, I'm a junkie.' So I had been relying on a guy who had been off his face for months, who at any moment could have caused me serious injury. From this I learnt that people are not always what they appear to be and it is not up to you to judge them. He was certainly not my image of a junkie, this calm and relaxed guy holding down a regular job. I never noticed any marks on his arms.

Given that people are made up of many layers not all of which are self-evident, we must always allow them time and space to reveal who they are. Also I learn that you mustn't prejudge people: after all, you do not walk in their shoes. In the final analysis, my junkie was a very decent bloke who patiently assisted and taught me to do what could have been a dangerous job. I hope he has lived long and well, though life took us in different directions and, really, I have no idea.

Firsts

The first time we do something in our lives it is always considered an act of great significance: inevitably, a life of any length embraces many firsts — some bound to have a greater impact than others, some best forgotten. A fitting place to start this little survey is my first birthday. On that day I was given a chocolate curl cake, which I put my fist through. Another occasion my parents understandably made a big deal of was my first day at school. This milestone did not trouble me but has caused my mother great trauma for over fifty years. I just walked into the schoolyard as content as could be. Unlike the other kids, I was so well adjusted to this radical transition that I didn't shed a tear. My mother has never forgiven me for that, treating it as a slight against her. Some firsts don't work out as we expect, and we must accept that.

There are so many firsts in my life I can't remember them all. People ask, 'Who was the first girl you kissed?' Hell, there were so many I can't remember — and, really, it doesn't matter. What does is that I liked it and indulged in the activity on many occasions. There are all sorts of teenage firsts, there's no point in going through them all. What is supposed to be 'the big one' is the first time you had sex. I will not deny I remember *that one* clearly! There will be no tale-telling here but you bet I enjoyed it and instantly decided this was an activity worth repeating.

Now I come to a first that's not nearly so common as kissing and the first act of sex. It's what I call my 'Fuckawi moment', harking back to the joke about a Pygmy tribe who lived in long grass that left them clueless as to their geographical whereabouts. Every so often they would leap up above the grass and shout: 'We're the fuck are we?'

That was the approximate sentiment I felt upon emerging from my coma after the car accident in WA. At that moment I had no understanding or knowledge of what had happened. Everyone assumed I knew what was going on but to me it was a world of amazement and bewilderment. I had no idea at all where I was. My injuries, the source of my pain and the extent of my incapacity all had to be explained to me. This was a first. The need to undergo a range of therapies was an unprecedented thing in my life. I was thrust into a new world — I would use Aldous Huxley's book title here but I was not brave in it. I struggled to comprehend it all. Previously everything had come fast to me. In a sense I had lived a comfortable life on the plains; now I had to climb all these mountains for the first time.

I am none the worse for having broken through all these starting lines; if anything, I may be a better person for it. I am glad that, after the initial shock had worn off, I got up and kept moving forward, not being shy to encounter more firsts. With hindsight, I feel I handled many of these challenges — such as involvement with lawyers and the court process leading to my compensation — well. There followed the need to manage a significant payout — and I am pleased that here, too, I was able to rise to the occasion and, in general, make what turned out to be good decisions. I am aware there will be many more firsts ahead of me in life, and hope to reach each of these milestones with peace of mind and a steady focus.

Camellia Day

The Royal Birthday (formerly the Queen's Birthday and now the King's) is an anachronism, a relic of the past with no relevance or meaning today. Public holidays are important because they add joy to people's often mundane existence. We must make the most of them — but they should be based in the reality of our lives.

If I cannot perceive worthwhile meaning in the naming of a public holiday, then it is up to me to construct some purpose around it. As for the Royal Birthday holiday, which in my state of Victoria falls on the second Monday of June, I long ago concluded that it is of great importance. A good time must be had as this is the last public holiday till spring. After this date there is a long cold wait in store until the next long weekend. For some, this is the high point of their year as it marks the beginning of the ski season: the time has come to resume their love affair with the snow. Personally, the ski fields are too cold and dangerous for me. They don't tick any of my boxes – but I do like a good party.

This time of year has another significance for me. It is about now that lovely white camellias appear on the tree next door — and I gain great delight from them. For a mate of mine, the King's Birthday holiday is special because it's when he starts his olive pick. He grew a grove of olive trees for the oil, so he waits for this time of year with keen anticipation. It holds an extra meaning for me, as it is when my elder sister celebrates her birthday and this often coincides with the Jewish festival of Shavuot – a harvest festival. This festival I do like as vegetarian food is supposed to be consumed then. The treat for this occasion is cheesecake, so how could I not approve? The only thing is that I must be careful not to overindulge, which is far too easily done. So, after due consideration, you can see that this long weekend is not simply a useless relic. Over it I have built layers of meaning, and in so doing laid the foundations for a life of richer purpose. King's Birthday, you are a leftover from a long-gone imperial banquet, but I am very glad to meet you. Till next year …!

Anzac Day

Anzac Day touches us in various ways. Instinctively I want to keep it at a distance. The last thing that I want to do as a very committed pacifist is glorify war. One thing I cannot avoid on April 25 is my little sister's birthday. Herein lies a real Jewish mother's story. In labour my mother noticed the clock and realised her child would be born on a public holiday if she held on for another few moments. What a gift to the child it would be, so she did that. …

Yet most of my sister's birthdays have been spent in places where Anzac Day wasn't a holiday so, in the end, she would curse

Mum for doing this. Hey, even with the best of intent some things backfire! I remember as a lad at primary school learning about the organisation known as Legacy and how it cared for the children of fallen soldiers. This touched me deeply. I was very keen to wear a rather expensive Legacy badge as the public holiday approached as a way of expressing my sympathy. When years passed and I learnt a great deal about war and what it did to people, this revolted me. With the spread of awareness, views change.

Once I visited an Anzac Day exhibition at the local Jewish Museum and this was an important learning experience as well. It astonished me to discover that a cousin had been held as a prisoner of war in Changi. This was the last thing I would have expected a relative of mine to have undergone. When I mentioned this to a good mate, he replied, 'Yes, that's interesting' and opened up about his grandfather who had been at Gallipoli and been forever damaged by it.

Various members of my family served in the armed forces — none, I hasten to add, for the glory of war. One, who had come here as a teenager, enlisted to serve his new homeland. Mum tells me of my grandfather coming home every weekend, an officer dressed in all his finery. I cannot imagine that the responsibility that came with high rank appealed to him. Many Australians joined up out of a conviction that it was the right thing to do. This sense of duty, and of comradeship in the Anzac tradition, runs deep in Australian culture and finds expression in the notion of volunteerism. *Don't sit back: contribute as you are able.* The residue of the Anzac spirit has seeped deep into our being and I have met no one who wants to eliminate it from our character.

After each of the large-scale wars Australia became involved in, it was rare to find people who had no connection to someone who had served. But millions of immigrants have built their lives here with no such connection, so the Anzac strand has grown thinner over time. Yet even they will have found it difficult to escape the connection altogether. I remember as a child being driven through many a country town with its avenue of trees dedicated to the soldiers who didn't return — and these were not their only memorials. Little wonder such sights made an impression on me. Without needing to be told, I absorbed the lesson that others had given their lives for the luxuries I enjoy — peace, freedom and democracy.

Living in Melbourne, it is very hard to escape the imposing presence of the Shrine of Remembrance, a constant reminder of those sacrifices. Every time I pass the Light Horse howitzers in St Kilda Road that were captured at the Battle of Beersheba — celebrated as history's last-ever cavalry charge, and one in which Australians rode to victory — a sort of chill passes down my spine. Times have moved on; horses have not been used in the military within living memory.

What I would like to know is: Where are the memorials to all the Aboriginal warriors and civilians who died in the so-called frontier wars? They should be part of our collective memory too. Could it be there are no memorials because the behaviour of our forebears was not illustrious — was nothing to be proud of? When I said at the beginning of this story that the Anzac spirit touches us all in various ways, I am mindful that one of these is the formation of a collective national myth as to who we are, built at least in part on a foundation of conflict and violence. That myth is at odds with another — that we are a peace-loving democratic people.

Theatre of Life

My parents learnt, or at least discovered, that you could get season tickets to Melbourne Theatre Company productions at a very affordable price. So they decided to indulge me as part of my education. I am very thankful for this act of good parenting: it has had broad ramifications in my life. For a number of seasons, along with a couple of girls from school, I was able to go and see every play the MTC put on and learnt to socialise at the same time. This was in the days before the Arts Centre opened. The MTC then was based in Russell Street; today it uses a number of locations.

Theatre going showed me that stories could be developed and played with imagination. The *Summer of the Seventeenth Doll* trilogy I found illuminating. It embedded in me a love of literature and inspired me to become a good reader. Going there with friends meant that after each show we would discuss and examine what we had seen, so the experience also sparked my intellectual growth and curiosity.

My adventures in the world of the stage did not stop with the MTC but expanded around this age in concert with a group of friends from the youth movement we all attended. Together we saw the original Australian production of *The Rocky Horror Picture Show*. It introduced us to a whole new concept of what theatre could be. Few shows I have been to since have produced such exhilaration. From that moment on I have had a love of musical theatre. I am fortunate to live in Melbourne where you get a wide choice of these shows, but my passion has not overflowed into a love of the opera. Yet my interest in theatre is broad and has led me into an exploration of the wider world of the arts.

Apart from the positive effects mentioned earlier, the theatre has given texture and meaning to life itself. And I take a broader view of what's theatrical than most people. One of the great theatrical spectacles in Australia is sport. Go to Australia's stadiums and you will see the sporting show embraced by an engaged audience. Go to the footy or cricket and you will see high drama expressed and played out. The same goes for the high drama and low farce performed on our national and state political stages. Passion and loss are not confined to playhouses.

I see theatre in many things around me; it helps me interpret the world I live in. As was truly said, all the world is a stage and we are but players. I would even go as far as to say that the course of my life has been a theatrical experience: like it or not, my life has not been short on drama.

When I have gone overseas, the 'theatre bug' has accompanied me. I've been to London a few times and indulged my taste for stage shows in its famous West End. I've never had the pleasure of going to New York and seeing Broadway plays but once, when in Israel, I was taken to see a marvellous production of *Cabaret*. Admittedly it was a bit hard to follow in rapid Hebrew but just being in a full theatre with its electric atmosphere was thrilling and told me that love of the theatre is a universal emotion.

I like to see live shows as often as I can. One of the delights of theatregoing is to watch the audiences as they file in. How they dress, the manner in which they socialise or stay aloof, is all part of the public show. I do think the crowd tells you quite a bit about a show even before the curtain goes up. One thing that always amazes me — no matter what production is on, the stalls are almost always full, which speaks volumes about the way theatre engages with people. It is far from being an elitist activity. It forms part of the way that people see and interact with life. Of course the full house also has its economic explanation because if there were no audience for its fare a theatre would go bust. But the primary reason for heading out to these seats of entertainment, whatever the weather outside, is that through the prism of the theatre we can enjoy, participate in, observe and better understand life.

Competition

By nature I am not a competitive person. I don't like to compare myself to others and this helps me be a relaxed person. On the other hand, I do like to compete against myself:

I take pride in achievement and consider this a very positive attribute. But, given my obsessive-compulsive personality, I have to try keeping this trait in check or it can do me real harm.

One sphere in which people develop their competitive instinct is sport. This didn't happen to me because I have no natural ability in that direction. From early on I understood that no matter how hard I competed, I would invariably come out the loser. So I saw no reason to harm my self-esteem by joining in these 'games' and contests. When I played sport it was purely for enjoyment and the focus was not on always being the winner.

Yet there were some endeavours where competitiveness is built into the structure and design of an institution — and there is no escaping it. The whole system of marking is a process that rates us against our peers and encourages us to outrank them. But the competitive urge failed to take root in me even in the school environment. I felt no need to put in a great effort to prove myself better than my classmates. No competitive streak emerged despite the system's tendency to develop it, so in this respect I failed to become fully socialised and ready to join the rat race of the adult world. Tangentially, it may have worked, though: measuring fresh accomplishments against earlier ones and against my personal goals is, after all, a form of competition. I was certainly anxious not to fall below the level I had set myself — and this applied in the ethical realm as in other parts of life. I set myself standards and was suitably severe on myself if I failed to reach them. Self-competition hurts no one and propels me on to a higher level. This impetus has stayed with me throughout my life, helping me achieve many things and shaping the person I am.

I had no great interest in school and did just enough to get by — just didn't bother. Not naturally indolent, I was, as my father would say, lazy to myself. But when I went to university my perspective and approach changed. I still didn't care what my marks were compared to other students: a pass was good enough for me. Gradually, though, I became aware that a bare pass was under-selling myself. If I really wanted to get a grip on what I was learning, I realised, I should be doing better than that. So I began to compete against myself, to expect more of myself, and would be disappointed if I gained anything less than top marks. This attitude — that my efforts should be directed at reaching the level I aspire to — has allowed me to circumvent an important objective of the capitalist world in which we live. The consumption principle is not for me: I have resisted the temptation to become acquisitive. The driver of capitalism is the notion of an unending cycle of growth. Some things obsess me — I fully concede that — but this is not one of them. I have found it funny that the thing some folk have missed most during Covid has been involvement in live sports competition. Since society thrives on competition, they find this hard to live without. As for me, I can live with it or without it.

Uni

University was significant in my life and I liked many aspects of it — but not all. Then, as now, I endeavoured to make the most of life and enjoy it, and I think I made a good fist of this. Far from unique in having no idea what I wanted to do with my life after finishing school, I was prepared to listen to my dear mother, who did have an idea of what academic subject would suit me best as preparation for a career. The one she chose —Town and Regional Planning — sounded interesting enough. That is, until I confronted the reality of it. Thrown in with a group with whom I had little in common, I can't say it was entirely negative. Gaining insights that would never have been open to me otherwise, I found myself on the receiving end of a good introduction to the world at large. But quickly I found the subject matter did not teach me things that I wished to learn. I stuck it out for a year and gave it my best shot.

Then, during second year, I dropped out and transferred to Arts, where I was much happier. As part of the course transfer I had to do one subject twice a week and chose politics. The lectures I attended began not long after a full day of work, so I often fell asleep during the lecture. A fellow student who was amused by this became friends with me, and to this day that friendship endures. He was instrumental in introducing me to some important people in my life, which was how I discovered that a key thing about uni is not what you learn so much as the connections you make there. Today they call it networking.

I was a good student but that doesn't mean I *liked* being a student. I never enjoyed having to produce work to deadlines. The exam is not my friend: I am prone to performance anxiety and rarely do well enough to demonstrate the knowledge I've acquired. Some students derive great joy from digging around in the bowels of libraries but I wasn't one of them. For one thing, I find the air in those places very unhealthy. But I worked out what needed to be done and did well. Some things I did enjoy such as following the flow of ideas, comprehending and applying complex thoughts, and gradually constructing a mental map of how the world operates.

University is also a time of social flowering, and I was not backward here. I knew how to work a room and, oh yes, engaged with a variety of women. I enjoyed mixing with people and learning about worlds and lives that were foreign to me. I feel this developed me as a person. I did not, however, take full advantage of what was on offer. There was a broad spectrum of clubs and organisations at uni but I wasn't interested in joining any — apart from some dealing with the Jewish students' body. I also mucked around on the fringes of the Newman Society as I found the Catholics an interesting 'mob'. But, all in all, my life at uni was very full, offering me a scintillating experience. You need robust energy to do all I did in those days; I wish I enjoyed today the health I had then.

Not unusual for those days, it was while at uni that I moved out of home. Happily, that turned out well. I moved in with a foreign student — now, that was unusual for the times. I was plunged into an amazing world — a diaspora but different to the

Jewish one I had grown up in. These were Zimbabweans: there was so much to learn about their world, I enjoyed it very much. Occasionally we had cross-cultural conflict but that was to be expected: the memories that last from that time are of the great times we had. Fortunately our share house was not far from uni so I could pop in and out with great ease. When I finished uni I didn't bother taking out my degree, seeing it as a meaningless piece of paper. As a matter of fact, in my well-educated family, no one has ever taken out a degree except my older sister, who gained her PhD from the Guildhall in London.

I left uni long ago but am still a student of life as it goes on around me — and so I should be. At one point after my accident I decided to return to university to do a few subjects. But it was not such a great time. I encountered great difficulty finding subjects that interested me, so that made it difficult from the get-go.

Commuting to and from uni I found very tiring and difficult also: no longer could I waltz in, play a bit, have a coffee and a chat, borrow an appropriate book to read and go home. Much of the satisfaction I previously gained from a tertiary education was now gone. No longer could I interact with people as I used to. At this point I had to realise it was more important to cherish the memory of happier times: it would be foolish to expect to relive them in any way. I was a new person faced with a new reality, and the life I lived needed to reflect that.

The Train Trip

Once upon a time I flew from Tel Aviv to Athens with very little money and somehow had to get myself from there to Paris so I could continue my journey and collect some money to live off from a family friend. Fortunately, I was able to buy myself an Interrail pass which would get me to Paris and all around Europe within a three-month period. But after buying that I was left very little change so I didn't see as much of Athens as I would have liked. Still, I remember a nice meal of okra in the Plaka. The trip to Paris was to take a few days. I had no idea what it would be like to sit on a train for that long penniless.

Well, the trip through Greece was wonderful: the mountains were so beautiful. Ultimately I got to the border with Yugoslavia where the Customs officers came aboard to check passports. When I handed mine over they freaked out because it was full of Israeli visas. They screamed and ranted for a while then, in a huff, they walked off with my passport. *Hell, what am I going to do?* my mind raced. *I'm in the middle of nowhere and now have no proof of identity.* I was shaking with terror. After one of the longer half hours of my young life, they returned. I had no idea what they would do but very politely they handed me back the all-important document, now bearing a Yugoslav visa. As you can imagine, I was very much relieved. Then the train trip began in earnest.

Across the countryside, past rugged mountains with snow on them, we flew. The peasants on the train were lovely: they all insisted that I eat and, not only that, share their food. Eventually this long journey brought us to Venice. I was so excited to be entering Europe. On stepping down to the platform, I beheld the most magnificent train station, like nothing I had ever seen before. It took me a few puzzling moments working out how to change trains but I was soon on my way to Paris, so excited I sat up overnight and got no sleep. Finally we pulled in to the famous Gare du Nord.

So what to do now? I had a solitary coin to ring the person I was supposed to contact. All day I rang but there was no answer. I was at my wits' end. Forced to spend time on some activity that cost no money, I took myself on a walk to have a look around. Under the Eiffel Tower I bumped into some Argentine friends who I'd lived with in Jerusalem. After I explained my situation to them, they gave me a little food and wished me all the best. Well into the evening I was able to contact the person I was after, an Australian living the expatriate life. He came and picked me up and took me to his flat. He was over the moon to have somebody to eat the Vegemite he had in the fridge. Nobody had bothered to tell me he was gay so when he and his friend went to their bedroom my jaw dropped. Not what I had expected! He looked after me well, showed and explained a bit of Paris to me and gave me enough money to get to London to meet my sister. While showing me around we bumped into my Argentine friends again, who were most pleased things had worked out for me.

The only request my sister had made of me was that I bring a couple of bottles of wine from Paris. Well, I was eighteen, I didn't know much, so I walked into a shop and bought a couple of bottles of very cheap wine without looking at them. When I turned up in London, my sister was furious that I'd brought her such cheap plonk. One of the bottles was even plastic! In a bid to quell her fury, I replied, 'Look, it's not so bad. Think of it as cask wine.' At first she hadn't recognised me because I had such long hair, which I hadn't cut during the previous year. This was just the start of a lifelong argument we have. I put my foot down and say, 'You must respect the choices I make with my body. It's my choice what happens to it.' She replies, 'You must look respectable.' Our notions of 'respectable' have differed.

With a couple of months' free travel I headed back to the Continent and ended up having a most enjoyable tour. So my European train travels, which had begun with great foreboding, left me no worse for wear. I have found over time that if you keep your focus and stay the course, with a bit of good fortune you will come out OK. I have two sayings that cover this: first, put your best foot forward — the hard part is choosing which is your best foot. The other one, stolen from Mao's *Little Red Book* is the journey of a thousand miles begins with the first step. ..but that step takes a mighty effort, I like to add.

Dear Comrade

Mum was a bridesmaid at a friend's wedding, so when I was born she made this women my godmother. Having read too many fairy tales and watched too many cartoons, I dubbed her my fairy godmother and used to joke that she rode around on a broom stick — actually she was anything but the scary type. Now her husband like many of my parents' friends was a progressive. He was also well known. When watching the news my parents would be pointing him out saying there he is, as he was at the head of the large moratorium marches which were the sensation of the day. Being the sort of man be was, in time he moved into Labor politics and became a member of of parliament. This impressed me no end. I thought it was the be-all-and-end-all and I thought very highly of this man who was always the most gentle of souls and softly spoken to accentuate it. As with everybody else, I was caught up and carried away with the enthusiasm and momentum of the Labor's 1972 *It's Time* campaign. I became very politically aware for a young boy and, of course, our friend was swept into parliament. Then came great joy and surprise — he was chosen to be a minister and was making his mark on Australia in a quiet way. He wasn't flamboyant and colourful like Al Grassby. He just did what he had to do. He knew that I was wrapped up in all that was going on and so to include me he started calling me comrade as a term of endearment — and he continued to do so until he died in 2022.

So our friend was in Canberra for many years. I remember I once went up to Canberra on a school excursion and he came to pick me up one night. He had no idea what to do with me and said — "Would you like to see my office?" "Great", I said. So he took me to see his office in Parliament House (now OPH and the Museum of Australian Democracy). It was a fairly small room that was crammed floor-to-ceiling with files and boxes. In those days members of parliament had to rough it a bit. On the way to his office he saw a few mates and gave their names and then he said with a wide smile — "Meet Comrade David!"

I learnt from him that people are not always what they appear to be at first sight. My father had a heart attack and they were going to give him major heart surgery, a bypass, which was a new thing in those days. I felt terribly sick— poor mum had enough on her hands and she wasn't able to deal with me. So she passed me on to our friend to look after me for the day. I turned to mum and said what use was that — he was just a politician. Mum said, hang on, he is more than that, he is real doctor so he can look after whatever ails you. I found it hard to reconcile that you could be two things at once. But eventually I understood that people are multi-facetted and they can be and do more than one thing. It was a worthwhile lesson.

My parents actually had a variety of friends who were progressives. Each expressed this in different ways. Dad had a best friend, in fact he was best man at their wedding and he was very close to the family. We all called him uncle. He was a uniquely brilliant man with a grasp of many subjects. When he was a young man he was an ardent, firebrand communist sprouting the virtues of fraternity and the brotherhood of man to everyone. He was a great believer in the rise of the working class. He was a math genius and went overseas to further his studies — so we only saw him infrequently when he visited Australia. Once, when a little boy, I went with dad by train to see him in Sydney. Going interstate was a very big thing and catching a flight was the stuff of dreams in those days, unlike today. Eventually he came to live in Melbourne as professor of math at Melbourne University. He had been sucked into the system and establishment in contrast to his political beliefs. He was no longer the radical working to bring down the system. He was a contrast to our comrade who was never subverted. Our comrade as an old man was still a starry-eyed idealist believing that change was possible. Eventually, for work reasons, my uncle was sucked into America to live. Even though he once had certain beliefs, amazingly, he became an American citizen. From what I have seen, it is very hard for progressives to keep what they believe going. This is why I place my comrade on a special level. He is not alone. I have met some others who kept their beliefs till death. One lovely man was Judah Watten, the author. I liked him because when I visited him with dad, he always gave me boiled lollies. He was a very old man when I knew him. Well it is hard to create beliefs and then sustain and hold them. I think when all is said and done the key thing is stay true to yourself— this is what I aspire to be.

Four

Bang—The Accident

After

At various points in our lives we all have dreams and fantasies that we hope will one day turn into realities. Well, in my earliest years I consider I was blessed. All that I did turned out much as I desired. Not only did many of my dreams come true, or show promise of doing so, but I enjoyed myself hugely in the act of growing to adulthood within a loving family who saw to it that I had an enviable education.

Then came 11 June 1984 — bang, the accident that turned everything upside down in an instant. The dreams that I had entertained and nurtured suddenly became unattainable realities. Well, sooner or later you have to adjust to this: there is no choice in the matter but to redesign your dreams and accept your brand new lived reality.

But no, it doesn't stop there. After creating new dreams begins the work of devising ways to attain them. It takes time — a long time — to come to terms with your new reality, the harsh beast that it is. Well, I had all the dreams that most people do: I wanted to find a nice partner, a woman with good looks, a good brain and similar politics to mine. Yes, I imagined a couple of kids and living where we would happily live life to the full. Like most people, I also dreamt of travel. I had already done my bit there, but I aspired to go back to Israel and live on a kibbutz where visualised myself being a productive member of a close-knit and mutually supportive community. I had no vocation. There was no job I dreamt of doing. I had done my academic studies and was satisfied with that. I knew that one day I would write something(I had no idea what). But all that I had dreamt evaporated on the fateful day of my accident. Redesigning your dream world is no simple task: it is hard to jettison thoughts that have been with you a lifetime and some portion of my old dreams survived to become incorporated into new imaginings. And, when I compare my redesigned and original dream worlds, there are considerable commonalities. I want to be happy, just as I used to; to live well and be a decent bloke, just as I dreamt of being before. The destinations remain largely unchanged, only the stepping stones are different.

Since all of us are social creatures it will not surprise you to learn that in my new dreams I saw myself living with a compatible woman. But, after some time in the new reality, I came to accept this was purely a dream. Much as it is natural to dislike living alone, my ability to find a partner and fulfil this part of the dream has been very limited. This was especially hard to accept, given the freedom I had in finding women before my accident. No one has been willing to help me surmount this barrier to complete happiness. But a measure of happiness is within our grasp. It is up to us to create the conditions for this. Our dreams must be moulded to fit in with the life we lead. We must first work out what makes us happy, so to have an attainable dream requires an act of self-investigation — and that is not always an easy task.

Dreams change, accident or no accident. Those I had as a little boy developed and were replaced by others as I grew older. Adapting to reality, I have long since ceased to dream of wearing the baggy green or running out onto the MCG as part of the mighty Hawks squad on Grand Final day. My dreams are not as grand as all that, but they possess the beauty of simplicity, like being able to use a knife and fork again; to speak and be understood; to lead a satisfying social life; to have a companion with whom I can practise the art of living well. That yearning, which nothing will drive from my brain, springs from the reality that I don't want to grow old alone. Well, I hope these dreams are not fantasies. I do what I can to keep them alive. I am determined to raise my quality of life and achieve them. In this I am little different to millions of others. All life's roads are connected, even if the one we are on is ours alone.

The Day

I remember it all in fine detail except, happily, the accident itself. I am very glad that is something my mind has not retained. The day was like any other at that time. I got up, had a bite to eat, packed my bag and paid the hotel bill, then hit the road for my next destination. I drove for several hours, came across a petrol station, stopped and filled up the car and had a stretch. On leaving the servo, I recall having a minor argument with the girl sitting next to me, telling her to put on her seat belt as it was something you should always do, no matter what. At some point after that, the accident occurred. Apparently my seat belt snapped and I flew out of the car, landing on my head. The girl's seat belt held: at least she was OK and was even able to save me. There are other details from that day I won't divulge.

Well, I am told the Flying Doctor Service airlifted me to Perth but I remember none of that. I was greeted by an amazing doctor on the tarmac who went to work saving my life, but remember nothing because I was out to the world. For many weeks I lay in the hospital in a deep coma. Now in a coma you are supposed to be unaware of the outside world but I discovered that is an urban myth. I was very aware of my family being around me. Apparently my elder sister, then living in Paris, flew straight to Perth on hearing of my accident. This caused me great confusion when I finally came out of the coma remembering that I had seen my sister while unconscious, which made me think I must now be somewhere in France. I understood that I had been badly injured but had no real idea of the magnitude or consequences of my injuries. As I had lain there in my coma much of the damage I had done myself mended. I have no memory of my collarbone having been broken but to this day it still twinges — just something I live with. With all my injuries I am eternally grateful to be able-bodied, not wheelchair-bound.

Brave New World

For six weeks I lay in a vegetative state. No one knew if I would ever come to. Apparently they took all sorts of actions to prod me back into consciousness. My sister even flew back to Australia from Paris, where she was living. But I was not ready to wake up. Eventually I had a fit and that brought me to — weird to think that epilepsy actually had a benefit for once. On coming to, you suddenly have to comprehend what has happened and are flooded by an onslaught of sense impressions about the new world you have entered. In fact, this process took years. It is a huge intellectual effort for a damaged brain even to attempt.

My whole lived reality was now superseded for good. Every prior understanding I had of the world had be thrown out. I literally had to learn how to live again. On the plus side of the ledger my intellectual capacities and training have not been greatly affected, and these have helped me survive. Apart from everything else, I faced such physical challenges as learning to walk again. I found being in a wheelchair the most awful of realities. I had to be forced to stay in it — the hospital orderlies would tie me into it. Friends who would come and visit used to laugh at how off my face I was on morphine. 'Look,' they would say, 'they need to tie him in his chair so he won't float away.' I freely confess to verbal dysentery: my speech was badly affected by the accident but nobody gave me any speech therapy. I have had to wait over thirty years for that blessing, and am very grateful that the day finally arrived.

Elephantosis

After my accident the doctors told my parents that given the nature of my injuries I probably had nothing left in the memory bank. But medical science is an imprecise thing and they got it badly wrong. It turns out that I have a syndrome I shall call elephantosis — not to be confused with the physical-enlargement ailment known as elephantiasis. I have an excellent memory, though I hasten to add that some gifts we have are not what we would choose for ourselves. To the extent that an excellent memory can be a drawback, my lifestyle is partly to blame: all the exercise I do strengthens the memory, plus all the reading I do exercises the mind and keeps it functioning well.

Having a good memory does have its benefits: you can sit through lectures without the need to take note because you can later recall all you require. With a sound memory you have no great need to make lists of things. Events, whether days or decades old, are at your beck and call. While all of this is a blessing it also means you get upset when your memory is less than perfect and it forgets something you were sure you could not forget.

The power of recollection is precious. To be travelling in and out of memory would be a frightening thing. This is what poor souls with dementia or Alzheimer's go through, and my heart goes out to them. My occasional *petit mal* seizures have given me a strong sense of the fear and upset those in the early stages of those diseases must live under. Upon the return of normal sensory awareness you simply don't know where you have been or what just happened. It freaks people out a bit: suddenly, mid-sentence, you're gone and a moment later you're back.

Now let's return to my elephantosis. I don't have a photographic memory, there's no instant recall in my toolkit and I am glad of that. But I can summon information when needed, a handy attribute in day-to-day life. Alas, my memory functions so well there are people who use me as their memory. I resent this because when pressure is piled on, sadly, it does not perform as well as I could desire. But it does mean I can speak with ease publicly without relying on notes.

Another drawback is storing too much information that is of no practical use. You have to train your mind to be selective. Even if there are plenty of facts and incidents that can safely be discarded, plenty of them stick in the memory that you would prefer didn't. In the social world you find you remember things that people have said, some of them quite off colour, and before long you have put together a catalogue of verbal misbehaviour.

In addition, you can recollect people's sub-par conduct or observations with pinpoint accuracy: even worse, every instance of someone letting you down when they didn't act as they ought to have or promised to act. This is one reason why if people come up to me socially and behave as if they were a good friend and I remember they have been anything but, I just walk away and ignore them. My good memory — of bad occasions as well as all the others — means I cannot put them out of my mind. I do admit I get some satisfaction out of such occasions, concluding it is better to absent myself than make a public scene and just as effective in making my point.

My childhood memories astound my mother. She never realised I was so observant. This is a key to having a good memory, picking up the detail of life. But the master key is being able to access what you want when you need it. The great cruelty of Alzheimer's is that this key has been lost, and along with it the self. I am not lost; I am very much the person I have always been, thanks to the retention of my memory. Not only that, I have had the good fortune to be able to develop it. Many have written about the nature of memory, notably Proust. While I am not in his league, memory is by and large something to be thankful for and to use wisely — when it lapses we encounter great problems in life. But it's important, whether you write like Proust or not, to focus on pleasant times past. If you dwell only on unpleasant events, you may end up telling yourself, 'I'm cursed with a good memory.'

Lonely

My wonderful parents brought me up to engage in life, to make the most of it, grab it by the neck and do all I can with it. I have tried to repay their gift to me by embracing this ethos.

From early on my life was active and full, with few spare moments. My natural obsessive-compulsive personality certainly helped. I was always with people powering through the day, in constant motion. This was my mindset too. Then, bang, suddenly one day all this was gone, my way of being evaporated into thin air. Adjusting to this was very hard. No longer was I out till four in the morning doing things. My life was toned right down. On top of this my physical capacity to do what my mind told it to do was greatly compromised. I fell out of the loop and the social world that I had known. That was the harsh reality, and remains so. Even though I feel I should be doing a thousand things, they simply cannot be done.

I missed a number of Melbourne's increasingly popular *White Nights* as I had no one to escort me and look out for my safety. By way of compensation, I have created a very full and busy life for myself. But there is one thing I can't escape, and that is the gnawing sensation of loneliness. I would very much like to have someone with whom I could enjoy 'the act of life', a vibrant presence alongside me, a true companion. This is easier wished for than achieved. I have no idea how to find such a person, not being into online dating. I want to meet a genuine, real, three-dimensional person in the flesh.

Previously my life was jam-packed, so much so that I begrudged having to sleep. Think of all those hours I could have spent doing something! The void of loneliness that exists where before there was a lively crowd of people in my life is a draining sensation. I fight it; I have sought to negate it in many different ways, with only limited success. To express myself properly, there must be another person sharing my days. This is a consequence of my upbringing: I cannot hide from it. Knowing from my studies that this need is a social construct stemming from our prevailing social system is all well and good, but knowing this doesn't help me fight it. I have found various techniques useful in waging the battle not to succumb to loneliness. But, when all is said and done, many evenings find me sitting in front of my television feeling the want of a warm human presence in the room — someone to distract me from this blue light.

If We Truly Care

Sometimes I reflect how lucky I am to have landed on my head, not my bum. I am not in a wheelchair for life and I am able-bodied, even if the body is rough around the edges. Should I want to, I can do things. Yes, I count my blessings: if I were better at maths, I would multiply them. True, I never had great co-ordination or good motor skills, so I can't expect them to be better or even near as good as they were before the knock on my head. This is a reality of life that I have to confront. But I am functional enough to live independently and manage most tasks, even if this is not achieved without a good deal of effort.

Getting dressed is no fun but I get there day after day. The ability to live by yourself as an autonomous human being possessing your own free will is a most undervalued and under-recognised boon, until for some reason this capacity is challenged or lost. Well, if I don't live by myself what is the alternative? Living in care? No, thanks. I want to decide what I do when I want to do it, to live and act as I desire, choose the food I eat — or don't eat. None of this is possible in care. I can take myself out for coffee or go out for lunch. The important thing is, life is what *I* make of it. If someone else makes these key decisions, then it is not *my* life.

In practice, I find 'care' — a word with such positive connotations — is demeaning: it undermines a sense of self. Most important, it provides little if any quality of life. Not long ago I witnessed someone dealing with care and it was not a pretty sight. The object of this care was a talented surgeon, my age, who had suffered a stroke and been placed in a care home. Give him credit, he was making the most of it — but it was an unrelenting battle. One day a friend and I picked him up to go to a lunch party: he was so excited he was about to engage in the world as desired. I must admit, at lunch he behaved well. The pleasure and satisfaction of being there were written on his face. Here was a lesson for me: we must extend what care we can to people and they will respond. It is up to us to make an effort and improve the lot of others. Strive as I do to achieve this aim in the way I conduct my day-to-day life, I do not always act as well as I would like.

My mother has instructed me that should we have to put her in a home I am to kill her. I can understand where she is coming from, but think that fulfilling this wish will be beyond me. My interaction with 'old-age' homes has not been good. When I was young, one of my grandmothers was put in one. She was left to rot, with little care provided. It was heartbreaking to see a woman I loved treated so inhumanely. Many years later, my other grandmother was put in a home. It destroyed her. A woman full of life was reduced to a corpse. A close friend of mine, an elderly lady, injured herself in a fall and could no longer live alone. There was no choice other than 'aged care'. To help her deal with the much reduced circumstances of her effective imprisonment, we would leave care packages — sadly, not often enough. When possible, we would take her out for lunch and the delight she got from these occasions was inspiring and uplifting. But the poor quality of 'care' at her 'home' – or, more accurately, the general lack of it — finally killed her.

When someone extends care to me in some form I take pains to acknowledge the act, and cherish their kindness. Many who I would have expected to reciprocate in my time of need have been seldom sighted and have shown no sign of concern. I bear no malice towards these less-than-quality people, but will not give them the time of day. They are dead to me. What is perhaps harder to understand is how others who provided me quality care for a while don't — for whatever reason —bother anymore. I can make up a variety of excuses for them, but all of them are hard to accept and none of them offer any excuses of their own accord.

If care beyond the person-to-person level is organised, it needs to be done properly. Throwing the vulnerable into mass accommodation does us, them and society no favours but is an instrument of harm.

In my view caring is a primary responsibility for each of us. Let's not kid ourselves, it is a burden at first, but the appreciation — often the proverbial light in the eyes — of the one you care for will swiftly make that burden feather-light. It is beyond our power to alleviate all suffering for any individual. But, if we truly care, we must try.

Hospitality

Over the years I have spent a lot of time in hospitals so I have learnt a fair bit about being in them and coping. The very first hospital I was in, as for most of us, is where I made my grand entrance into the world. As I mentioned earlier, I was born in the middle of a heatwave. In those days air conditioning was far from a common thing so to keep babies cool they held them under a cold water tap. I credit the season of my birth for my love of heat, or as one friend of mine puts it my thermostat has been out of kilter all my life. After that I had a charmed childhood and life. Growing up, I only ever spent one night in hospital — that was for what they called growing pains. I remember being terribly bored there and just wanting to escape. I never broke a bone and suffered no serious cuts, nothing like that. It seems I saved everything up for one occasion — my car crash, in which I did more than enough to make up for a life of largely avoiding time in hospital. Since then I have been a frequent bed user.

My accident occurred on a lonely road in northern Australia. From there I was taken in a very bad state by the flying doctor to the deservedly famous Sir Charles Gairdner Hospital in Perth. I was greeted on the tarmac by a surgeon and looked after closely and well until after it became clear I was on the road to recovery. I can't say as I remember much of this hospital as I lay there in a coma for many weeks. Given the things they did to me, that might have been for the best, though I did learnt that even in a coma you do have some degree of perception, even though it is limited.

Being unable to recall the things I went through may even have saved me from getting PTSD. By the time I came to from my weeks-long coma, many of my injuries had already healed. I do recollect being taught to walk again. That was difficult and no fun. They were very strict with me: the thing is, once I could walk I became a terror. I would move around and create havoc. From the viewpoint of hospital staff, I was a total nightmare; from my viewpoint, I felt well and could see no reason why I should be confined to a room, let alone a bed, one second longer. I just wanted to get out and engage in life again: it took me a while to realise that life as I had known it no longer existed. Now I was starting from scratch, like a newborn babe. Eventually they got fed up with such a difficult patient — nowhere more difficult than in the worst hospitals — and let me go back to Melbourne. There a new round of hospital roulette awaited me, but being so close to my home made my mental state more acute. It was then I entered what I now consider clinical depression but no one really picked up on it so it went untreated.

Deliverance to my hometown came with the rude shock that it wasn't just in the west that you don't always get what you wish for in hospitals. They put me in a room with a guy who had meningitis. Conscious that it was a highly contagious disease, I thought I already had enough problems and didn't really need to run the risk of one more.

One thing I learnt from these extended hospital stays was that drawn-out days waiting for a visitor to turn up can be soul-destroying. So now if a friend of mine is in hospital I do my best to go and visit them even if for only a few minutes. It breaks the oppressive monotony of hospital life for them but another consideration, people are not always up to receiving visitors. This you have to accept even if it took great effort to get there.

Hospitals are institutions so there is no escaping their power structure, in which you are the weakest element. You must obey their logic and way of doing things so they will be telling you what to do and how to behave — not once but many times a day, every day. This required me to deploy all the skills I attained in my education. Without them I would have unravelled completely.

Moving from a few weeks at The Austin to my next hospital was like going from backpacker accommodation into a luxury hotel — a real shock to the system. I had to have my gall bladder out. This wasn't an after-effect of my accident but a genetic malady: the whole family has had it. For this I went to Cabrini Hospital in Malvern. This was a whole new world. It smelled nice and was well staffed. You did not have to wait half an hour for a nurse to come. The food was better than edible and choosing your meal from a menu made it feel nothing at all like a hospital. But no matter how nice it was, when all is said and done, it was still a hospital. I was still locked up, deprived of my liberty and free will, things I greatly value.

My next hospital experience was mind-boggling. I had a heart attack and was taken to The Alfred, one of the best of our public hospitals. While they deal with hundreds of patients smoothly and efficiently, it's a far cry from the comfort of a hospital like Cabrini. What upset me most about being there was that it is the hospital where my father had undergone bypass surgery many years earlier. That surgery was a wonderful success but upset me very much at the time. I learnt later that my coronary was the culmination of many factors, a critical one being genetic, so it would have been hard to avoid in any case. I didn't mind being in a public ward as there I met people I would never normally have come into contact with, and got an insight into who they were — making this hospital stay an educative experience.

Amazingly, the doctor chosen to do my operation was part of the team that had attended my father. It is rare they get to do both father and son. It also turned out that my grandfather used to give him lifts when he was a boy. The world of events weaves itself into the most wonderful and complex formations. While The Alfred was not overly stressful it's an unpleasant operation to undergo wherever you are. There was (and I understand still is) a shortage of rehab beds in Melbourne so finding a place to recuperate, as opposed to just being turfed out and sent home still in pain, proved a serious challenge. In the end, I had the good fortune to be sent to a very comfortable rehab centre in Brighton. More like a comfortable motel than a hospital, a couple of weeks' confinement there was all I had to accept before regaining my liberty. The only real downside was that Brighton being at a bit of a distance from home meant there were few visitors, so the days passed slowly.

Having seen more of hospitals than most people encounter in a long lifetime, I thought that was it — but my genetics 'had other ideas'. Years ago, when my mother contracted colon cancer and I tagged along when she was taken to a specialist for a consultation. He decided that because of my high likelihood of finding family history repeating itself I should have a colonoscopy, just to be safe — but that procedure brought on a fit and a bout of dehydration, giving me another night in hospital. Well, just my luck they found polyps on my colon, which means I now have to undergo regular colonoscopies — which, you guessed it, means more time in hospital. Then, just to make my health more interesting, I underwent a fit while the doctor was lasering out the polyps. This risk, at least, is unavoidable as the danger to my health from letting the polyps grow would certainly be much greater.

Enough already, I hear you sigh — but that's not the end of it. On holiday in Israel I was staying at a friend's place one hot night when I ventured out of my bedroom in the dark 'looking for' a light switch and tumbled down a wooden staircase, banging my head about so badly it was off to hospital again. There I promptly got pneumonia and — I know you're thinking it couldn't possibly get worse but — the knock to my head triggered a minor stroke. Let me say at once, Israeli hospitals are great — they will save your life — but they are also, in my experience, rough around the edges. Also, I had to deal with everything in Hebrew, which the medicos spoke way above my level. Added to this was the bad luck of timing. Just when I was there this hospital had been largely taken over by injured Syrians from the civil war, so the attention given to individual patients was not as great as it would have been in normal times. One day I'm lying in my room with a lovely view of the Mediterranean enjoying my holiday in the sun; the next, I get stuck in a room looking out on the Mediterranean *without* being able to enjoy it. Go figure!

From there I was transferred to a holding hospital in Tel Aviv until it was time to send me home. They refused to send me to a quality rehab hospital there as they decided it would be cheaper to sort me out in Melbourne. The holding hospital wasn't so bad but I would rather be home. I learnt in these hospitals that they were largely staffed by Russians and Arabs. As an act of decency I tried to speak to the Arabs with the limited Arabic at my command. They loved this as it gave them a degree of respect. I learnt from them that hospital work was considered a safe, secure job and a good place to be in Israeli society. Regrettably, in all hospitals you will find people working there who are on the fringe of society. What could have been a tedious time in the holding hospital was enlivened by a friend who visited me every week with his laptop, enabling us to watch cricket live from England and even footy finals from Australia. I even recall a decent party or two attended by friends. The food was not great — but I survived. ...

So at last it was back to Melbourne, to a nice small hospital where they taught me — one more time — to walk again. Not many people learn the skill on three separate occasions, which when I think about it makes me rather special, not that I would wish it on anyone.

Five

Health

Each to Their Own

Living with a number of health conditions, I have discovered that I am far from alone. Often a debilitating condition is not noticeable to the naked eye. To manage my own wellbeing I have found it helps to observe and digest how others handle their particular malady (or maladies). Most interesting of all is to watch how people handle an acquired affliction and the changes it brings to their perspective of the world — there being no better example than Covid19's impact.

The origin of people's health complaints can be genetic or acquired. I have both types. Not too much can be done about the genetic: that is the roll of the dice. Brain damage, such as I have, is tricky. It's where genetic and acquired conditions intersect. I am very pleased there are some conditions I don't have to deal with — Type 1 diabetes, for example. I am also blessed not to suffer hay fever or sinusitis. I see people living with the affliction of diabetes and not handling it at all well. Oddly, I see people consult doctors and even undergo operations in an attempt to cure it while continuing to eat sugar-filled snacks and carry out other behaviours that can only aggravate their condition. I sigh deeply and feel like crying out, 'You can't have it both ways! If you have an issue and know what exacerbates it, you need to shun that substance, however tempting it may be to your taste buds.' I stay far from this club of fools, focus on my own battles and live within the parameters set by them. Let me get on with my life sensibly or, to borrow a cliché, far from the madding crowd.

Near Life Experience

Often we hear people talking about a near death experience and what this has done for them. To a degree I treat this sort of discussion with scorn. I now have had a number of close calls, what could be called near-death instances. But I will not pretend these moments have delivered me deep insights, let alone acute clarity of mind and comprehension of the world. Thinking about it, I don't see why they should.

Despite the closeness of the calls, I cannot say they brought me to the point of confronting my mortality. I always thought I would survive and was in good hands. So I feel terribly robbed to have gone through these episodes without experiencing any special inspirational moments. After my original accident I went into a coma for weeks: when I finally awoke it had to be explained to me what had happened. No white lights or tunnel travel for me! Then when I had my heart attack and was taken to hospital, on coming to I was told I was going to have bypass surgery. Familiar enough with that, I just sat back and submitted to it. Once again, I was not preoccupied with my mortality. Ditto when I had my fall and a minor stroke. All this came to a head for me when a friend got Covid and I was trying to assist him through by writing encouraging sentiments. Suddenly I realised he was facing imminent death and I was unable to offer any useful advice based on my own experience, simply because I had not had to deal with this plight before. But, on balance, far from bemoaning my lack of knowledge I regard it in a positive light, as one less burden for me to carry.

The Doctor Won't See You Now

The idea for this story came to me as a result of an email from a friend who was sitting through what I will dub the agony of the waiting room. Understanding what he was going through, I had empathy for his plight and replied in that spirit. That got me thinking, I have spent a lot of time in doctors' waiting rooms, so I do have a bit to say about them. To manage my various health conditions I have to see a range of doctors so I spend much of my life on the medical merry-go-round. It never stops so I can get off it. As a result I spend countless hours waiting on doctors, something that is hard to digest but I have had to learn to swallow it to preserve my sanity.

What really gets up my nose is that I always make sure to be on time for doctors, knowing better than to muck them around. They are busy people who run to a tight schedule. But, even though I am always there on the dot, it is rare that I am seen at the allotted time. 'If I am punctual,' I exclaim, 'why can't you be?' I understand that sometimes there are extenuating circumstances but these can't occur every time I visit a doctor. Getting no reasonable response, I put it another way: 'I consider my time is valuable to me, why don't you? Why do you insult me by wasting it?' It all boils down to a case of bad manners (well, that is my non-medical diagnosis, anyway).

So many hours of my life pass this way. I must see these people: I have no choice. What options do I have while I am in the room just waiting? I could pick up an out-of-date magazine I am not interested in. At one point I used to take a book along with me. But I soon found these are not the most comfortable places to read, and with distractions every other minute — from receptionists shouting down the phone to sick babies wailing — they are not conducive to reading. Or I would get to a critical point in a book where I was engrossed and that would be always be the moment the doctor would call me in.

It is possible, of course, to sit there twiddling your thumbs and counting the minutes but that is very draining. I use the time to go through a routine of hand and leg exercises. I look around the room and count various things. You see many people seriously engaged with their phones but as I don't have one that is not an option for me. So I have learnt to relax, calm myself and survive.

Is all this waiting worth it? Eventually I go into the doctor's clinic where they might do a test on me before asking different questions about how I am. Perhaps they will fiddle with my medication; hand me a blood test form; send me on to someone else to check something — for example a stress test, which involves another visit (so make that two stress tests!). When all is done, I walk out, not overly satisfied.

I go to reception, pay my bill and book another appointment. Specialists can be booked out a year ahead. It seems I can never get a time that suits me. How glad I am that many of these doctors I only have to see once a year: if they want to see you more than that, you know your health condition is far from good. I walk out the door ready to jump back on the carousel once more. Up and down I go. Will it never stop?

Fitness Testing

Genetically I am not sporty, athletic or fit: I don't think forebears on either side of my family devoted much of their time to exercise. I feel it helps to have an understanding of our genetics if we are to be aware of our limitations — but it mustn't stop us living well. I suppose you can see it as an ongoing battle between the person you would like to be and the knowledge of your constraints and you act accordingly. There are many genetic bonuses that I value and cherish but at the same time I live with a number of genetic deficiencies such as the tendency to talk too much.

As a child I played in cricket and footy teams, also learning to play tennis and swim, after a fashion. I even dabbled in a bit of squash and other activities but was not particularly adept at any of them, due to poor hand-eye co-ordination. To repeat, I understood my limitations and accepted them as my genetic lot. I was better suited to mental recreations such as chess. I enjoyed these activities, and still do, but even so they didn't bring home any prizes, awards or ribbons. Still I was not jealous of the boys who did.

I had a normal sort of childhood. Walking to and home from school, cycling round to my friends' homes, all this keeps you fit and healthy to a degree. They were different times. Many of the worries we have now were not as bad then and this allowed me freedom of movement and activity. My diet didn't undo all the good conferred by that level of activity: I had a strong sweet tooth but at about the age of sixteen I became a vegetarian. If you don't eat properly as a vegetarian you get sick so my way of life kept me essentially fit and healthy without the obsessive effort of a sporty fitness freak. I did try a gym for a while at my father's insistence but that didn't turn me on. On becoming an adult, I realised that staying fit was going to require a more conscious effort.

For the first half of my gap year, the bulk of which was spent in Israel, I didn't get to eat much. Vegetarian food wasn't abundant in Jerusalem and the group I was with was very active. As a result of all this I lost a lot of weight. The next six months was spent on a kibbutz where, by my standards, I became super fit. Toiling in the I avocado orchid was hard physical work, then I would spend the afternoon swimming and playing in the pool. This built up my body strength and fitness levels. A very nice surprise came my way at the end of the year when I went to buy myself some jeans and couldn't believe my smaller size.

Returning home from Israel I looked and felt great, a sight to behold, if I say so myself. I maintained condition without great difficulty and with no involvement in structured sport, unless you count a rather active sex life. Burning off a lot of energy made good sense to me. My vegetarian diet, not spoilt by too much indulgence in junk food, kept me in trim, and I took on a number of store jobs that contributed to this. For a while I was a storeman in Myer's furniture warehouse. But not all the influences trended in the healthy direction; at the same time I was also your typical slothful university student, a bit of a lounge lizard.

I have no doubt my general fitness saved my life on the day of the car accident that changed it forever, and that fitness also assisted my recuperation from it. But while recovering I went on the ultimate chocolate binge — most enjoyable but with long-term consequences, transforming me from skinny to large. The battle to keep my weight down was lost years ago but, although unhealthily large, I have remained rather fit which has aided my recovery from every health setback along the road without too much difficulty.

The tummy I developed since Israel has been a pain. I have tried to get rid of it. The fruit diet, for example, was a waste of time: I put on weight with it. Bike riding seemed a natural — and, what's more, I like it. At one point I was covering a hundred kilometres a week. It was making me strong but even that much cycling wasn't enough to burn off the paunch. I subsequently learnt that riding is good but you need to do weights to complement it. Unfortunately they are potentially very dangerous with my epilepsy and only advisable under supervision.

Eventually I gave up riding after doing thousands of kilometres, and the risk of overstraining my heart was only one reason: excessively windy weather, congested roads and clogged bike paths were others. In time, I got myself an exercise bike with all the bells and whistles. Using my brain damage to positive effect, obsessive application was not an issue. I rode at a fair speed for good periods of time, covering huge distances and losing ten kilos — though the effort-to-weight-loss ratio petered out right there. I still do a fair bit of spinning on the exercise bike: I think it's great.

Soon enough I settled into a new daily routine. I would perform exercises for ten minutes or so, which developed into an hour over time. This gave my body flexibility and got my metabolism moving. Recognising the need for expert advice on the right mix of exercises led to a great inclusion in my life, the hiring of a personal trainer. It is an indulgence, I agree, but one that has turned out most beneficial for me.

The inspiration came from a brainstorming session with a guy from Jewish Care who was assisting me as part of my care-agency package. Discussing what would be the best exercise mix, he piped up, 'What about a personal trainer?' I said, 'Are you serious?' He replied, 'If we can improve your quality of life, that's what we do.' I leapt at the idea — but finding the right trainer is easier said than done. He fished around with no success but I persisted and finally he said, 'I have a gym just a couple of minutes from here that is rather good. Go ask there.' Having never been there before I didn't know it was open to the public so I waltzed in and asked if I could speak to a trainer. They introduced me to a bloke who said, 'Come back and we'll have a chat'. As luck would have it, I had struck gold. This guy had a diversity of experience with people who had a variety of brain issues so he was perfectly equipped to deal with the likes of me. With all his training and practice, he was and is able to pull all my various therapies into a coherent block. After discussion we agreed two-hour sessions weekly would be the ideal regimen in my case. Happily for me, my care organisation saw fit to fund these so we've got a lot done.

He's a true gem, my trainer, because his professional insights are touched with ingenuity. Given what I had been through, I had convinced myself that one attribute to survive unscathed was my self-esteem. Well, my trainer quickly smashed this illusion, graphically demonstrating that my posture was all wrong, which led to my discovering, like Eliza Doolittle in *My Fair Lady*, that achieving good posture is surprisingly difficult. I had been standing with a tilt to the left, an obvious consequence of my head injuries, but also slumped over — reflecting the state of my self-confidence and the image of my self-worth. He even pointed out that I was walking around duck-footed, with my feet and toes facing incorrectly. This has proved very difficult to remedy but identifying that there is a problem is the first step on the road to any solution. The trainer has also been working on correcting my left-side neglect: better posture broadens my field of vision, so I notice more things in my way and bump into fewer of them.

With the trainer I can do things that previously were too risky, such as working with weights. These exercises help repair my hand so we are building muscle to burn core fat — but it is not very flattering because muscle weighs more than fat. The big thing my trainer has got me into is serious walking. The more you walk, the more fat you burn off so I have taken this up with a passion. Instead of the ritual '10,000 steps a day', I do kilometres. My trainer works on my breathing and general posture, so walking and talking both benefit. Admittedly, I have gone a bit crazy on walking but on the upside I am blessed to be living in a suburb with a good range of walking options. The only issues are finding time and having good weather to do it in.

Since my natural inclination is to be an intellectual couch potato, I also count myself lucky to have sustained a reasonable level of fitness throughout my life —derived not from any special focus on the goal of being fit but the natural outcome of the way I have chosen to live.

Health Care

Nobody chooses to interact with the health care system, and my dealings with it have been extensive. I consider myself lucky to be in Australia where the system more or less works, and where good outcomes are the norm.

First, we all benefit from Medicare, the universal health care that covers us every time we have to see a doctor. The benefits don't end there: we have the PBS, the pharmaceutical benefits scheme, which subsidises the cost of medications and makes them affordable. In other countries I've been in for a time, I couldn't afford all my medications. To complement this safety net, we have well-subsidised private health insurance.

So if you're thrown into the health care system you will find it looks after you: the big issue is knowing how to navigate it. This I have learnt to do well through constant access to it breeding familiarity. Those who fail to handle the system don't do well. Even in their case, though, the NDIS when doing the job it was set up to do is a great blessing. Every time my health has taken a serious turn our hospitals and medical staff have done an admirable job of getting me well enough to return to the business of life. I don't think I could ask more from the system than it provides me. Its only failing has been in not guaranteeing me continuous good health but I must take my share of the blame for that.

Taking A Break

After finishing high school, many people take a year off before moving on to the next stage of their life. This is called their gap year and I was no exception. To this day I look back on it as the most wonderful and worthwhile thing I ever did.

It set me up to progress in life. Alas, Covid has put stringent limits on what young people today can do in their gap year, but moving straight on to further education is also fraught with problems for these no-longer-children-but-not-quite-adults. A gap is a moment in which to pause and rest, to collect yourself and assess who and where you are. Such a moment paves the way for a critical step forward in personal development. It goes by different names but the value of it is just the same: some call it a sabbatical, others long-service leave or simply an extended holiday. In my experience, some people cannot go on with life unless they have this circuit-breaker.

In some ways my life has robbed me of the opportunity to recharge my batteries. How can you take a break from work when you don't work? So I have had to search for other methods of renewal. Turning myself into a fitness junkie gave me new understandings about my body and its relation to the world at large. I have definitely gained. Another more creative approach I have chosen is this writing project, which is very demanding but also affords great scope for personal investigation. I do hope it results in giving me a clearer perspective on myself and, yes, I do enjoy producing work that others consider valuable and useful.

Overriding My Instincts

The mind is often willing but the body is not always happy to go along with it. This conundrum comes in various forms and it is up to us to recognise it and overcome it. Getting the mind-body duality in balance can be a great intellectual task. But when we can manage this terrible balancing act the world sings with a deep baritone.

Too often for my liking, I end up being tone-deaf when the world sings, and this is much to my personal detriment. I first became acutely aware of this in my early sexual encounters but, with my disability and the ageing process at play, being aware of this conundrum has enabled me to pursue a better quality of life. As a young man I found on a number of occasions that women very much liked the idea and thought of being with me but when the intimate moment arose suddenly they were not up for it. In other words, their mind was willing but their body wasn't. Inevitably, this left me with a degree of confusion. To understand this disconnect further, I looked to examples of it in my own life and the perspective I gained thereby has helped me navigate the path I have travelled over the years.

As a younger man I was loath to miss out on any aspect of life. So I used to begrudge sleep because during that time I could be doing something else, couldn't I? This state of mind would often lead me to a point of exhaustion. A valuable lesson ultimately had to be learnt: how to match my willingness to do things with my ability to do them. There is wisdom in the saying you can't burn the candle at both ends, but my desire to do all that I could was ingrained in me and my view of myself. This approach to life was encouraged by my parents as I grew up. I was expected to exert myself to my full potential. In fact, it was frowned upon if I didn't manage to do things. I always saw this as a healthy thing. It meant I got things done and lived life to the full. Thanks, Mum and Dad.

The old freedom of action I had before my accident was gone, along with a large part of my brain. My thinking took a lot of time to adapt, to recognise that my new health status was like a series of bollards on the perimeter of a no-go zone. Learning to reconcile mental will with bodily capacity has been very difficult. It makes the task of daily life like walking on a tightrope and straining every sinew not to fall off. If I overbalance one way, I fall off deep into the abyss.

While I can think of a thousand things I should be doing, the reality is I cannot do so many of them merely for lack of energy. Tiring easily, I must juggle my day around my rest. If I don't, I'm cactus and a danger to myself. It won't do to get so knackered that I walk under a tram! The mind is very willing to be the powerhouse it once was, of course, but reality tells it to take a cold shower. It has taken time but I am now a good judge of what I can and cannot do. My belief system, which owes a lot to the Protestant work ethic, rebels against it. But even beliefs must bow to reality. So, although willingness to be productive is in my DNA, and the conviction remains that indolence is a crime, I must override my instincts if I am to manage my life reasonably well.

The Drink of Life

Our lives are brimful of lost moments. Covid and lockdowns have accentuated this. To many people's distress, things anticipated or longed for suddenly vanish as lockdowns or even just social distancing fall upon us. People have had to learn to deal with this, although they might not have been equipped to do so. For many, being deprived of the acts of life has created great anxiety.

For me it is a bit like water off a duck's back, after years rehearsing the art of dealing with lost opportunity. That is something that waltzes hand in hand with disability. With the advent of disability, wishes and aspirations for one's life that were previously held dear simply vanish. Zap, they're gone. This leaves the person fresh to disability forced to recalibrate their expectations of what is to come. What once seemed set in concrete has now been washed away like a sandcastle at high tide.

My life is a case in point. Before the accident I had plans and expectations of undertaking a wonderful tour of the world, seeing its greatest sights and enjoying the finest pleasures it had to offer. These plans and expectations evaporated overnight: they were no longer even the stuff of dreams. I learnt to accept this, painful though it was. More recently, a mate of mine took long-service leave and was about to do a tour of Europe. Then Covid swept in. With his fixed schedule in tatters, he had to recalibrate, so he focused on two other goals: he got himself fit and pursued an interest in jazz. He possessed the key aptitude for flexibility. Somehow he knew that in any storm the trees that survive are those that bend with the wind.

I have found the deferment of enjoyable activities makes them even sweeter, once they become possible down the track. Witness the joy many people have had on seeing once again the friends they couldn't see during lockdown.

And, as I am writing this, we are in lockdown again — so once again I peer over the barrier of deferred gratification to the jubilation and euphoria that will follow. If the glass is half full, take my advice and top it up whenever possible.

Body Image

Our body image affects who we are and how others see us — and it changes over time. Also, it influences our social being and, speaking for myself, one's mental health more than I would ever have imagined.

As a little boy I was just skin and bones, and proud of this as little boys are. Being active and busy from daylight till after dark kept me in shape — that fine thin shape — just as it exhausted my parents. They couldn't take me out shopping as I ran off in all directions. No ADHD as they call it today, just a normal little boy excited to be in the world. So I viewed myself and my body with quiet satisfaction, except on one point. I was always the smallest child in class — but even this fact didn't enter my consciousness much or detract from my wellbeing. And so I reached high school content with who I was. I just realised I was not cut out to be an athlete. My body wasn't made that way, and this I happily accepted. Then came my teenage years.

While the other boys shot up and filled out, I didn't. I accepted this in my usual relaxed manner but over the years without realising it I put on a few inches and in the end was tall enough to see over a crowd — and that satisfied me. While not actually tall, I was tall enough and this nurtured my self-esteem. Over the years I developed a strong persona and exuded a presence. You could see it in the way I walked and in how I held myself. When I entered a room, people took notice: this guy is not the shy and retiring type. Without wishing to appear conceited, it was the body and the mind people would respond to, so altogether I presented as, and felt like, a very collected package as a teenage boy should be.

Through my teenage years I considered myself a bit tubby so I wasn't happy to walk around shirtless, or even in a T-shirt. Not a good look, as they say. I realised I didn't carry a natural six-pack — the outline of my ribs was covered by a layer of flesh — and this hurt my ego a bit. So I wasn't exactly the spunk I would like to have been.

When I turned eighteen and headed off to Israel to study in the Machon (Zionist youth training regime), food was far from plentiful there and at the same time my sweet tooth subsided a bit. In no time at all, the flab I'd been carrying went and now I'd become what you might call a hot property. On finishing at the Machon it was off to a kibbutz to live and work. There I engaged in real physical labour. Before long I was fit and trim, both mentally and physically, even a bit light for my height. It's amazing what a bit of weight loss can do for you. Fortunately, I did not relapse for years afterwards, but I did still carry a residual roll of flesh, which always upset me.

By the time I started uni the full package had come together and, if I may say so in all modesty, I was an awesome and imposing sight. I had a great time at uni, both socially and intellectually, and this was reflected in my appearance. Clothes fitted me well and to some degree I was a snappy dresser. Looking back, I was at the top of my game and people responded to this accordingly.

Well, the accident turned my world upside down, and led to many a calibration and contortion until my body reached the condition it is in today. Every stage of life's journey leads me to where I am today, which I hope is standing tall and erect.

After six weeks in a coma I awoke with a very altered body. This gave me a terrible shock and I reacted badly. Any paunch I had before the accident had been stripped from me. I was now back to just flesh and bones — a shadow of my former self. To make matters worse, I was not counselled well. Somehow I got it into my mind that I was on the verge of becoming anorexic and the only way to save my life was to put on weight. (To this day I suffer from this belief.)

Determined to embark on the ultimate chocolate binge, I put out the word that any visitor was to come with a Mars bar for me and got upset with people who turned up without one. As you can guess, the binge — combined with being bedridden — brought the kilos back on in a substantial way, adding a rotund belly to my frame which I carry to this day. This has done significant damage to my self-image and self-respect over the years, with a long train of consequences.

My mind kept insisting that my new body was not *me*, and the worst of all things was and is that clothes would no longer fit me. I was not the first or last person to discover that a tummy is a lot easier to put on than take off. I have reduced it to some degree but never been able to get rid of it and never reduced it enough to satisfy me. What upsets me most is that I can't get pants that fit properly: they always slide down and this is most uncomfortable and embarrassing. I do a lot better in shorts than pants but you can't wear shorts all year long.

I have already written about how the way people speak to you and react to you affects your feelings, and this applies to self-image as well. This has been brought home to me dramatically in a number of ways since my accident. We often hear on the news of young children whose self-image has been so compromised, for whatever reason, that they end up committing suicide.

Take it from me, people can be awfully rude, even malicious: they tend not to care about your self-image, only their own. There are even low-quality types out there who boost their self-image by undermining yours. As they say, there is a special place for those people — hell. People will happily and carelessly point out that you have a stomach — as if I didn't already know. Do the idiots think I carry it by choice? They are just revealing their own crass stupidity. The endless stream of pregnancy jokes is not in the least humorous and certainly not designed to help me. Rather, I see these jests as utterances used to cover people's fears about themselves. I have not allowed these cruel onslaughts to distort the perception I have of myself. My body type just happens to be on the large side: it takes all types to make the world.

The Longest Journey

The longest journey begins with the first step, as Chairman Mao once wrote. I have been walking — step after step after step — for as long as I can recall. It has never bothered me having to walk from one point to another.

I wasn't driven to school: I walked there and back, though admittedly in my case it wasn't too far. But (one way at least) it was uphill! If I went around to see my mates, my feet would carry me there. Walking gave me freedom and independence. I enjoyed it — but, oddly enough, bushwalking and orienteering held no appeal. As I grew into my teens, I would walk on the streets on Saturday nights with my mates, either to visit someone or to head off to parties. Since none of us was old enough to drive, to us it was a natural thing to do. So you could say walking was ingrained in my being.

Then came my accident, and I could no longer drive, so walking became even more important than it had been. Whether it was visiting the chemist's, or shopping at the supermarket, if I were to be capable of doing anything, I would have to get about on foot. After coming out of my coma, I had to relearn to walk

— not that that took very long. Soon I was off and running, you might say! Decades later, walking remains an integral part of my daily routine. Far from being a drag on my time, it offers the perfect opportunity to sort out my thoughts. Living not far from Albert Park Lake, for years I daydreamed of walking there and around it. An elderly neighbour of mine was a regular on that circuit. This man is a serious walker. I will never be a touch on him.

When I began working out at a gym under the guidance of a personal trainer, he explained that walking was actually the best way to burn off fat but to get real benefit out of it you need to walk for a decent period of time. This prompted me to turn my lake-circuit walking dream into a reality, and I have got great enjoyment out of it. It is such a lovely stroll and I reward myself with a coffee at a café that offers a wonderful vista across the water in a world-class location.

Before long, the trainer had talked me into buying a pedometer so that I count out the proverbial '10,000 steps a day'. Quickly discovering that this exercise was a bit too easy, I soon turned 10,000 steps into ten kilometres a day. That, too, is not such a difficult feat: I just have to find the time to do the walking. Not too many days had passed before I noticed I was doing sixty or more kilometres a week.

Adding my weekly totals together, I have now covered a tremendous distance, and am determined to keep this up. Contrary to what people who have never followed the route might think, the hours spent walking around this lake are anything but tedious. En route, you can watch swans do ballet; and my neighbour will come back from his outing having counted the different bird species he has seen that day. He is what's called a twitcher.

Delightful as it is, the lake is not my only destination. I also walk down to the beach and along it — a relaxing stroll. But sometimes the pavement is a little crowded for my liking, and then it is best avoided as I don't want to be walking into things. My vision problem (technically left-side neglect) puts me at risk of doing this. But improved posture, which my trainer has been working on, has reduced the risk to some degree since following his instructions has enhanced my field of vision.

You would be right to say that for me walking has become a passion and obsession. My obsessive-compulsive personality, which accentuates a tendency to perseveration, has found an outlet in this typical human act. I can honestly say I've covered a lot of ground, both figuratively and literally — but it's not something you can do every day. I won't trudge around the lake if it's too wet or windy: there is sense in being risk-averse. But, given a fine or benignly cloudy day, you will find me on the well-worn trail. Afforded plenty of thinking time, I regard my walks as not only physically therapeutic but good for my mental health.

Walking is a great way to see the world around you and how people behave when they are at their most unselfconscious. To glide along the waterside taking in the joys of nature has taken walking beyond the status of a necessary activity to being a linchpin of my existence. At times my walking self is so blissfully happy that I feel I could easily keep going and end up walking around

Australia — though even I am realistic enough to admit that will take a bit of time. Such is life.

Back to the axiom that the longest journey starts with the first step. This is a wonderful way to approach the world at large. To achieve anything we need to propel ourselves into motion from a standing start. That first step is not always easy to take but I feel it is the only way that I can get anywhere. As I've told you, all I have to do is put my best foot forward (having worked out which one that is). Sometimes in my life I have had to lift my foot and branch out in a new direction. I won't be at ease with myself until I have done that.

Yes, walking is a good metaphor for the act of living. It is far better to step through life than sleep through it or be propelled along in a wheelchair. My issue here is simple: to find people with whom I can walk forward. Acting on this philosophy, I have stepped forward and sought out a new social base. I have seized the opportunity presented by new therapies whenever the chance has arisen. I didn't just walk, I jumped at the prospect of speech therapy. The same applies to recruiting a personal trainer. I will never settle for being a lesser person than I can be.

Striding through life on two legs sets us apart from other animals and represents the way that I live life. Sometimes we have to summon a special effort and call on reserves of energy but it is a worthwhile object.

The Cone of Silence

At some point we all end up in the dentist's chair. I end up there far too often. A combination of factors has given me poor teeth and this has been exacerbated by my accident. Once you're propped up in the dentist chair you are totally disempowered and all control is handed over to the dentist. It is they who call the shots and all control rests in their hands. So sitting there is like being in the proverbial cone of silence. You are not allowed to speak. For someone like me, that is the worst of all situations. Inevitably you get an itchy nose. You can't scratch and you just need to sit there and suffer it as well as you can. What magnifies this discomfort is my dentist who is worth talking to. Conversation with him is not just polite small talk. So my mind is rushing with conversation but there is no outlet for it. To me this is a form of torture. So I only enter the dentists chair if there is real need. Needles and other things are not an issue for me. The real pain is being shoved into the cone of silence

My dentist is gentle and deft of hand. He is very skilled and causes little pain — full credit to him. In that regard, a visit there is not so bad, I can cope. One thing I recognise — I am lucky to have access to a dentist at all. In many parts of Melbourne this is a forlorn dream. If in great need, people have to go to the dental hospital and suffer in agony. Being thrown into the cone of silence is another dimension for them, one that they would endure if they had the opportunity. So I should count my good fortune, not whinge. But as I travel through life it is critical I understand the treatments I have and what they do to me. By comprehending this, I can understand myself and my general predicament. To my dentist I say, whilst the cone is lifted and I am allowed to speak — many thanks for all you have done for me over the years.

Isolation

We are living through groundbreaking days. Hardly anyone alive has seen anything like this before. This makes it hard to digest, but digest it we must. Somehow we have to reconcile our expectations with our lived reality — what is going on around us. Our perspective was shaped by what much of the world was going through as earlier Australia had few Covid cases. In many other places it has been a serious public emergency. Seeing the impact elsewhere, we didn't want it to be replicated here so severe measures were imposed. These measures had various serious implications for the way we live our lives — not all bad, I feel. As we begin to emerge from this great disruption to our lives, I feel it is time to reflect. As I am trained in reflective history, I hope to pull a few of these threads together and observe in real time what has gone on all around me.

Two of the main repercussions Covid has had on us are isolation and quarantine. Isolation happens to be a very strong feature of the way people live in the modern world. We had already found various ways of dealing with it — but this period of extended isolation was abrupt and not something that you can come to terms with easily. My circumstances having given me a degree of insight into how to live with isolation, I can readily relate to the sudden shock that heavy-duty isolation imposes on you.

Imagine one day all your social discourse, your connection with the world, just vanished. You have no choice, your daily routines are shattered, and now you are left to find ways to deal with it. This happened to me three and a half decades ago. Waking from my coma, I felt the full force of my isolation. Like my contemporaries today, I had to come to grips with a new and somewhat grim world — and fast. I am familiar with this situation:it cuts to the core and if you are not careful it can burn and destroy. So people have to be creative and learn how to cope from day one. If isolation is an abyss, quarantine is one step further into the abyss. It is as if you have been thrown in jail. Left to your own devices, you know that survival depends on your mental strength. You also know that not everyone possesses that strength of mind; not everyone is going to make it through. My heart goes out to these people: they are where they are through no fault of their own. Dumb luck has brought them there. It need not lead to a dire outcome. Look at great literature: some wonderful works have been written in incarceration — but it takes an exceptional person to do it.

So, what is isolation? Very simply, the separation of you from everything to be found outside your front door — other people, shopping, life in general. Obtaining food is obviously very important. For the tech-savvy younger generation, this needn't be an insuperable difficulty: they can order everything online. In large part, this is how Wuhan survived. But, for older people who are not tech-savvy, getting enough to eat, to stay alive, can be a real problem. One solution is Meals on Wheels but in Melbourne the supply was overwhelmed by demand. The advantage of this service, to those it does reach, is that it regularly enables deliverers to check up on people's wellbeing.

At its very core, isolation is a question of power: the very first thing it does is take away your power over yourself, your free will. No longer can you do as you wish when you wish to do it. The world has been determined for you and is out of your control. The challenge, within the confines of your own home, is not to let it rule you. To the extent you can do so, you must resist its force. My personal objection to drugs and addiction is based on the same principle: what you do and how you live your life must be under your control. Master your domain; don't let your conditions determine who you are; determine your conditions instead. Smoking had me in its grips for many years but I am very glad I took control of it and rid myself of the evil it was doing to me. I assume we all want to be people with free will and control over our lives so it is up to us to emerge from the period of bondage with our spirits and that all-important sense of self unimpaired. In lockdown it is helpful to remain as active as possible, physically and mentally, so as not to sink into oblivion.

Daily routine must be established so that you don't get swept away by the swirling torrents and undertow. Emotional instability must not be allowed to envelop you — that way, come to the worst, lies suicide. This occurs when an individual can no longer see a way out. I have not been there so I have an uncomprehending here. For me, there is always a path to a better world and sometimes you must forge it yourself out of whatever materials come to hand. When events threatened me with oblivion, I needed not just to keep up with the flow of life, which was now taking me in a radically different direction, but to find some joy in what I was doing. Searing experiences of this type lead one to appreciate the simple things and to embrace the small but good things that life has to offer.

A clear-eyed perspective helps. When it comes to Covid isolation, remind yourself: *in this time I am not alone. There are many others like me who have to travel down this road*. Well, the first time I confronted isolation I did it all alone. There was no one to accompany me on the path to oblivion. Many find their spirit refreshed because, faced with adversity, they begin to communicate from the heart with the person they live with. This can lead to great personal enrichment. But I live alone, deprived of any opportunity to engage in such joys. Many others take the easy way out and binge on mind-numbing Netflix. Yes, modernity provides us with multiple ways of circumventing the solitude of isolation: Skype, FaceTime, WhatsApp — all linking us to the wider world. More active types try to turn hardship to their advantage by using this time to get fit. During people's lockdown exercise hours, what do they see? A posse of poor over-walked dogs out on the streets and people doing themselves irreparable damage jogging. Plus you must be careful not to get run down by cyclists, so if some bizarre good can come out of all this it may be that those minds not overcome by the woes of prolonged confinement are actually made more vigorous and alert by the need to exercise.

So, now I am isolated in this brave new world, how am I to fill my days? How can I know what will be the right path to take? I was confronted with the same doubts and uncertainties early on in my recovery, and still to a degree later on. From the outset I decided I had to have faith in my decision-making process, to be confident that what I determined must be the course to follow would be correct for me to do. I knew that in the end I would live or die by the decisions I took, but dwelling on that fact would only increase the burden. I wanted to respond in the way I would have done before my accident: would it be possible, I wondered, to find and retrieve my true natural self? As I still saw myself in that mould I must not let the label and realities of disability take hold of me and determine who I was. So many years later, this battle goes on. I am me, not what others say I am. This is much the same battle an addict of any sort faces, much the same battle anyone facing a long period of lockdown must wage. Thrust into this void as so many have recently been, they need to dig deep within themselves to discover who they are. Fortunately for me, I had become well acquainted with my core self during that earlier battle. Knowing yourself is one thing; recognising the limitations your post-accident body imposes on your activities is the other half of the battle. One activity I could return to and did — very time-consuming, when for once that was a good thing because I had so much time on my hands — was reading. This glass was more than half full, and I grasped it with open arms, telling myself: *Now I have the opportunity to read things I have never previously had time for. I shall use my isolation as a bonus and, yes, relish it.*

Here my policy is: take what you know and turn it to your advantage. Some reading habits I persisted with. There are certain genres I won't touch: science fiction and crime novels, for example. I can't bear these types of book: I would rather try to digest astrophysics, as I did.

Reading took up a good portion of the day: then it was time to look after the body. I had always done some exercise but not large amounts — you would not call me a fitness fanatic. My favourite pre-accident exercise — partying, even flirting — was off the agenda now, but I channelled the will to be fitter and healthier so determinedly that before too long I was. Working on my fitness would take up a large part of my day and still does. The void of hours, of purpose itself, cries out to be filled. This slots in well with my view of life – that it is a task and we must do it well.

Another activity I chose to fill the void – and one I enjoy inordinately – is gardening. It doesn't take up so much time but lends a continuous thread to my day and, as the seasons come and go, a sublime sense of continuity to my existence. As a wise friend who is a well-known gardener explained to me, the garden should only take half an hour a day, maximum. If you are doing more than that with it, you are just wasting your time. My personal battle with isolation from the get-go has been significantly magnified by people who gave up on me after the accident. At times this has cut deep and it has been very hard not to become bitter and angry about it, and even aggressively rude. I do my best to avoid these responses. I am naturally gregarious: I thrive on human interaction, but as much as participating in it I love to watch and listen as people go about their lives. I soon learnt that I could no longer indulge myself in this activity as I used to do. With my social mobility restricted, it cut me to the quick to find that people no longer sought me out to join in their activities. Now, instead of often being the instigator of social engagement, I found myself forced to beg for company. The indignity stemmed from the unavoidable realisation that people who used to include you in their plans suddenly had no space for you in their lives. It took me a while to realise that complaining or requesting people include you in their activities was demeaning. Constant rejection does nothing for your self-esteem and the soul; all it does is amplify one's sense of aloneness. Eventually I reached the point where I decided if certain people didn't bother to welcome me into their busy social round I would consign them to what I call the 'graveyard of life'. Should I come across them socially I would give them short shrift — and I did., for the sake of my self-respect.

In time I found my isolation had another consequence in my attitude to society. If somebody had been kind and good to me for a period, I would expect this to continue. Then when it stopped I would be left in a mess and wonder what had gone awry. Eventually, the way I came to see it, the fact someone had been good to me once did not elevate them to a higher position of worth than if they had treated me poorly all along. The people I treat well and value are those who have sustained contact with me, and remained considerate of me, over the long haul.

Those who are new to the impact of isolation, take note: certain times of day are harder than others. Commuting can be tough. Denied the stimulation of activities that occupy your mind at other times of the day, you don't have the diversion of phone calls or emails while you keep your eyes on the road. If, as I do, you believe time ought to be used productively, there is almost something criminal about passing the hours with little to show for it.

One thing that accentuates isolation is my speech. At times I can be hard to follow and, as some people cannot be bothered to make the effort to deal with that, they don't bother with me. You might think they're being slothful (I definitely do), but I cannot do much about that. I recognise that some people automatically 'tune out' certain accents — I am guilty of this myself sometimes — but isolation can also have the opposite effect of increasing tolerance. I have found myself hyper-aware of other people's isolation in the light of my own, Moved by their suffering, I want to be there for these people, to add a little something to their world. Sometimes I act on this impulse, doing a good turn like regularly ringing an old lady in an aged-care home to relieve her sense of isolation. If I were a better person, I would visit her in person more often. But I feel I have no right to criticise others' behaviour if my own is not exemplary. So you could say that in this way my condition has made me a better person. But this ethos also stems from the way my parents brought me up.

Looking after my own mental health is a priority. Sitting home alone all day every day, engaging with no one, is soul-destroying. So I make a point of ensuring that I keep up social contact with someone every weekend. This is not always easy to do but it is vitally important. I guess my various therapists and caregivers provide social contact to a degree and, as mentioned before, communications technology is there to reduce isolation — Zoom being the latest weapon in my arsenal — but I do find there's one snag to that 'solution'. You need to be in front of a device at the same time as another person, and if that other person doesn't have, or know how to use, the device in question, it might as well not exist. I have found that watching children can be illuminating. You see some who can occupy themselves without a care: they are always busy, content with their own company; while others need to be entertained all the time. So it is with adults. Some of them love nothing better than to have time on their hands. They actually relish isolation and, for them, Covid has been a godsend. For better or worse, I'm not that kind of person myself. I need some stimulus to keep my mind ticking over: else it idles and atrophies.

When Covid arrived I was more than ready to deal with it. But, the way I live, it has had no great impact on me. It's just that my already quiet social life has become a touch quieter and getting to and from places, with public transport and taxi travel both compromising my health, I rely more on lifts than I did, and would have spent more time at home than before even if lockdowns had given me no choice.

Six

disABILITY

All Is Not Lost

We lose all manner of things in life, more than I have space to list here. It's how one deals with loss that counts. Where possible, I try to turn a negative into a positive. This cannot be done all the time — the loss of one's parents being the most harrowing example — but it can be done enough of the time to make the aim worthwhile.

If I lose something, I say to myself, 'David, relax, you will be happy when you find it. No need to get upset.' Usually I can say 'No worries, it can be replaced.' Sadly, this is not the case with abilities: some capacities, when lost, can never be recovered. Then true wisdom takes the form of acceptance, making do. There is nothing to be gained by stressing. On occasion I have lost things in my house that turned up years later — and their rediscovery was pure delight. So, even though it is annoying to lose things, there can be joy and even satisfaction in what follows.

For example, take learning new capabilities to which I had previously given no thought. The sour side of disability consists in those things that cannot be replaced or regained because the loss is permanent. The key to happiness is learning to live without the ability that will not return.

Here a key word is 'compensate'. Quite often you can substitute a new way of doing something you cannot do in the old way. I lost the ability to handle a knife and fork so now I've retrained my right hand to do everything that's required. I've enjoyed an increase in dexterity, both literally and figuratively.

My accident blunted the sharpness of my mind: its fine-tuning began to drop away, if you will. I feared this, and that years of learning would be laid waste. I had to do something about it: this was something too important to lose forever. Using techniques that had assisted me in the past, I rekindled my passion for reading, to increase my knowledge and regain mental acuity. Reading also helped me to counteract another lost aspect of my faculties — my attention span. To complement this I watched large amounts of TV. This I combined with neurogenesis, the growth of new nerve tissue, which is hastened by building new brain pathways through exercise. Much has been achieved through these workarounds but some abilities still fall short of the desired levels, such as the use of my left hand. But, with the help of my hand physio, I will keep on trying to improve.

Whenever something is lost, it will take time and some consideration to comprehend the ramifications. But over time new potentials are created. I lost the social world that once existed for me, but via the detour my life was forced to take I have been led to find a better one, a true social world. In so doing I dispensed with the shallowness of my earlier years. As the great saying goes: two steps forward, one step back. All is not lost. As I fight for a better life, I am not a loser: I feel I gain.

Just Because

Just because I am disabled in some ways, that does not mean I am disabled in others. To treat me as more disabled than I am diminishes me. This is something I go on about a bit, simply because it cuts to the bone. As it is, I suffer enough: to make me suffer more is an ignoble act. With my disability there is a battle for self-respect and self-esteem. So anybody who does something to compromise that is wilfully hurting me. Yes, I accept that some people do this unintentionally but, whether deliberate or not, it inflicts pain on me.

In this situation I feel I must stand up for myself. Personally, my intention is to reach beyond my disability, to be or become a good and decent person. This is my goal, flawed as I am. I have always prided myself on the quality and development of my intelligence. So, when I am treated as a fool or an idiot, outrage is a natural reaction.

There are those whose behaviour works in the opposite direction, helping me rise above the flaws that inhibit me. Bless these kind souls, people who see what is in me and encourage its full expression. One such person was my old professor from university, who taught me much at that time and even more afterwards. He had great faith in my abilities and encouraged me to write. He would be most pleased with my current project. His reminder to me, still ringing in my ears — *If there is an empty page in front of you, it must be filled.* Every time I am treated as an incapacitated moron I grind my teeth and out comes a demand born of self-assertion: 'I am not like that. Give me a chance.'

To those people who help me rise above my disabilities and be the person I would like to be I record my undying gratitude — to my speech therapist, my hand physio and my personal trainer. I thank each of you for your assistance and for treating me as I ought to be treated. The battle is never easy but it is winnable if I'm well treated. Put it another way: what have I done to deserve anyone's disrespect?

Therapies

By nature I am a very independent person, and also a bit stubborn. I like to be able to do things myself, with no one telling me what to do or assisting me. But due to my condition I have had to learn to moderate these tendencies and learn to behave sometimes in conflict with my own nature. Not only have I had to learn how to accept help but even to ask for it if needed. It has been a very hard thing to swallow my pride and, at times, my self-esteem so that I can progress on the journey to be a better me.

One of the axioms I live by is that I don't want to be a lesser person than I can be. To attain this goal I have had to partake in a wide range of therapies imposed on me by others. This has been a bumpy road to travel, and I will be on it till my last breath, as I doubt that I can ever fully be what I aspire to be. Getting as close as I can will have to be the measure of my success.

Straight after my accident I threw out any social worker they assigned to me. I had nothing but disgust and disdain for these middle-class meddlers. The sort of 'help' they offered was the last thing I wanted. To a degree my instinctive reaction was right; though on reflection I think some help from a knowledgeable person could have been useful. In my opinion the problem with the profession is the people who staff it. They are so sure they know what's best for you that if you submitted to their every direction you would end up living a life of complete dependence – the exact opposite of my goal.

Now I am more selective, not rejecting them entirely. Stepping up to the plate and applying myself to useful therapies is how it should be done, even though this can be very demanding. In fact, I have found that the various therapies consolidate each other's worth. Therapies, rightly regarded, not only enable me to live my life in a better way but also integrate me into the social swing of things, enabling me to interact with the outside world. Take, for example, home help in looking after my place: at first I resisted it. I felt it hurt my pride to admit that I wasn't able to look after my home as I should. Eventually I gave in — and now I think it's wonderful that someone can come in and be trusted to do those things well that otherwise would get done badly or not at all. Plus, it is important that I live in a clean, hygienic environment and this does not detract from my pride but adds to it. I was lucky to obtain such a service but it took time to sort out. Originally, the home help was provided via my local council but it was not up to scratch. Now it's provided through the NDIS and, after some fine-tuning, the system is running like a well-oiled machine.

During the act of therapy I am constantly asked to do things I have difficulty doing, but that is the point of the exercise. Ultimately, in most cases, I will be able to do what is needed without problems but when I come up against these barriers for the first time I get flustered and don't perform as well as I should. My initial recoil from the set task has me feeling that my inability to master it is demeaning. But walk through this valley of personal humiliation I must if I want to become the person I would like to be.

My likely reaction, of course, is factored into the equation by the therapist, who must possess great sensitivity to the client's emotional state. Not all therapists are aware of, or up to, this component of their duties. This I have to understand and accept. At the same time, a good therapist will sometimes need to be strict, even tough on me, if I am to make progress. I do recognise that at times I am not the easiest person to work with. This can be due to my disabilities compounding the nature of my complex personality.

I have been very fortunate to find one therapist who tries to link in and harmonise all the therapies I am undergoing: this is my personal trainer, who was gifted by the person in charge of me at Jewish Care, the community care network that was looking after me for some time. For that act I am very grateful. He designs my training to focus on my weaknesses. There is a lot of much needed work on my hand. As well as a healthy concentration on posture and breathing, this significantly assists my speech, not just the quality of my walking. My trainer has put hours into 'repacking' my posture so that I present as I should. The exercises he orders to make my hand stronger and more supple tie in well with the work of my hand physio. Working on my shoulder also has benefits for my hand movement.

Whatever effort a therapist puts into my exercise regime, I need to be on my game to make the most of it. I cannot be distracted or mentally not there. Maintaining focus is not always easy. Sometimes I'm simply not in the mood. I need to see the value in it to be motivated. Also it helps if I like the person I am working with; it's a waste of time for both of us if the person turns me off in some way.

So therapy is a two-way street: success with it depends on the skill level of the therapist and the receptivity of the patient. Therapy doesn't stop at the therapist's door. For it to be of any value at all what is done in the room must be carried through to the act of daily life. After a long and not always patient struggle I am very thankful for what I receive and thank the NDIS for making it all possible. Without it my quality of life would be much poorer.

Let Me Ask

One of the hardest aspects of disability is losing the capacity to do things. This hurts: it cuts to the very core of my being. When someone infringes in this space it is as if they are inflicting a personal injury on me. I have enough of them to be going on with, thank you very much.

This brings me to a sore point that even well-meaning people in my orbit often fail to understand. Often the degree of my incapacity to do something is not great and, given time, I will find — or have already found — a way to get around it. To survive I need to be able to do things for myself. I find myself often put in a situation where, without my asking, people do things for me. They feel they are helping and don't understand when I get angry and push them away. Even in my calmer moments I have a firm message for them. Please don't compromise my limited independence. By doing that you undermine my mental health and in fact set me back by stopping me from learning to do things myself. I am not a shy person: should I need assistance I am capable of asking. Don't just assume I can't do things and belittle me. My ego is like a riverbank in the outback – it can do without further erosion.

Often I find this is an expression of a power game where the other side takes power off me, trying to make me dependent on them. Taking my limited power from me I find to be an unkind act. As my personal space is one of the few things I have left to me,

I guard it zealously. To add indignity to debilitation is the same as adding insult to injury.

DISabling

There are some things I cannot do or find difficult — but to be disabled further by the mindset of others upsets me and makes life more difficult, an experience I call disabling. It can be accidental or intentional: when it is intended I consider this a very low act. Why would anyone take satisfaction in making a lesser person of a fellow human being? There is evil in that act.

More often than not, the disabling is an unintended outcome of a certain course of action, and it often relates to a person's speech disability. Repeated incomprehension of what someone is saying — repeatedly asking them to repeat themselves — is very disabling. See it from where I sit: the person I am trying to reach is telling me that I am not up to scratch and cannot communicate as I should or as an able-bodied person would. Not only do I now feel a lesser person but I feel excluded from being part of the functioning world. I do see it from the other side: the listener is having problems understanding what I am saying and they would *like* to understand. The critical point here, though, is the way the disabled person gets treated. In this standoff, are they treated like an idiot with an intellectual disability or just someone having a bit of trouble getting out what they have to say? The way the uncomprehending listener responds will amount to one of two things: an act of empowerment or of disempowerment. The listener can choose to treat you well and with compassion or step on who you are and belittle you.

I will never accept that people should be made to feel anything less than human. Whenever they are, it offends my politics and ethics. People should be treated well and with value unless they have proved themselves unworthy of such treatment. All the disabled person asks for is to be treated with respect and equality, on a par with other people wherever possible. Well-intentioned acts can be very disabling. The pain runs deep. How does this come about? People like to do things for me, assuming I can't do them. They are saying very loudly, if not using the actual words, 'David, you're not up to scratch.' In the act of doing something to spare me the effort, people disable me in ways the accident never succeeded in doing. Opening a sugar stick for me without my having asked someone to do it gets me nowhere. This is something I need to do myself. If I am going out for a coffee, shutting my car door gets me nowhere: it might require some effort but I can do it. These are particular instances: the general rule is that if you do something for me when I haven't asked for your assistance, you are pushing me backwards into the world of the disabled. This is a hindrance and, by the way, completely unnecessary. You needn't worry: I have no false pride. If I need help, I am only too happy to ask for it.

More instances of avoidable disablement: to ask someone in the street a question and be fobbed off as a less-than-adequate person is disabling. For a waiter in a café not to understand me is problematic. For someone in an information or ticket booth to look at me in consternation because they can't follow what I am saying is disabling. All this occurs and the responsibility for handling it lies with the disabled person. Nobody wants to be treated as a second-class citizen or a second-rate human. Then, when some well-intentioned body butts in and speaks — unsolicited — on my behalf it is disabling in the extreme and, in a word, humiliating.

Finally, our health condition can disable us: that is, it can stop us living life as we would choose. But the limitations imposed on us by our state of health should be the beginning and end of any loss of *ableness*. So my final plea is directed to others with a disability, whatever its nature. We are participants who, up to a point, can determine how disabled we are. I don't want my disability to define who I am and what I can do. I mark the boundaries beyond which it must not step. I will master my condition and must not let my condition master me. In day-to-day life I now recommend you commit yourself to a suite of therapies that are right for you and make the most of them. You are playing a serious game, but you don't have to obey the rules set by those on the sidelines. I understand that I start on an uneven playing field but woe betide anyone who in any way makes the game harder to win, success in it harder to attain.

Disability Never Leaves You

Once you have a disability, it never leaves you. You never wake up one morning to find it's gone. The difference between a disability and a bad smell is that eventually the bad smell goes away. The only choice open to me is to learn to live with it.

A useful first step is to recognise that disability is disempowering and that the struggle to restore power will be an ongoing one. Fight to master your disability; do not let it dominate you. As I see it, this is a fight for independence and self-respect. My stance is that I must not allow my disability (which is what the world convinces me I cannot do) to disable me (— a fusion of strengths combined in the person I remain). If possible I aim to turn the tables and seek for my disability to *enable* me. One avenue that takes me in this direction is to focus on the time my disability gives me to consider the right way to treat people. This way I can use disability to become the person I want to be. The spur my disability has given to making me a fitness fanatic is another example of its power to enable me.

The workarounds I have engineered to overcome my inability to use a knife and fork and the repercussions of that missing nerve in my lip are proof of disability's power in motivating me to relearn skills. So I get very pissed off and offended when people point out to me that I literally cannot do something. Hey, it's not as though I can forget it! To conquer a disability takes unremitting toil, 24/7. It's exhausting and I would love a break but sadly there never will be one. But now you know the upside of that.

DISempowerment

It is obvious that once you don't have full command of yourself you lose a high degree of control over your circumstances and hence become disempowered. It is totally demeaning to need others to do tasks for you that you think you should be able to do yourself. So, to put it figuratively, you're behind the eight ball in the struggle to reach your goal: becoming, as you once were, an empowered person with integrity. And one very sad thing I have observed is the reality that most people prefer to disempower you — and one of the reasons they do so stems from their own deficiencies.

A related discovery that lived reality has taught me is that disability is about power relations. It helps to be aware when someone is using your disability to empower themselves. This happens all the time, most often not as a deliberate thing but when it is done deliberately I consider this the lowest of the low. You would be amazed the depths that some people will sink to for their own advantage: I no longer am.

Voice is one common way that people use to dominate you. If speech between any two people fails to serve the purpose of genuine communication, a healthy power relationship between people is disrupted. It is common for people to hear an altered intonation and shut off completely. This occurs with both familiar and unfamiliar people. If you ask a person in the street for some assistance and they treat you as if you were a drug addict, this belittles you and is disempowering. It may occur that you are treated less than OK in a shop or a café — or even at an information desk of all places! — and in my experience the dismissive or impatient response can end up making your speech even worse.

As soon as someone hears your voice is distorted in some way, they alter the way in which they speak to you. This I consider theft. It means they are not treating you with the full respect any person deserves — in other words, robbing you not just of the empowerment that speech confers on you but of your whole public persona. Constant belittling is exhausting in the extreme and — I would argue — further disables you. Speech is a two-way street: it can be used to disempower but also to empower — even if it is distorted. It is all about the ebb and flow of communication. If we have something worth saying, then the listener will often make an effort and the speaker — even with distorted diction — can have a commanding presence. For a moment, consider Martin Luther King if he had spoken with a stutter. People would have listened because of what he said no matter how it was delivered.

So if you have a message to get across and make some effort, you are far from powerless, tiring though it can be. Even so, no matter how good you are at the mastery of conversation it is very easy for the person you are trying to communicate with to take control of the situation. I would say more often than not the disabled person is at a disadvantage and this is used against them. In this case, for that person awareness is their best weapon of choice. If they understand the power plays at work they can seize the initiative and achieve their purpose, whether it be something as simple as ordering a coffee or the more complex task of having a satisfying conversation.

The disabled are always at a disadvantage because they are not in full command of what is going on. Or rather they are not in as much command of the power flow as they could be. One thing that really gets up my nose is when people choose to disempower you in order to make them feel better about themselves. As far as I am concerned I have enough problems and am not willing to take on more because the other person is lacking in some way. The recurrence of such demeaning encounters makes the café or restaurant a place fraught with danger. Instead of allowing you to choose or speak for yourself the other party speaks and decides for you as if you were not capable of doing so. They feel stronger but at the expense of your dignity and making you weaker. Dignity is something worth fighting for, else you will find the person opposite you oozing delight as they order the worst things for you and sitting there with mirth while you eat them.

Controlling how you get about, at what pace and where you go is another form of disempowerment. Taking over, or failing to understand your preferences, is a common way in which people steal power from you. People who place demands on how you get about are using their strength to take possession of you. Some people who see you have a taxi concession card expect you to take taxis everywhere, but they forget a few things. Even half-price taxis are not so cheap, and the actual act of getting a cab is far from easy. I have found from my place it is not so hard to get a taxi but getting one home is often very difficult. I prefer not to overuse my taxi card. Many cabbies scare me; far too many are not good drivers and getting across town with these jokers can be very stressful. With my mobility compromised I can't pop in and out of places as I once did. You may want to go somewhere and somebody offers you a lift. Often they have a hold over you, forcing you to go at the speed they fancy.

One important area where power is exerted is the realm of food: any small child will tell you that. Making food decisions in your own right is an act of control over the world in which you live. Many a parent has battled long and hard over this so if you go out to a café or restaurant and someone is telling you what you can and cannot eat because of your size or shape, that is deeply demeaning. At a café when someone is encouraging you to eat a cake or something that is not good for you, they may wish to keep you in the state you are or they may feel more powerful by not indulging themselves. When a disabled and an able person are playing this game, the playing field is never on the level. So it behoves the disabled to be aware of what is going on and the part they are playing in the game. Much easier said than done, of course, but being aware that all dialogue involves an exchange of power is a good starting point. Let's face it: nobody wants to be the eternal loser in these games.

G & D

G and D, which stands for guts and determination, is considered a highly desirable attribute, and is the ultimate praise given for a top-level footballer. I feel this virtue is not confined to sport but an essential feature of a quality life. In my opinion the G could equally stand for grit. G and d has the ability to propel a life forward: it has mine. I have met people who feel that what propels them forward is not g and d but g and t — that is, gin and tonic. I am not of their persuasion, though. My head is fogged enough: I like to try keeping it as clear as possible.

On reflection I feel it takes guts to determine what actions you need to take; and determination to carry those actions through to their completion regardless of the obstacles you must confront along the way. To do this requires focus and persistence: the two are inextricably linked. I do consider myself lucky that my natural personality inclines me to g and d, plus in an obscure way my brain damage has come to the party. If things must be done I like to get a move on and do them.

One of my challenges is create some balance in the way I approach matters. This is easier said than done. Once I embark on something I want to make sure I get to the end of it. I freely admit this determination to see things through may be because of my obsessive-compulsive personality — but also that determination can morph into bloody-mindedness. This is compounded by an aspect of my brain damage that I mention elsewhere — perseverance, which means I latch onto things, ideas or activities, and then cannot let them go.

I have come to accept that g and d isn't all it takes: I will never manage everything. But what I do give g and d credit for is ensuring that, whatever I do, I will always give it my best shot.

The Voice

When I was younger there was a popular song called '*The Voice*'.* Not that I paid much attention to it. I didn't like the singer or the music, so I just put it aside. Since then this song has been immersed in Australian popular culture and is still often heard, thirty-five years on. It is now the anthem for the Aboriginal and Torres Strait Islander Voice to Parliament to which I say — sing it loud and sing it strong and good on Johnny for belting it out in such a cause and one that I share wholeheartedly. I realise now that I may have made a mistake about the song and should have paid more attention to it at the time, even explore what it was about.

Since those days I have learnt from life experience that having a voice is critical to progressing one's needs. When the voice is 'on song', then it is possible to express one's needs and, all being well, to have them fulfilled. When it falls silent, a passive victim emerges.

I feel my voice is essential to my being. Yet the moment a person is disabled their voice is stolen from them. Instead of letting them speak for themselves other people speak for them. This infuriates me because I was born with the gift of the gab. Through my Irish heritage, I 'kissed the blarney', as they say, and if there's one thing that defines me it is that I can speak for myself. After many years of enforced quiet, I have found my voice again through the medium of writing. I am not what you would call a shy, retiring person. But even for me, when people treat me less than well, I find it hard to blurt out what they deserve to hear: 'Hey, you're treating me poorly. I demand your respect.' The thing is, if I don't blurt this out people do not understand what they are doing to me.

Be the offence sexism, racism or the exploitation of power relationships, we need to *dig deep* and find the resources within us to express our refusal to put up with degrading remarks. It is good to see others step up and speak out, making it easier for us to do likewise — people like Grace Tame on sexual violence or football stars Eddie Betts and Adam Goodes on racism.

I have yet to see a disabled person with a high public profile whose voice has resonated as powerfully. I will not hesitate to contribute my two bits even if my voice lacks the resonance to carry this off. I have never been able to sing but am capable of considered and modulated thought. So my voice can certainly broadcast the ills that have been done to me and that I see done to others.

When I went in for the big meeting to get my initial NDIS plan worked out, I was able to express myself articulately and describe my issues. Here, my voice enabled me — or, as the Centrelink mantra has it, identifies me. Sadly many others in need don't —

and they cannot rely on others to do it for them. Here is where the system falls short.

*That is what the song was popularly known as. Its actual title is *You're the Voice*, the singer John Farnham.

The Trick

Life gives each of us our burdens to bear. The trick is to learn how to live with them, how to carry them without collapsing under their weight. Mine have been a bit unusual, granted, and no complaints. But, looking at how I have borne the burdens my life has heaped on me, which I have learnt to accept and live with, I cannot imagine how I would have managed them without a modicum of intelligence and an even larger serving of humour. These are the weapons I have wielded to hack my way through the jungle of life.

Mindset counts for a lot, in my view. I feel it is OK to accept that I will never be wealthy, live the good life as most people understand that term or travel as desired. This is all fine by me: I respect my limitations — and so I simply redefine the good life and endeavour to lead that. The nice thing about this acceptance is that it enables me to escape falling into the trap of conspicuous consumption. I value the world I live in, and don't want to abuse it just because I can. This mindset of mine consists of a mixed bag of refusals and inevitabilities. Much as I would like to drive again, the ever-present risk of epilepsy rules it out. Getting dressed is a hassle and will be all my days, but some therapies hint at improvements to my life down the track. For example, I am confident that one day, just as I have now trained myself to open the front door with my left hand, I will be able to use a knife and fork; my speech will become increasingly comprehensible; and when I am better understood this will assist my social integration.

But the big thing that I will never accept is that my health condition defines me. There is a lot more to me as a person and to how I behave than being the survivor of a car crash and health emergencies. I need not list these other facets of myself here: people acquainted with me know my virtues. The most important thing to accept — and I do — is that I am a good person and conduct myself well. I can be satisfied with that.

Care Worker

I am often asked, 'What do you do for a living?' Before responding I pause a moment and then reply, 'The work I do is unusual. I am a care worker. ... I work on looking after and caring for my health. For this the government pays me a disability support pension and funds the NDIS.'

I take my work seriously. It is time-consuming, tiring, constantly demanding. The nature of the work can be depicted in many ways: this is my version of it. Given the diverse ways in which jobs can be carried out, I find it very hard to compare one person's work to another's, or to judge who works hard and who works less hard. Who knows what is hard? Is the key factor the time spent on a job, the ergonomic effort expended physically — and how does one even begin to calculate mental effort? Everyone responds in different ways to the rigours of a task or set of tasks. The job can be your tyrant or give you pleasure. Among my acquaintances are retired people who say my work is living the good life. I see what they mean. Since I don't have a formally designated job, people assume my life is one unending period of pleasure and leisure. If only that were true! The way I see it, disability is full on, very engaged, work and you can never take a break from it.

People achieve identity through the work they do. So and so *is* a doctor, a lawyer or perhaps a sparky. What they do becomes who they are. Since I don't work I just get labelled disabled. Well, I find this very insulting and disparaging. I am far more than the level of my ability and resent having my identity reduced to that. I wish to be labelled a good, thinking human being. There, I have defined it: my full-time occupation.

People who undertake physical work, perhaps implementing skills they have been trained along with others to master, gain satisfaction from these activities. Being unemployed, I am denied these expressions of self and forced to find other ways of fulfilling my potential. This is not always easily achieved. But my large portion of free time has given me the chance to reflect that even if I were employed I would still strive to behave in a good and decent way, because that is an identity to be proud of. And, even if having to work makes your life busier than mine, I don't accept it as any reason to thwart your ambition — or that of any person, working or not — to behave well.

Thanks NDIS

These days we hear much about the NDIS, how it fails people and doesn't work. Well, for me it does: I can't sing its praises loudly enough. It has made a wonderful contribution to my life.

Initially, I thought there was little a disability insurance scheme could do for me so I need not get involved. But I try not to close my ears to well-intentioned friends with direct evidence of what they tell me, so gradually I overcame those initial misgivings and did become involved in the process. Today my life would suffer a great loss without it.

The NDIS's mission statement is to improve the quality of life and social interaction for the disabled. Well, it achieves all this for me in spades. It helps me to function in the wider world, despite my disabilities; and, although it is there to increase my social interaction, I am aware that perhaps I should make more of an effort. Overall, it's not hard for me to see why it's the ant's pants.

I suppose I am lucky that what I require from the NDIS is just services, not specialised equipment. That is where I understand people do find it wanting. But even on this level the equipment that I do need has been provided. There are some things I am expected to pay for, and that's fine by me. I'm not greedy.

There is a fine line between availing oneself of what the system can provide and rorting it. I don't want to do that. I have seen some people go after stuff for the sake of it whether they really need it or not. They create a wish list and chase every item on it. I have no desire to be like these people. All I ask is that objects which add real value to my life be included, and so far they have been.

I fear what will happen to me in a few years when I move from the NDIS to being looked after by aged care. My hope is that it won't be difficult to obtain the care package I will need.

Seven

Being Me

Songlines

I am a member of a very old and developed culture, Judaism. Luckily, I have been planted on top of another very old and developed culture — that of the Australian Aboriginal. The two cohabit within who I am and my understanding of the world. I am very pleased about this as this interaction gives me insight into the operation of the world. This planting within me is one of many different gardens that I tend. Let them combine and thrive in me.

Like the Aboriginal culture, the Jewish one is built generation on generation. It has evolved cumulatively over time; it is not stagnant but dynamic, creative and exploring. These are things I applaud. Judaism is built around its calendar and the various festivals that reside in it. Each festival is a story in itself, with many diverse storylines. Put these together and a place in the meaning and scheme of life is developed. From my understanding of Aboriginal culture, herein lies a great similarity between the two cultures. The whole meaning of what Indigenous people are is transmitted through the process of storytelling. This, in all its complexity, is expressed in word, dance and art. This is constantly evolving and re-creating itself — no unchanging Bible for Aboriginal people. Their culture is ongoing, lived and a delight to witness or to try to comprehend. Through its sense of community, Judaism has developed in similar ways. To both cultures the sense of family — or let me say 'our mob' — is critical. So here my garden beds in and spreads its roots. We cross-fertilise and become a strong plant, full of flavour, grown in the Australian soil. I like to think of this as our very own produce: let me call it contemporary bush tucker.

Both cultures cherish and sprout from the land, whose rhythms and the cycle of nature bind the people who live on it to it. This is their lived world. Judaism is built into the cycles of the land of Israel and Aboriginal society is bound in with the concept of 'country', wherever they have occupied this vast land. To those who know and love it as their own, the topography of this land can be read, listened to and tasted.

As an urban white male I have had only occasional contact with the Aboriginal population, incidental at best. It could be said I am a voyeur, but not all our interactions in modern life are face-to-face. The opportunity may not come my way to be in the same room as them but observation is a form of interaction as well: I can watch an Aboriginal star in a game of footy. Only Covid restrictions can stop me going to see a show by someone like Jack Charles or watching Bangarra Dance Theatre company. If I want to immerse myself more I can go to the gallery or museum and view some of the Indigenous art there. All these activities are well and good but they don't build a deep relationship. Nonetheless I would say seeds are sown and cross-fertilisation is occurring. The blending of this Other with me is building a healthy biodiversity. So I would not snarl and turn my nose up at this. If being a voyeur is all I can do, it is still a contribution.

Jews, like Aboriginals, sit on the periphery of society. I am not greeted with open arms, there is always a lingering prejudice. Stereotypes are forever at play. This applies to Aboriginal peoples as much as it does to me so I have to feel for them. There is no reason either of us should be a victim of prejudice, but the reality is we are.

My people — that is, the Jews — seeded into modern Australia. Initial planting came with the First Fleet, which included a number of Jews, and has flourished from century to century. And flourished to great heights: the first Australian-born Governor-General happened to be a Jew; our greatest general, John Monash, also was. As was our first environment minister. As time goes by, much will be added as our roots have sunk deep into the soil. My wish is that all the First Nations peoples will achieve this flowering: a process that has has begun with the Albanese Government's commitment to holding a referendum on enshrining a First Nations' Voice into the Australian Constitution.

So what can a white man do, even one from a visible minority? Not much, really. I can and do participate in large demonstrations supporting the political empowerment of Aboriginals over their lives. I can and do call out racism if I hear it. I keep myself informed and applaud things like the lovely Uluru Statement from the Heart. Jewish roots, entwined with Australia's Aboriginal roots, have made a strong environmentalist of me: I have great respect for the land we live on and cherish. I would like it looked after and feel it should flourish under the tender care of its natural custodians. Deep family respect for elders strikes a chord with me — elders past, present and emerging, as it is so wonderfully put.

My ancient culture has come and now lives alongside another ancient culture with which it bears great similarities. I feel it is my role to taste and be nourished by the fruits of this ancient culture. I admire you, first of the Australians, and how you have survived so long in this harsh land. May we till the soil together into the future.

First Nations

As I write this it is NAIDOC week — National Aborigines and Islanders Day Observance Committee week 3-10 July 2022 — so I thought I would explore further how the Aboriginal presence has touched me. I do accept that it does in profound ways. As an urban Australian living in Melbourne I have never come into contact with an Aboriginal, so to people like me the Aboriginal has become the proverbial Other.

This makes it necessary for me to seek out where the Aboriginal presence has touched my life, perhaps without my being aware of it. On reflection I discover that Aboriginality has made a profound impact on me. First, as a white Australian, this puts me into the position of oppressor, which is not something I would ever want to be. To be honest, I find it impossible to separate or exclude myself from what has gone on since the arrival of the First Fleet. Where I feel most touched is in the relationship Aboriginal people have with the land. This is a layered relationship of which I, as an outsider, can only understand certain elements. But the land, and the forms of the landscape, are clearly considered to be the source and expression of all life — and this all-embracing view of the world touches me deeply. *We are the land and the land is us.* To understand truly what this means is to see ourselves as environmentalists with a personal obligation to care for the land. It is an obligation that must be expressed through actions, not just speech.

'Reading' the world I live in through the twists and turns of Nature I regard as a valuable addition to my life. The other aspect of Aboriginal life that touches me profoundly is their ancient and continuous tradition of storytelling, particularly through the notion of songlines. This appeals to me greatly, the idea that all the knowledge we need can is transmitted. As the fabric is passed down across generations, the stories themselves are carried forward and develop more layers of meaning: the enriching of story makes it self-evident to the youngest inheritors of Indigenous tradition — and all this feeds into the perceptions of Australians like me who, though not Aboriginal, can enmesh them in the observations that go to make up their understanding of what it means to live here — and, in my case, to enrich my written work.

So in NAIDOC Week it is time to pay high tribute to the first peoples of this country and to salute their fine cultural practices. Long may they persist.

The Dreamtime

When I cast my gaze back on life before my accident I see it as the life of what and who I am by nationality, an Australian. So I have concluded that for me life before the accident was the Dreamtime. During this period meaning and myth were imported into my life, the world fitted into its place and I fitted into it. I walked around — no, I glided with ease. The Dreaming has had a great influence on who I am. But this has been replaced by the great moment of rupture that was my accident. Let's call that the Invasion.

The Invasion turned my world upside down, and it has been up to me to adapt to it. My story in the wider sense is that of my adaptation to life after the accident. Both my body and my mind have been invaded by what happened to me and sadly my Dreamtime is under constant attack. My task is trying to preserve what I was and let it flower in the new conditions under which it lives. Important as my Dreaming is, I have to fight for it not to be compromised and frittered away. During my Dreaming I enjoyed robust good health. It was not an issue for me. I had not so much as broken a bone. It's hard for me to remember visiting the doctor: the only illness of significance I had as a teenager was glandular fever. From birth to adulthood I had spent only one night in hospital — for what they called growing pains. So in my dreams I was Superman, able to do whatever I wished. Then, bang, in one shot the dream was blown asunder. Multiple bones broke, I needed a tracheotomy, so severe were the injuries to my skull and brain: yes, it could be said I don't do things by half measures. At that point I yearned for a full return to the Dreaming but sadly that wasn't to be.

Reality and my genetics intervened. First my gall bladder had to come out. Within a month of that operation, my mind had returned to the Dreaming and I was off overseas, to Africa. Later I had a heart attack and bypass surgery. This was largely genetic in origin. As my descent continued, I found I had issues with my colon. Then, I had a fall and ended up in hospital for many months. This was repeated when stomach cancer struck and then another fall. But, when all is said and done, sitting here today, how I perceive myself is what matters. Despite all this history I revert to the feeling and the story as they were at the beginning. I consider myself to be in robust health, albeit in a modified form. The dream has not evaporated: it persists. My personal Dreaming and current lived reality are reconciled. I do feel that this is what it means to be healthy.

The story of meaning and knowledge were present in my earliest dreams. One grandfather was a doctor, the other had spent a lifetime as an educator; my parents were teachers and we resided in an educated society. Able to read and write by the time I went to school, these skills were complemented by television, which seeped a love of storytelling into my soul. My favourite was Davy

Crockett. Like any small boy wishing to emulate his hero, I called myself Crockett. One day when Mum came to pick me up from kindergarten the woman in charge of me greeted her with 'Hello, Mrs Crockett.'

Fast-forward nearly a decade and I was captivated by the stories of a better world that Gough Whitlam with his It's Time campaign promised to give us. I was crestfallen when the Dismissal happened. It seemed to me my dreams of a better world were shattered. In the heyday of my Dreaming, I had no idea what I wanted to do with my life, beyond living in the Marxist Utopia that was the destiny of my parents' Dreaming, a dream world that influences me to this day.

In my university years I acquired the skills and knowledge necessary to dissect and construct the world of the Dreaming, nebulous as that might be. I was thus also enabled to comprehend and navigate the world into which I have been thrown. But only now have I begun to draw on these resources as I should, to reveal — through these many stories of mine — the world in which I live and travel.

Book Shops

I was brought up to believe books are to be valued and prized, the repositories of knowledge and imagination — great and wonderful things.

In fact I was taught to read before I went to school. Reading was an expectation my parents had of me. This high opinion of books was elevated further by my dad having been an author. I guess it has always been considered part of my destiny that I would become an author — of what, I had no idea. I tried writing fiction but failed badly. Storytelling was my niche, but true stories not fiction. With all this background, it is no great surprise that bookshops have always felt like a second home to me, a friendly and favoured habitat. At university I visited them to get the texts I needed. One of my favourite leisure activities at that time was hunting in shops for rare books that would add to my wealth of knowledge. On a visit to London I got great joy from visiting bookshops in Charing Cross Road, where you don't buy by the title but by the inch. I made a special trip to Oxford to look at bookshops there, and in one of them — called Blackwell's — found myself in something close to heaven. It was like a precursor to Amazon. From there books were sent all over the world. Of course, while there I bought more volumes than I could possibly carry home to Australia.

Earlier in the same overseas sojourn, but this time in Israel, I entered a delightfully cool cave on a very hot day. In it sat an old man at a desk with air conditioning at full blast while he listened to classical music. All this was like a waiting room for heaven. The old man knew his stuff and directed me to a number of books of great interest, a most satisfying meal. While I was there it happened to be Book Week, and in town late on Saturday night I was taken to a bookshop where there was such a crush of people I had to be careful not to get knocked over. Coinciding with Book

Week, this was the first night of discount specials. To see books being held with such desire and reverence warmed my soul.

After the accident, reading returned me to my true self, and was central to my recovery and ongoing life. The biggest problem has been keeping supplied with enough reading material. While it was good to spread my favours around, books are not so cheap so, at one point. I began to frequent that ultimate bookshop, the local library. A by-product of this was that it left my house less cluttered, (finding space for books I have read was always a problem). At one point I got a dream job working in a bookshop but, alas, this was not to become a career. I was exploited as free labour and the promised full-time paid position never materialised. But books — unlike certain people — never let me down. They provide the furniture in every room of my imagination, as well as the texture and colour that brighten up the darkest recesses of my mind. Through them I have travelled the world and these days I cannot walk past a book shop. I even know of those that double as a café and consider this a sublime blend of pleasures. A final point: there is no substitute for a book's tactile delight. E-books don't do it for me. I have no desire to use a Kindle. The feel, the smell, the heft of a book: these cannot be replaced by technology. Knowing I am not alone in this attitude, I feel confident the era of the bookshop has many years to run.

My Word

All I have of value in this world is my word. So, as I see it, my chief task is to ensure that it's worth something. If I attach value to my word, I become of worth myself. So how do I confer value on my word? That is very simple — through my actions. I need to back up what I say with what I do.

The problem — if I may put it this way — is that many things are easier said than done. But the goal is worth striving for. Far too often have I discovered that what people say and what they do are far removed from each other. This has caused me great disappointment and upset. I don't look for guile and deceit. Some may regard me as naïve, a sucker for expecting people to actually tell the truth. Maybe I am. Far too many people over the years have promised to stand by me and assist me but have never been seen again. In my eyes they are lesser human beings.

Don't think I am harsh on them. I always give people the opportunity to prove themselves by their actions. If they fall short, they fall short. But for me to treat them as they deserve requires of me that I live up to the standards I set. I must be true to my word, so if I say I will do something I must go ahead and do it. No idle promises from me.

When I see people living true to their beliefs — whatever they may be, and even if those beliefs are the polar opposite of mine — they will receive great attention from me. For example, I have cousins with whom I disagree in almost every regard. But they have created and live a life consistent with their beliefs.

Talk means little to them; it is action that counts. As a result I have great respect for them and we converse freely (we just avoid the topics of religion and politics). On the other hand, I know a number of folk who beat their chests when it comes to environmental issues but whose lived reality is in stark contrast to the views they espouse. These people's words are so much hot air and show. I refuse to accept that anything they say or do has any value.

One aspect of a person's behaviour helps me assess their worth — and that is whether or not they're punctual. If someone turns up at the time we have arranged, it shows that they value who I am and the importance of my time to me. Habitual latecomers are of little worth as they are showing no respect for me and who I am. In my world there is no such thing as being fashionably late. Yes, I do understand that life can intervene and delay a person's movements but someone of worth will do their best to avoid such occurrences. I usually aim to arrive a few minutes early, to be on the safe side. Language content is another guide to character, I find. What I say needs to be something of substance, and — if it is a matter of opinion — it must be an opinion honestly held. If I judge this well, my listener will want to hear what I say, digest it and feel I have made a valuable contribution. When my word is respected, I am respected too. This is where I want to be: at the nexus of human interaction.

My Brain

A few times neurologists have asked me to undergo an MRI scan. When they look at the results they say, 'Wow, your mind is a cave. There's not much in there. How do you manage? You should not be able to live by yourself.' I smile sweetly and reply, 'Well, I do.' Here I arrive at a point that bedevils me. My mind does not operate as people expect it would. This is nothing new; it has always been the case. Even before my accident my brain and the way it worked were unusual. This is what made me a unique person, an original character, and these aspects of me survived the accident. They live on powerfully. Or rather, I should say, the person I was lives on powerfully.

Many people find this hard to accept. They expect me to be different and to act like a damaged, altered person. Yes, I am in some ways, but in many others I am not. Out to preserve as much of what I was as possible, and if possible enhance it, this is how I will have my revenge. To *Dig Deep(*er), I am not what I appear to be, in fact never was; appearances easily deceive and the delta that flows from this reality runs deep. One aspect of me that is unchanged from when I was younger is that I like to reinvent myself, regarding myself as a chameleon of sorts. The only difference may be that I have gained a little in certain respects, due to the passage of time.

Pardon a little immodesty but I was always bright and gifted. I used these abilities to turn the serious business of social interaction into a fun game. I was able to master social analysis through my studies and reach a high level of intellectual thought. I enjoyed these intellectual gymnastics and was able to use them in my day-to-day life. I would allow my imagination to wander and play, in a way not always appreciated by my peers. A brief example: one Anzac Day I convinced a group of friends that Simpson and his donkey had been part of the Zion Mule Corps, an outfit of Jewish volunteers that fought at the Gallipoli campaign in 1915. Simpson had probably never met a Jew. One of this group, upon finding out this was pure fiction, was most upset with me. But even then I was developing storytelling as a way of conducting life, carrying parallel worlds in my brain. The accident did not remove the ability or tendency to cast an illusion — and in doing that I am often functioning far better than I am feeling. People don't always understand what I am doing but usually there is a reason behind it.

Sadly, my brain now is not at the pinnacle it once reached. This is not due to the injuries *per se* but to the impact on how my life operates. The quality and fine-tuning of my brain have diminished. At one point I did return to university but found that what was required was now physically beyond me. I couldn't enjoy university as I once had. Yet wonderfully, with all the damage I incurred, my learning and intellectual development were largely maintained. The level of comprehension about the world that I had attained with my studies remains unimpaired, and you bet I am delighted with that. But people find it hard to believe that in such a badly damaged body as I have these abilities can be retained. I am so grateful they have, since my learning and natural personality combined have enabled me to survive many long dark days.

One of the hardest things to accept is having a functioning mind in a less-than-able body. This reality compromises everything I do or say. My opinion is not given the weight and respect it deserves. To stand and accept this daily would undermine any person's self-esteem no matter how strong it was. I felt I had dealt with this rather well and at least had sustained my dignity until it was pointed out to me that the way I stand reveals otherwise. I did not stand erect; my posture did not exude the confidence I would have claimed for myself. But I will not let the effects of my injuries determine who I am. So with the assistance of my personal trainer and speech therapist my aim is to overcome these barriers to the expression of my complete self.

My intellect is still strong: it rages in my head. Thoughts and ideas are constantly flowing but my speech issues cut me off from the world, denying me the opportunity to express and externalise this flux. I do end up having some good-quality conversations with myself but the unfortunate consequence of this is that when I see people it all blurts out. My mouth becomes a rapid-fire machine gun, making it difficult for anyone to follow, let alone respond to, my utterances. In turn this limits the quality of conversation I can have with people. They get frustrated talking to me: it is all far too much and too intense. I have to rely on people knowing me, understanding me and making allowance for this.

It can be very difficult with strangers or meeting people at a social event. It's all very well having an active brain but mine operates as if on steroids. It is hard to credit that this flux of words is issuing from a virtually non-existent brain. My theory is that the part of my brain that was damaged is at some distance from the seat of my intellect. I have developed workarounds for these issues of mine. Through email conversation I can express what's going on in my head and people can choose to respond as they wish. FaceTime and Skype also enable me to 'let off the steam' in my head.

So how do things lie now? Due to my command of language and the content of my speech, people are easily deceived. They do not comprehend the hidden complexities. Brilliantly as my mind appears to function, they don't see that I am unable to use a knife and fork and that many simple tasks elude me or are achievable only with great difficulty. My distorted speech, though I am working on it as best I can, still leads to great offence. People hearing it will speak to me as if I am an idiot or react as if I'm on drugs. When someone speaks to me as if I am a child or mentally deficient, it hurts: it is like cutting me with a knife. The complexities of me lie beneath the surface but due to my sensitivities I get upset when people make little effort to perceive who I am. I suppose this is the lot of all people in one way or another but my condition makes me hyper-alert to it. It has taught me to size people up more carefully. Using skills I was trained in at university, I tune in closely to people's underlying narrative. At the same time I take care not to be too judgmental. So, to the extent that my condition has made me a better person, I must be thankful for it. Well, it's only right that there be some compensation for all that I suffer.

Smoking

Smoking is something that has permeated my life. I am a lot better off without it. Let me tell you how it has wreathed its insidious way through my being. To begin, my grandfather was an exceptionally heavy smoker known for always having a cigarette in his mouth even though he was a doctor. Sadly, he died of lung cancer when I was very young. I was robbed of his input into my life.

My other grandfather also smoked but as a religious man he gave it up at the end of every week, for Shabbat. I am sure smoking contributed to the stroke that killed him. Again this denied me a timely opportunity to be taught what I needed to know in life.

My dear father had a heart attack with a smoke in one hand and a coffee in the other. Happily he survived another forty-five years after that. My grandmother, the doctor's wife, was a colourful character who also smoked heavily. Many people did in those days: it was not only socially acceptable, if you can believe it, but in some circles socially expected. I can see my grandmother now with a smoke in one hand and a whisky in the other at one of those famous parties she used to attend at Rippon Lea. When a doctor said to her in her eighties he might have to give her a puffer, she replied grandly, 'The only thing I want to puff is a cigarette.'

An aunty I was very close to only smoked two or three a day but she got lung cancer and died. This was a terrible loss to me as not only was I close to her but she had helped me reclaim myself after my accident.

Being a modern child — and given my family history — it will not surprise you to learn that I grew up a committed anti-smoker. I remember being deeply shocked when a student of Dad's had a smoke after one of his lessons. As far as I was concerned that was not the done thing. As a young boy I lectured my special uncle about smoking. If only he had listened to me ... he ultimately died of lung cancer too, another loss created by this curse.

I didn't start smoking till I was twenty-one, and look back on it as a terrible act of folly. With a personality like mine, there was no chance of becoming a moderate, occasional smoker. As I did with everything else, I smoked with a passion. Two packs a day filled a number of voids in my life. I did try to be polite about it and not upset people.

My sister gave up the habit, using hypnotherapy. Urged to follow suit, I refused. Playing with the little brain I had left was a no-go area. My personal objection to smoking was not its health consequences or the filth it created but from the angle of addiction. I loathed being under the control of an external force, deprived of my free will. As I have stated before, my disability has robbed me of a significant part of my life and I have found it very hard to come to terms with this. Giving up even more of it undermined my inner being. Being a smoker upset me, but I was an addict so — caught in the vicious circle — I continued to puff my life away.

What finally cured me of my addiction was that harsh taskmaster, circumstance. I had a heart attack. Lying in hospital without access to smokes, I was able to break free of the claws that had gripped me. 'Why start again?' I asked myself, and could find no good answer. I haven't lit up since then and dare not as I know the consequences. Freed from the jaws of addiction, I gained greater insight into the conditions under which I live, and that's a worthwhile benefit in itself.

Chatterbox

My mouth is constantly in motion – not because I'm eating but because I am talking. Always with something to say, I barely take a breath. This impedes the quality of my speech, something I have had to relearn to master. For someone like me not to be understood or for people to have difficulty understanding me is a cruel turn of events.

This has been a post-accident reality I've had to learn to manage. I want people to comprehend the sounds that come out of my mouth, as naturally I consider them meaningful. Call me a chatterbox or a victim of verbal dysentery, but the need to speak is magnified by the isolation I suffer. So when I get the opportunity to speak, I go hell for leather. This ability of mine is well known: I even enjoy having conversations with myself. And, yes, I see the humorous side of this.

My constant babble is generally accepted as simply part of who I am: most people seem able to digest it as a healthy portion of what I talk about they regard as being of value and interest. I apply the various skills developed over a lifetime to deliver a considered opinion about the world around us. This has led me to the point where I am determined to create an interactive blog. I feel I can only develop these opinions with input from other people, recognising that there are limits to the quality of discussion I can have just with myself! When I was in rehab hospital after my fall and minor stroke, the medicos thought it wonderful how I chatted with myself and thereby enabled me to do what was desired. No mere babble, my speech had purpose. No wonder I get so frustrated when people can't understand me as well as I would like them to. Conversation is my air; I need it to breathe.

When my speech gets interrupted by silence, people grow very worried: it is not something they are used to. If I take a moment out to listen to people (which I like to do) or even just allow someone a chance to speak, I get asked with keen concern, 'Are you OK?' Once upon a time I used to have absences — epileptic fits I used medication to control. (It works: I have fewer of them nowadays.) Typically of these gaps in my 'presence', I would stop mid-sentence and simply tune out. This would greatly upset anyone who happened to see it. Then I would continue as if nothing had happened. This is a mild form of epilepsy but others often don't know that. Happily, with this now being a rare occurrence, people have become very used to the relentless flow of words that come from me. A situation arose recently that amused me, that gave me a feeling of value and that yielded the welcome revelation that some people do listen to me.

Well, my trusty iPad had died on me. In a split second I became a non-citizen of the cyberworld. This didn't last just a day or two, which is what generally happens when I have a techno problem; it went on for close to a week. Once I was back on air I found out that friends and acquaintances had been checking with each other: 'Have you heard from David?' They started to get extremely anxious as the last time I'd fallen silent for this length of time was when I had my fall and ended up in hospital. After several days I started getting phone calls asking if I was all right. Calls even came from overseas. Given my personal history, I could well understand their concern. I remember after I had my heart attack a wise friend told his wife, 'If you don't hear from David for a few days it's important to check up on him.' From this I conclude that, even though my constant babbling can be annoying and irritating, at least some people see a certain value in it — and this makes me feel good about myself, I can tell you.

I Like to Spiel

Why have I chosen storytelling as a medium for the things I have to say? Well, first, I am inspired by the example of the First Nations people on whose land we live. Through storytelling they handed the thread of their culture along, from generation to generation for tens of thousands of years. Painted into their storylines — their songlines — were the subtleties and depths of knowledge that are needed to navigate this world. So it is that I learnt I could weld my ethos and conceptions of life through story. Layered onto this learning from the First Nations, I come from another culture that conveys meaning through story. These stories are told annually and within them, also, is embedded the knowledge that is needed to navigate life.

I refer, of course, to Jewish culture. To use a Yiddish term, I like to *spiel*, that is, to make up and tell stories. This is how I communicate. When at university, to pull all my previous studies together I studied ethnography, this taught me the art and wonders of storytelling. If done well, so much can be conveyed in a satisfying and digestible manner. It is these skills and knowledge I have employed in my writing. They have been key to my survival and coming to terms with my disability. My storytelling gives people access to the kaleidoscope that is my mind.

To my surprise I have discovered that there is a degree of universality to my storytelling, and this has delighted me. But, when all is said and done, I feel I haven't done anything special, I have executed no great achievement. My daily existence is in many ways mundane. I have just tried to live as a person should. Yes, if my reader has enjoyed the musings in these pages I will be thrilled. In telling the stories of our lives there is no right or wrong way, I feel. To restore real meaning to a much misused cliché of our times, it is what it is.

The Good Walk

At the very best of times I am quite an uncoordinated person. But my accident has made it a lot worse. Aspects of my brain damage and other consequences of my accident affect how the world exists for me now. Let me begin with a simple example. By inclination I am a daydreamer, what some call a space cadet. I walk around with my head in the clouds, not paying as much attention to the world around me as I should. This is a great way to put my mind into neutral and develop clarity of thought but it comes with many real dangers. Walking anywhere, I need to be as mindful as possible of my safety. Now this aspect of me gets magnified by an aspect of my brain damage called *petits absences*, also known as *petit mal* seizures or absence seizures. In short, this means I miss moments: I go away for a minute then come back. It is a form of epilepsy that I now have under fairly good control thanks to a special medication. It is easy to see how this is a very dangerous condition. But when it is layered on to being a natural daydreamer the danger is amplified. This is one of the reasons I don't drive. I would hate to have an absence, miss a moment and injure someone. I would find it very hard to live with myself, so it is taxis and lifts for me. This constraint on my freedom of movement amounts to a serious loss of liberty.

Another aspect of my brain damage that endangers me is a thing called left-side neglect. I am delighted that my eyesight was not affected except for this one thing. It means I don't see or pick up things in my left field of vision. As a result, I walk into things or people I simply don't notice. They are at risk and it is so easy to hurt myself. I am always bumping into poles or street signs as I walk. I try not to walk too fast so as not to injure myself.

Last, there is a repercussion of my accident that was revealed to me by my trainer. My posture is far from ideal. Partly this is because of brain damage: I slope to the left instead of standing erect.

Then another factor comes into play: because of the life I have lived my self-esteem and confidence are far from what they should be so I slouch. Put these things together and the result is to magnify my left-field neglect. This is no idle matter as I like walking and do a lot of it. You could say it is my primary 'mode of transport'. Over a year I cover thousands of kilometres and, not surprisingly, I have the occasional fall. It is a worry because I don't want to hurt myself and spend days out of circulation to recover. I have an idea of what will cause a fall and do my best to avoid precipitating one but, sadly, it is sometimes unavoidable. When I do fall my natural inclination is to somehow get myself up and continue on my way home. But I can hurt myself trying to get up. My greatest fear is that I would have a fit out on the street that would cause a fall and I would be unable to make it home. Thankfully that has never happened, but the fear is ever-present.

Happily my fits are under control. Even when they did occur that was only when I was at home. Some things have to go my way! Uneven footpaths and obstacles in the road pose a danger too: I don't always see them and tend to trip over them. I forgot to mention earlier that my sense of balance has been compromised which just occasionally gets me into strife. One thing I have discovered when I do fall is the lovely nature of people, which has given me faith in humanity. Someone always comes to my assistance — but they don't leave it at that. They always want to be assured that I am OK before I go on my way.

To all these very nice people I owe, and offer, great gratitude, and hope I need never call on their services again.

Life's Perpetual Challenge

From the moment we are born life is a challenge, the same for all of us. Our story is about how we confront each challenge that comes along. Each of us does this in a way that expresses who we are. We can't avoid doing this.

I have been thrown many challenges that other people have not had to confront. It is my desire that what I have to relate in these my stories has to some degree been entertaining. Now it is time to explore the notion of challenge in greater detail.

The first big challenges we all face are to walk and talk. When I learnt to walk I never expected I would have to learn how to do it two more times. I was a lively little boy and ran everywhere — worrying my parents terribly that I would get lost or be hit by a car. Each of us does it differently. I know one bloke who didn't walk till he was three years old but ended up being a champion runner. I have seen some children walk at eight months.

As for talking, from the moment I could speak I have barely stopped for breath. That is because my mind is constantly engaged, always in action. The joke became, the good thing about my coma was that I was silent for once. Actually, if I fall silent for a few minutes people get worried and concerned. Since my accident, the quality and sound of my speech have never returned to what they were. That has caused me many ongoing challenges in interacting with the world and, till this day, it is something I am working on. For my speech to be less than it should be is a very high wall that I find difficult to climb. It pisses me off badly when I am treated differently because of my speech, just as it does when people cannot comprehend what I am saying.

In short, school was not a challenge for me, just something that must be done to progress in life. I have never been a driven person, happily so. From what I have seen of them, driven people are in a constant state of stress. Until my accident, life came easy to me. I was not confronted by great obstacles and could remain true to myself. But then — bang! — the whole picture book changed — and I was suddenly confronted by countless challenges. Surmounting these challenges, I decided, was going to depend on how I tackled them. I wanted to remain true to myself and to approach each obstacle with consideration and reasoned thought. I would like to think I have done this.

After years of lived experience, I have concluded the challenges of disability arise from two directions — a double-edged sword, as it were. There are the physical challenges and, just as sharp and penetrating, the social ones. Both types are inescapable and unrelenting.

Before my accident, the social world was my oyster, and I avidly devoured it. For me, life was an ongoing party. But from the moment I awoke from my coma I had to learn to adjust to a different reality. Nearly forty years on, the adjustment doesn't get easier. I need to be constantly on my toes, aware of what I am doing in a wide variety of ways that are operating concurrently.

First of all, to conquer the speech barrier so that I can function and be understood requires great attention and concentration. My utterances do not gush and flow as they once did but with due attention I can manage — I just wish it was a more natural thing. The various ways in which hindrances to social interaction inhibit my life are revealed in the reflections you encounter in these pages. The efforts, conscious and constant, that I make to communicate and socialise have one end in view: How can I live and create the life I desire?

This edge of the sword twists and turns, cutting very deep and causing great pain. Turning to the other edge — the reality of living with a disability — I think the hardest part comes from having lived without a disability in my earlier life. This means I have full comprehension of what it is to be abled so I know very well what I am missing out on. The disability must be comprehended afresh every day and this is no easy task. I am still learning about it and what it means almost four decades after my accident. You bet the pain of it all is still raw.

Let's look at my disability a bit. I have found there are a number of things I cannot do, so it is up to my ingenuity to find ways to get done what I need to do. My left hand is as good as useless. But I must be careful not to over-blame my injuries for this. It was always very weak; I have always been right-dominant. While not much used before, the left was functional to some degree. Now, if I need to do something that requires two hands, I have to think my way around the problem. Some things are beyond me. I am not able to use a knife and fork, which can be very embarrassing. I also have to work out how to eat without making a mess. In the end, I use my dominant right hand for everything, and this generally gets me by. There are other eating problems. In my lip there is a non-functioning nerve. This means my mouth does not seal a cup properly. So when I drink there is a fine dribble down the side of the cup. I must be aware of this so that it does not make a mess and dirty my clothes. Making and drinking coffee is a problem. Opening up sugar sticks is hard. Sometimes I just give up or spill sugar everywhere. I hate doing that. As I have said before, the battle is relentless — and a lesser quality of life in abstract terms translates at a practical level to diminished pleasure in sitting at a café table.

My handwriting was always poor but the loss of dexterity has made it even worse. Things like iPads are my salvation. Opening bottles and jars requires two hands, so this is out — I must ask someone to do it for me. Home help is a godsend. Doing buttons up correctly is a no go, so I choose all my shirts without buttons. It is embarrassing to walk around with your buttons done up incorrectly.

Yes, a lot of these problems relate to the social sphere and there is no escaping that. Just getting dressed is a daily trauma — the worst of it being that I can't find clothes to fit me. The result: I appear to be a bit of a slob — not at all what I desire. Smartphones are beyond me, putting me outside the social network. Please don't get me wrong: I am not whingeing: I do manage to get by. I aspire to getting a measure of left-hand functioning and undertake hand physio to help in that quest. Slowly there are things I can now do, such as opening my front door with my left hand — a very important skill if the right hand is full. Perhaps one day I will be able to use a knife and fork again. Until then, there's no reason to feel sorry for me. I am getting by. I manage.

Dig Deeper

I don't look disabled, it is not a self-evident thing but far more subtle. Truth be told, I have had a privileged and charmed life: I am white, middle-class and educated. None of this is a disability. Further, I live in a comfortable house in a desirable part of Melbourne, so in the overall scheme of things I have done rather well. This is the perceived reality that is veiled by the impact of disabilities on my life.

When someone takes a glance at me, my disability isn't clear. In fact I look sort of abled. I am not in a wheelchair, don't use a cane, none of my limbs are missing. The only obvious sign is my distorted voice. To discover my disability requires closer inspection of how my life functions and operates. Far from picturing myself as a disabled person, I see myself as an able functioning soul with a few limitations. What makes it especially hard for an onlooker to see the veil under which I live is that I have retained many of my cerebral functions and, while they don't appear damaged, they are far below what they once were. To some extent, that reduced function disables me even further. Having insight into the nature of my disability makes it harder to live with: I am constantly reminded of my shortcomings.

So the lived reality is that my mind and body are not in sync. When I get it wrong and don't listen to my body, just attempting what my mind feels is possible, I can do myself some real harm (though I suppose this applies to all of us in our day-to-day lives). But there is an extra imposition on me. Inattention poses a particular danger: I don't want to be walking into trams or in front of cars, I need to be constantly aware of what I am doing. Given that, tiredness is a health hazard for me so I dutifully have my rest during the day, which allows me to function and make it to the end of the day. I need to take special care to keep myself presentable rather than appearing to the world as a dishevelled slob. Since I don't see myself as disabled, I don't want to appear to others in that light.

Even with my speech — the most obvious sign of my disability — a number of factors come into play that the casual observer does not pick up. I am not as I seem but a performer with many different guises, all, operating at once. The complex difficulties affecting my speech can be largely overcome and I can be comprehensible but it involves much effort and sadly I don't always manage to pull it together as well as I would like. One aspect of the damage is that my concentration span is not what it once was. This makes it hard to gather the factors needed for a sustained period of clear communication. Compounding the disability is my personality. By nature I am a very plain-spoken person and this, accentuated by brain damage, makes me appear very over the top. It's hard to dissect what is in operation: me or my brain damage. We witness here a very tricky thing.

As I said a little earlier, I am not what I appear to be. But — here's the rub — no one else is either. Everyone is layered and the composite result of these layers creates who they are. You can't take people at face value. Dig a bit deeper and you can discover the truth behind the facade of the people around us and deal with them for who they are.

I Am Valuable

Being disabled undermines your sense of self. With your ego coming under constant attack, the most crippled facet of a personality is your sense of worth. All of us need to feel valued and wanted by people. This becomes hard to feel when the people you know run away and hide, or decide not to bother with you anymore. All that I had done prior to my accident seemed to have gone out the window and been forgotten. So my solution was to start from scratch and find new ways to be of worth. One aim I found was to turn myself into a type of human search engine providing people with what they need to know. To be attuned to people's needs requires listening and really getting to know them. It helps to be good company but brain damage makes you less than good company, so even being aware of this doesn't make it easy to achieve in practice. All sorts of things compromise my sense of worth, such as people treating me poorly as if I were a drug addict, all because of the distortions in my speech. As if this weren't enough to be dealing with, in steps the government tells me I am of lesser worth simply by giving more money to people as wage supports during the Covid crisis than they give me regularly. They are telling me my needs are not as great, that I am less deserving than the average person. I do not see how that can be justified. When Kevin and Julia raised the pension they were telling me I was of value, that I deserved a certain quality of life. In fact Julia underscored the point with the creation of the NDIS.

In the sea where I swim there are plenty of warning markers to point out the limits to my worth but not enough lifebuoys to keep me afloat in choppy water. I need to be sure of who I am and not be cast adrift from the qualities I carry with me. Without comprehension of why I am of value, I will surely sink. Strong as I am, there is an ever-present risk of getting sucked into the vortex of depression: the risk is renewed as a result of the battering I receive in various forms on a daily basis. I have previously mentioned that my compromised posture no longer reflects the way I see myself — as someone of true worth, of stature. My healthy ego will always accept a boost. I cherish and value the NDIS because, not only does it assist me in the act of life but it also builds on — and encourages me to express — my true value. It all comes down to self-perception. The mirror you hold up to yourself never lies. It shows you your worth; and your job is to be worthy of it.

Complain —Why bother?

How we react to adversity, in my opinion, serves as a reliable barometer of personal character. I feel it's important not to be excessively sentimental when faced with hardship. My advice to most people suddenly having a hard time would be, 'Come on, deal with it.'

The most common cause of popular complaints is the weather. You hear folk whingeing about it all the time: it's either too hot or too cold. I don't see the point of it. Why moan about something when there's no way to change it? Some things in the course of nature need to be accepted as the way things are: the existence of seasons is a fact wise people accept. I have no right to expect balmy spring temperatures all year round. People grumble and whine about all sorts of things, and far too often about matters that are beyond their power to alter. If you are going to do so, complain about something you can have a degree of control over.

When I was young and would complain about something, the typical response that would come back was, 'What are you going to do about it?' This question taught me valuable lessons that have stayed with me. It influenced the way I have conducted myself ever since, so I am grateful for the wisdom that the balance of my life resides in my own hands. I am not a passive observer but must be an active participant in my life. The onus is on me to get involved.

This has been key to my rehabilitation. I have only progressed because I have participated in my own therapy. When opportunities arise I grab them with both hands and they have proved most beneficial. Let me give a couple of examples. Somebody who was working with me once asked, 'David, is there anything you'd like?' After pondering a moment, I replied, 'I would like to do some speech therapy: it has been over thirty years [without any]. I've always thought it wasn't worth complaining, that this was my lot.' My questioner took this answer in his stride, saying: 'OK, let's find you one.' This he did, and the benefits have been clear and enduring. There's still no point in complaining my speech isn't up to scratch, but it's a lot better than it was. Within my capacities, I have been availing myself of expert advice to improve my situation. The lesson here's quite basic but so often not heeded: grab your opportunities and run with them. My second example also concerns the bloke who assisted me in acquiring a speech therapist. For many years I have been trying to do something about my body shape. Well, one day this bloke flippantly suggested I get a personal trainer. I listened to what he said, ignoring the tone, and answered him: 'Is that possible?' It was, as it turned out. I pounced on the opportunity as soon as the idea was floated, pressing until I got the right person for the job — and it has turned into one of the best decisions I ever took. To benefit from it, I've had to put my share of effort into what I am told to do. It all harks back to a simple childhood lesson: don't let life happen to you; you must happen to it.

Several people I know have every right to complain because life has dealt them a bum deal. But I never hear them do so. At most

I hear them speaking up about how they will deal with whatever situation they are in. On the other hand, I come across many others who bewail their plight, in a seemingly endless lament at how cruel life has been to them. Very often, they have little reason to adopt this attitude — and I have noticed a remarkable thing: more often than not, these are people who haven't been confronted with their own mortality.

All praise to life's stoics. I had one dear friend, a woman who was good to me and a frequent visitor to my home. The poor lady developed asbestosis as a result of having hung around her dad when he built a garden shed crammed full of the deadly material when she was young. It is a very painful condition, in many cases a death sentence. But she took the attitude that what had happened was out of her hands. In effect, her attitude was, *There's no point in complaining: I shall live my life as well as I can while I can.* So with part of the compensation she was awarded she bought herself a sports car for no other reason than that she had always wanted one. Sadly, after a few years, she succumbed to the illness, and although I still feel the loss of her strength and optimistic outlook in my life she did teach me plenty about the art of living — and I never forget that. A friend of mine has a mate who has gone through a long battle with blood illnesses. After years of being subjected to different therapies, his immune system is destroyed and there is little he can now do, so I asked my friend, 'Does this bloke ever complain?' 'Not once,' was his answer, 'except when I told him I was going out with the lads' — and he knew he couldn't do that. The key point here is deprivation —

the loss of contact with our fellow human beings. This would drive anybody to the edge.

Otherwise, people tend to be accepting of their lot if they understand that changing it is out of their hands. Lastly, let me mention a young teenage friend of mine for whom I have great respect. The poor lass is beset by several health problems, all concurrently. She has diabetes, is a coeliac and, to top it off, she also suffers from Crohn's disease. This means her life, sustained by a very limited diet, is one long ordeal of unremitting pain. Much as she would like to, she cannot go out and live the life other teenagers do, yet when chatting to her I have never heard a breath of complaint pass her lips. When I ask, 'How do you manage these health conditions in a way that allows you to live the life you want to?' her response reveals that she has become very philosophical about the limits that hem her in. I am very happy to report that she has it together and, by any reasonable definition, is living life well.

Life is the full deck of cards. As for me, while I will happily jest about my poor genetic inheritance, which bequeathed me a number of health issues such as heart problems, a dodgy colon and defective gall bladder, I also have genetics to thank for a number of benefits ranging from intelligence to a lack of allergies – no hay fever, asthma or anything in that line. It also appears that Alzheimer's and other forms of dementia do not reside in my family.

With so much to be thankful for, I am not going to cavil about my accident. I have lived long enough to know you can't re-run the past. When asked, as I sometimes am, 'Why don't you complain?' I often utter a wonderful Australian saying that I feel sums it up in a nutshell. It comprises just two words: 'Shit happens.' Not accepting it doesn't help, it blocks the road to better health.

Giving It A Crack

What appeals to me about some people, and repels me about others? Why do some people turn me on or make me want to be friends with them, while others make me want to run and hide or even be rude to them? My behaviour is often considered confronting — a result of my brain damage. When I treat people badly, the reality is not a failing of my personality but a very considered move on my part.

What I like to see in people, and what makes them interesting to me, is whether they appear to be having a good crack at life, that they are trying to live life in all its dimensions the best way they can. The slothful and those who don't bother I have no time for and no interest in. I want to mix with people who choose to engage with the world in a positive way. The catchphrase I use is: Life is an active event: live it. I have also found that those who won't have a go tend to display other unappealing qualities as well. I have no time to waste on those who are less than well behaved.

I have become close friends with a former acquaintance from university and her husband because they give life as good a go as they can. They are not passive observers who let life happen to them but engage with it. Their life is so full that they can be annoyingly hard to catch. But when life throws curveballs they don't dodge them but take the extra challenge on as they should. Between the two of them they have a number of brothers who are in a less than good way but they are involved with them and assist them to travel through life as best they can. This is what I like to see: people behaving decently as a critical aspect of giving life their best shot.

Accordingly, the husband did a degree and then followed up with a, diploma. This strategy has served him well, keeping him in work for many years — a good crack at it, I would say. They had three kids whom they've kept in constant motion and as a result *they* now have a love of life. Their eldest has been a delight to watch flower: she has talent as a cyclist and pursued it with all the energy at her disposal. If she fails it won't be for want of effort. Along with this she has included all the activities a young person should pursue in life. It is so nice to sit and observe a person in the act of doing this. I have the same pleasure in watching another young lady I know as she prepares to become an opera singer. No moment in the day is wasted; she is throwing everything at it. I watch in awe and gain great delight in seeing people like her giving of their best, and deserved success coming their way. It is fair to say that I live vicariously through them.

I have a very good mate. Via email we keep in close contact. Part of this discussion involves each of us making sure the other is making the most of life. It's not so hard: we are both naturally inclined that way, and that's one reason we enjoy each other's company. Another mate with whom I keep up a similar discussion calls me his life coach. I feel he needs no help from me: in many ways he is having a better shot at it than me. I get jealous of all he does, wishing I were able to emulate some of his pursuits. Well, with the first mate I mentioned — the emailer — we both like to get out and do things together. Over time we have accrued many shared memories, the basis of a quality friendship. We care for and look after each other. To build this further we have even created our own rituals, certain things that we go out and do. This, I feel, is the whole goal and purpose of things — to help each other live the best life we can. I am very blessed to have him as part of my life.

When we engage in life and give it a crack, we are better off doing it together. As I live alone, there are limitations in achieving this aim. For example, it's no fun eating out alone. My travel limitations restrict my capacity to live as I think I should, but I won't accept being forced into passivity: I need to lift my game and make sure I am doing everything I possibly can. There is nothing to stop me from going to the gallery alone, doing exercise or reading a book. All these things, among others, are examples of having a good shot at life.

As they say in Yiddish, you should live life as a mensch. My guiding principle in this regard is very simply to try treating others as I would like to be treated myself. If someone falls below this standard you might think my behaviour to them is less than kind and generous; I like to consider myself tough but fair. I see nothing wrong in dishing it out. This way life gets my best shot and I keep my self-respect, something that I never want to compromise. My studies, reinforced by the behaviour and teaching of my parents, prioritise the importance of seeking to aid people wherever possible; not to sit, forget and do nothing.

Patience

Patience is an acquired art. My life has forced me to take strong possession of it and use it well. Some say it is a virtue. What a load of crap. Patience only becomes a virtue if used in a positive way. Sometimes it is a necessary evil. In the end it is a reality, nothing more than a tool with which we construct our concept of time.

By my nature I am a little boy. If things are going to happen I want them to happen now, not some time in the indefinite unreachable future. I don't want to have to wait for anything, so patience — the art of waiting — is a very hard thing to master. Yet the effort (again it is a necessity) does have the merit of being a powerful aid in preserving one's sanity. This is a reality that my disability forced me to confront. After my accident there was no shortcut: I needed to wait for my injuries to heal so I could progress on my journey. Luckily for me, a good part of my recovery took place while I was comatose. When I came to, I had no idea various bones in my body had been broken as they were already mended. Yet, of course, there was much that had not mended, and this is what we now call my disability. I have often been told that time will heal. Being a trusting sort of fellow, my initial reaction to this upbeat news was, 'Sounds good to me. How long will I have to wait?' To this there is no set answer, and with some things no matter how long you wait they simply won't heal — at least, not on their own.

At a certain point I had to involve myself in the process by adopting what I call proactive patience. With time, it is true, some things have rectified themselves but, sadly for me, many things haven't. I must live with this reality, no matter how patient or impatient I may be. Yes, this shook the faith I had in a full recovery, and the hardest thing to accept was that the extent of my recovery was out of my hands. But it didn't mean I should stop waiting altogether, or lose all hope. I still believe that if I take a constructive view the end results I desire will arrive at some point, but this is only the opening move in the patience game.

I have no control over when things happen. They happen to me, if they do, at a time not of my choosing. Waiting is something I get plenty of practice at doing: much of my week and of every day is spent waiting for people to come and assist me, or waiting in offices to see them. Sitting waiting for someone to appear is rather an awful experience. You soon realise that waiting is a mindset: it can be done standing as easily as sitting, or pottering in the garden — but no further away as I don't want to miss the sound of the doorbell. There is no point in getting fully engrossed in a book, either, only to be interrupted. So what have I found comes in handy to occupy myself and help me be patient? This might be watching TV, reading something light or writing an email. There are various things I can do on my iPad to pass the time. But I feel this only alleviates the pressure of waiting; it does not eliminate the need for it altogether. I would much rather be engaged in the world than waiting for things to happen to me. My whole life seems to be built around waiting for things. Much of this is worthwhile, like waiting for home help or my trainer, or even for my speech therapist to appear on FaceTime.

All this makes up the art of patience. It is an art of navigation requiring great delicacy. I must be a participant in my life, not an observer of clocks. Life must not pass me by while I sit and watch for the next development. Technology has been a blessing. Even as I am patient, I can simultaneously be proactive: communicating with people via email, writing down my thoughts and sharing them; expending my knowledge and understanding of the world by reading newspaper and magazine articles and viewing everything from documentaries to YouTube clips. Through all these pursuits, and others, I feel I have turned the need to be patient into a healthy and constructive way of life. To turn the evil necessity of patience into a virtue, the trick is not to focus on the sin of wasting the valuable gift of time but to use it well so that its value is maximised.

Eight

Friendship

Our Friends

'Friend' is a term we use very loosely. When we are small, everyone we meet and come across is a friend. We know no better, we have no idea of what the term and the reality behind it mean. This is something that develops over time — a lifetime, in fact. By the time we are mature adults our idea of what is a friend has been transformed by our life experiences until it becomes something very different from what it was when we were small.

So happy are young kids to have and make friends that often a child who feels they haven't enough friends will create imaginary ones. These often disappear once their social circle expands. I think this is reflective of an innate need for friends and companionship. It is only as time goes on that our thinking about what a friend should be evolves.

Early on, we develop the notion of 'best friend'. Inherent in this is the appreciation of a priority among friends: some mean more to us than others. We learn that not everyone is our friend and that in being a friend there are certain roles to play. This is for us to work out: it is not a clear-cut, finely delineated thing.

I think our idea of friendship develops as we come to need the things that friendship can offer. Sadly, for a variety of reasons, not everyone is capable of supplying these requirements. As I have traversed life I have found that many people fall well short of fulfilling the requirements of friendship. This reality has motivated me to act on a higher level. I want to be there for my friends — what I consider the core of friendship — and not to sink to the level of false pretenders. There are no hard and fast rules, but I have concluded over time that it is up to me to set my own standards to live by, to uphold expectations of my own behaviour — and what others do is up to them. I have learnt not to get upset when others don't meet my standards. It is wrong of me to expect that others should live life as I do. When others don't meet the standards I set for myself I need to accept that we are human, with feet of clay. I have seen that friendship should be forged and worked at; it is not something that is just given but a two-way street requiring effort on my part.

When it comes to those who call themselves my friends but whose actions proved they are not, I offer no free rides; so a few people have been shocked when I turn my back and walk away from them. Yes, to be concise, they are not worth my time of day and will not get it. This can be tricky at times but you must stick to your guns.

The first and most important requirement in a friend, to my way of understanding, is to be there. This does not mean being there in the moment of need — which is usually easy enough.

Friendship is not an occasional thing; you need to be there for your friends at an ongoing everyday level.

Real friendship involves a degree of mutual respect, not always easily attained. Sentimentalists may dispute this but it is also a power relationship: it is important to watch how the transfer of power occurs. This is where the disabled often become victims. They don't hold the cards and so have little power over what occurs. They are often put in a very demeaning position where they are asking for the friendship to be reciprocated in some way. But it is at the discretion of the so-called friend whether this occurs and, if it isn't, the result can be both alienating and demoralising. Better not to chase people; rather, let them chase you. This brings us to a basic tenet of friendship: it is built on shared experience. So, if one side is unwilling to share, I feel the friendship is null and void. Which is why those who have acted less than well towards me are liable to receive in return, if anything, a bit of abuse and terse words.

True friends go out of their way and do things for people: they don't ignore them.

The Tram Girl

Every day I used to go to school by tram. It was easy enough, I felt. I would walk up to the corner near our place to catch the tram. Thousands like me did the same thing all over Melbourne. Trams are a good mode of transport and riding my bike to school and back would have been an effort. I had to catch one tram, then another after it, to get to school. Now my tramline was not the most reliable so I always had to wait for the tram. Sometimes it was quicker to walk to the second tram stop so I would.

I soon noticed that I was far from alone at my tram stop. Others caught the tram to the stop nearest their own school: that's nothing unusual in Melbourne. Soon I became aware of a girl standing there every day just as I did. Being a bit shy, I didn't chat with her. Also, I noticed she was wearing the uniform of a good Catholic school which meant we were off limits to each other. So we stood there, observing everything but never communicating. My folly, I would say, looking back on it now. Often I would chuckle: a car would pull up near the tram stop and a line of young girls of various heights would tumble out of it and walk up to us at the tram stop. These little girls would walk up to their big sister. I would smile and think, *This is a seriously Catholic family* — not a thing of myth but a reality. This little dance went on for years with no conversation at all.

A few years later, when I was at university, some friends of mine said they would like to introduce me to a girl who lived near me. I said, 'Fine, I am up for it.' Well, lo and behold, it was the girl from the tram stop. We smiled at each other nicely and said 'Hi, time we had a conversation.' We ended up becoming good friends and instead of waiting at a tram stop with her I started giving her lifts to uni in my car. In time we even had a very close and intimate relationship, probably something we should have done when younger. But, as they say, this is how the world turns. It was very funny that when I went to visit her she would try to shield me from the mayhem that was her home life. She was one of seven kids. If you chose the wrong moment to arrive, you would encounter pandemonium full on. I didn't mind but she wanted to shelter me from this. It was ridiculous that we didn't become friends earlier: she was only a five-minute walk from my parents' place. But she was right to point out that hers was another world, in which I had a lot to learn.

When I was recovering at my parents' place after my accident, the tram girl came over to visit. She could see I was being lethargic and that this was bad for me. So she got me up and made me walk to her parents' house with her. This turned out to be just the kick in the pants that I needed. I had been deprived of social interaction and, being a very social animal, this was getting to me. It turned out I became very good friends with her many siblings, even her parents. I ended up going there often so that I had someone to chat to. With so many kids in the family there was always someone there. I also needed the exercise. It was not much but it did get me moving and engaging in life, so the tram girl turned out to be a gift.

In the blink of an eye, the tram girl got a job, got married and had children. The act of life kept her busy. Preoccupied by the business of life, she found it difficult to find time to see me. I accept that this is the way life goes. Yet she had clearly not forgotten me: at one point she even moved in, living in my house for a while. When she did that, it worked well for her. Now she lives on the other side of Melbourne, almost an hour's drive from here, so we only manage to see each other very infrequently. But when we do it is always good. We have a natural rapport but, unlike many others I know, she does find time to slot me in here and there. She is not in what I call 'the graveyard of life', which is what I call the natural residence of many others. Who was to know that someone you shared a tram stop for a few minutes a day would be engaged in your life for over forty years?

The Gnome

When I was sixteen I went to *hadracha* camp, which was great. Hadracha – Hebrew for 'the art of youth leadership' – is the technique and the way to act as a youth leader. There was a large group of us from a number of youth movements. We all got on well and many friendships were made. In fact, some of these people I am still in contact with to this day.

One such person I will call 'The Gnome'. He was and is a wild redhead yet with a very tranquil and charming nature — a lovely juxtaposition. He is on the small side so in his own way looks like a vibrant gnome, always fun and a worthwhile person to be around. Being a person of acute self-perception, at one point he started to collect gnomes. To the observer this made good sense. He even found a mould to make his own, which bore his individual stamp. We became solid mates and he has been there for me when so many others who professed to be friends haven't. So now let me share a few tales of my interaction with his unique magic.

One day I saw him at university so he said, 'Please come have a coffee with me.' I replied. 'Sorry I can't, I have to go to a lecture.' His reply was beautiful with its delivery. With a sparkle in his blue eyes he said, 'Don't be foolish. Don't do that. You might actually learn something!' This made it very hard to refuse his invitation but the reason I was on campus was for the lecture so I went since it's not wise to miss too many of them. On seeing my resolve he smiled and said, 'OK', adding with a twinkle, 'Next time'. No insult was felt. He was a gentle being.

When The Gnome finished his course, he went and lived his dream, establishing a kibbutz in the north of Israel at a place with an amazing view. It is always my delight to visit there. I have a wonderful time and drink in all the view has to offer. At one point he house-sat a glorious property in the Dandenongs. I would go to visit and recall toasting jaffles in an open fireplace and our spending whole nights in thoughtful discussion. At that time it seemed to me that being a human gnome was a happy existence, certainly judging by appearances. But our Gnome had horrors in his past that I never entered into. As a close friend I could not be unaware of them but I thought they were best left alone. It was as if his tranquillity was a way of rejecting the horrors he had been subjected to. This seems to me a wonderful way to resolve problems: rise above them, just will yourself to become a good human being.

At one point my parents went overseas on holiday, leaving me to look after their house. I had to go away and do something for a bit so I got The Gnome to house-sit for me. During this time my little sister snuck into the house to get some clothes. Well, she found a mouldy pizza in the oven and then The Gnome, asleep in her bed, in one of her nighties. It all seemed so natural. No harm was done to the house.

It will come as no surprise that The Gnome was brilliant. While doing a PhD once he came to me for some help. I understood precisely what he wanted but it was above my ability to deliver. My solution was to put him in contact with an old professor of mine. After seeing him for the first time, The Gnome came to me and said, 'He was great but he gave me a list of fifty books to read.' So I chuckled, 'Then you will have to read them all.' I later learnt that, despite the prodigious reading list, the main feature of his visits to the professor was discussing footy. They had a mutual interest in the Saints.

After I returned home from my hospital stay in Perth, The Gnome was spending some months in Melbourne on a visit. Swiftly he saw my situation and needs. He could see I was in a bad way, starved of social interaction and friendship. So, although he had a lot he needed to do each day, he would drop in and sit with me. He did a lot more than many so-called lifetime friends. Whereas others never bothered, he cared — persistently. Their behaviour has never changed; nor has his. His living at such a distance is a loss I cannot help feeling but, well, that's the way it is so I must accept it. The spirit of The Gnome has been absorbed into my being and this helps give me the serenity to confront life.

The Sunset

I have a close and dear friend who inspires me by the way he conducts his life in the face of adversity. I wish I could come to terms with life as he has. My friend was born with the curse of a genetic disorder, which has determined and structured his life. You will never see any ill will from him. In fact he is the nicest of all people. I have never heard a bad word about him and can't see how anyone could say one. He is universally loved but not, I feel, well treated. Given our respective health conditions, we relate to each other in a way others cannot relate to us.

My mate, who lives in Israel, has now been in a wheelchair for over thirty years. I know, from a few experiences of my own, that it's no great fun to be in one. They are very uncomfortable: getting around and doing things in a wheelchair can be a logistical nightmare, among other issues. But my mate has adapted to the sedentary life. Never once have I heard him complain. Fortunately, he has a carer who comes in the morning to get him up and the same bloke at night puts him to bed. He has developed a good relationship with this bloke, even taken him on trips. When his condition was better, his two children — with whom he is very close — would care for him. With the stress of everything he divorced his wife but, in an exceptional situation, she still lives in his place and cares for him. So I would say he is well looked after and this puts me at ease.

Living as he does near the beachfront, every day he rolls down there in his chair. He looks out over the crowd but his great joy is to observe the sunset which is lovely there as the beach faces due west. For many years unable to live in the world as he would wish, this act has brought him a sense of liberation. Even when rockets were landing on Tel Aviv from Gaza he kept going to watch the sunset. It revitalises him.

One memory in particular I cherish. Once, on the longest day of the year, we sat at a restaurant on the beach, ate a good meal and watched the sun go down. He made it an uplifting moment. Over the years, people he thought he knew have forgotten and deserted him as they have me. He doesn't mind, as long as he has the sunset to gaze at. His daughter once made a brief trip to Melbourne so I got to play good uncle. To make her comfortable I took her to watch the sun setting over St Kilda pier. It turned into a lovely evening. I was very glad to see her because she could tell him about where I live. After all, he will never be able to visit me.

After I had my fall, pneumonia and a minor stroke I was put in a holding hospital in Tel Aviv where he would often roll in and visit me. While the benefit wasn't all one way — it was great for him to have some company — I always had to let him leave to allow him time to get home and see the sunset. This was the priority of his life. One day he was especially chipper and I asked him, 'Why are you feeling so good?' He explained that it was Yom Kippur and the streets were empty so coming here was easy for him. It gave him the same sensation of freedom of movement that other people derive from walking about. Lying in the hospital, learning many things about the way he was forced to live made my own misery more bearable as I would not have swapped places with him.

I make sure we keep in close contact since I want him to know there is someone who cares for him. The sun can set over the Mediterranean every day of his life but it need not set on his life. Whenever I see a sunset now I think of the great fortune that is mine, and it reminds me I must engage in the act of living. Bad as life sometimes gets for me, I always know there is someone worse off. One of my greatest hopes is that one day I will get to visit this great mate of mine and go down the beach with him again.

Modern Man

I have a mate I call a great dad, simply because the sole purpose of each breath he takes is to be with his children, enjoying with them the acts that make life worthwhile. My own dad was rather good at this endeavour but this mate takes it up to another level. Observing the things he does, I stand in awe. Once, for his birthday, his wife gave him the present of a night away for the two of them. On receipt of this news he said, 'Great! What about the kids? Are they coming?' His wife stood there and shook her head in disbelief. I just chuckled when she told me about it.

His eldest child was a son you could say was built in his own image. No need to gaze in a pond and fall in love with himself, as the Greek story goes. All he ever needed to do was look at his boy to be lost in self-adulation. As the boy grew he became the ultimate sports nut, just as his dad had been. Any sport he could do he would. No child I have seen participated in so many sports as this one did. Dad was there for his every activity. So solid a grip did the child have on him that he even got dragged out to the rugby during an early Covid scare. He didn't mind: the joy of seeing his son on the field was his paramount concern. If you visited him at home of an evening you would witness him reading to his children collectively. He was involved in every facet of their lives: for him all this was pure joy. I have seen him take all three of them away on holidays by himself and manage. I would say that in him his wife picked up a real gem.

Well, as time passed, the boy and his sisters grew and slowly they became less in need of an involved parent: they wanted to spread their wings, to be free and independent. This was very hard for my mate to accept and deal with. He wanted to be there for every moment of their developing lives but dads can't do that. They can't be there for the first kiss and other key times so as time went on he had to adjust his compass. But, even as he found this difficult to deal with, reward for all his previous effort was winging its way towards him. The children — who by now were close friends with him — would come home to Dad and tell him the latest intimate details of their blossoming lives. He found that he was involved in them but at arm's length. The loss he had felt through their greater distance from him was now counter-balanced — remedied — with a gain, the discovery of even greater closeness to them.

He collected himself and redefined who he was. No, he was not falling into an abyss after all. Why? Because he had done his job well. He had helped create three strong, well-balanced, thinking and independent people. All he had to do now was watch their lives unfold. At last he had time to sit at a bar with his mates and have a quiet drink without feeling the urge to rush off and do something for the kids. He found something in himself that we all seek — contentment. I have no profound message for my mate; I simply say, 'Well done. You have lived well.'

The Road Not Taken

One day while driving round with a friend I exclaimed, 'Spring has sprung. I need a new girlfriend, this is serious!' The friend pondered a moment, then said, 'I know, I have just the woman for you.' He directed me to a large house. We went in, it was bustling with many people. A large Catholic family lived there and I quickly discovered silence was a rare commodity in that place.

Well, she introduced me to a lovely creature, a blonde blue-eyed beauty. I was captivated at first sight, as I am sure many boys were. So we took her out for a spin in the car, and she and I hit if off straightaway. Being keen, I arranged to see her again, and then again. Things were soon going along nicely. One night after a party I popped a kiss and she accepted. It was a done deal – boyfriend and girlfriend, two united as one. My spring crisis was resolved. Happy me.

Only later did I discover that she came from one of Melbourne's foremost Catholic families. Her father was a pillar of the community and consequently, at that time, she shared many of his beliefs.

I understood that I had to be gentle and careful with her, respect who she was and where she came from. A bit frustratingly, she was doing residential nursing so I could only see her late at night after her shifts. As the residential quarters were all-female, I was not allowed into her rooms. This was a substantial barrier to courtship in days when there were no mobile phones to lessen the strain.

A very intense relationship developed. I'm not one to kiss and tell, so there is no need to go into details except to say I took things no further than was warranted given the strict Catholic ethos of her upbringing. That said, I did find it hard to swallow her involvement in anti-abortion groups. Today she has relinquished those beliefs; she has exchanged them for what I regard as a better stance.

My relationship with her was strong and meaningful, and my family — rightly — approved of her as a good influence on me. On the other hand, I don't think her father accepted me at all until he found out that my grandfather was a doctor. Wonderful as things between us were — and yes, she made me blissfully happy — I saw that the cultural divide was too great and felt a bit young for her. So, very foolishly, I ended the relationship, which brings me to the topic of remorse.

I should have had more backbone, I should have risen above our differences. Over the years since my accident, she is one person who has been unfailingly good and true to me. In that respect we have travelled the path of life together. Many times I have regretted my stupidity as I have seen what a quality life partner she would have been. Our intimacy will never subside; even after all these years, we care for each other dearly and are involved in each other's life.

To her I extend a gentle kiss and apologise for my short-sightedness. This is the woman I should have married, with whom I would have been happy for life. We cannot waste years waiting for perfection: it will never come.

The Schnitz

Once upon a time I was a member of a wide-ranging social group. We all enjoyed each other's company and had a great time. Our ideas about life and the world generally coincided. This collective derived a high from being together, and they gave this high a name: the Schnitz (a little like the Irish term '*craic*', for a good time had by all). It was like a recreational drug. We envisioned spending life together and moving forward, an element of this 'high' travelling with them.

Well, as time went on, members of the group coupled, married and entered on life's journey, had children and holidayed together. To many it appeared this was how life ought to be and the Schnitz would continue to be with them, why shouldn't it? But over time the darker side of life intruded. One friend, integral to the group. got cancer and died. He was mourned but superficially and his memory was not cherished well. Life wields its wand, and sometimes the magic disappears! People went through difficult divorces, some took sides instead of being supportive. The Schnitz became a forlorn dream for some. One member of 'the gang' came out as gay; another had a terrible accident. These people were left by the wayside. As people aged, new challenges arose – and the Schnitz was unprepared for them.

As a former member, all I can do is look on and contemplate how shallow people can be. It has not undermined my faith in humanity, simply rid me of my naïvety. Somewhere, for a new generation perhaps, the Schnitz lives. I smile at the thought.

The Reindeer

This story is about a young lady I knew who had a shiny red nose. Since this gave her a similarity to the renowned Rudolf, I shall call her The Reindeer.

Well, I met this young lady in one of my university tutorials. She was a plain type, subdued, never too loud, but I could see she had a real interest in the world and wanted to be involved in it. I was on polite talking terms with her. There was no special level of intimacy and none of the sparkle and magic that other young ladies evoked in me. This didn't bother me: I was happy to be friends with anyone and learn what they were about, considering that to be an important part of my studies and pursuit of knowledge.

One day at dusk I was driving along one of the roads that run by the university and saw The Reindeer walking. Thinking it was a bit dangerous for a young woman to be alone in that place at that hour, I stopped, uttered a few common courtesies, asked where she was going and the young lady replied that she was on her way home. Naturally I offered her a lift and, happily, she accepted. Home was a boarding house of sorts, tucked away from more prominent buildings. She had just a small basic room, her haven from the outside world. We had a pleasant conversation. After leaving I felt concerned for her living in this isolated spot, so took it upon myself to deliver her some care and company — thinking perhaps in the process I could learn a few things.

So on my way home I got into the habit of dropping in to see how things were going. This involved only a minor detour for me. In her small room we would have good long talks and I would witness how a poor student committed to her studies lived. The frugality of her life made me feel privileged and guilty that I lived so well. With all the benefits I had, I was not as committed to the pursuit of study as she was.

I notice things in odd ways. It didn't strike me that this room had no amenities in it, no shower or kitchen area. But one evening I suddenly realised: she pulled out a little hotplate and began to cook dinner on it. Just how humble a life she was leading hit me between the eyes. Bang! She had little, I had taken much for granted, and my heart went out to her. I feel guilty in hindsight that I didn't take her out for the dinner she so richly deserved. I wasn't flush but I shouldn't have been so cheap. I still feel very bad for not acting as I should have. Slowly I built a nice relationship with this young lady; we enjoyed each other's company. A country girl, she came from a world I did not comprehend. But it was from this world that her grand capacity for self-sacrifice sprang.

It so happened that one night, even though I had no intention or design of doing so, I ended up sleeping with her. This came as a total shock to both of us. Being who I was, I did enjoy this but when I discovered the mattress she slept on I was horrified. Never had I seen any bedding in such a poor state: full of lumps, it was ready for the tip. I cannot believe this poor young lady ever enjoyed a good sleep on it. While I did continue to visit her after that one night, the romance was at an end as neither of us had inclination in that direction. At the end of the year I headed off on an overseas trip and when I returned she was gone. I never saw her again. Sad as I was about that, having grown fond of her, I felt she had taught me a lot — about my middle-class privilege.

Being able to study is not a right but a privilege that must be fought for. And this requires sacrifices. In fact all things of value require that we give a bit of ourselves. What else did she teach me? Real poverty is often hidden away: a stranger to poverty has to dig to uncover it and the daily reality is frightening. Where possible I should lend a helping hand. Today when I see a woman with a shiny red nose I know that deep down in her I will find not just some sentimental reminder but a heart that beats truth.

My Mates

I have written a lot about friends and friendship, usually in a less than positive light because so many who call themselves our friends let us down. I was saddened to find that many people I considered true friends who rallied round in the initial period after my accident soon lifted their gaze and evaporated into the atmosphere. The glow of their affection was replaced by a gnawing nothingness. Only the odd decent person hung around and behaved well to me.

Friends are like balloons keeping us afloat during troubled times that threaten to drag us down. So, I'm happy to say, over time I have developed a number of friendships with people I scarcely knew — or in some cases hadn't met — in those days. These people have travelled my journey with me. Through all its ups and down they have sustained me. I have often heard the saying that you can't choose your family but you can choose your friends. If you choose wisely and well, your friends themselves form a family of sorts. But I wouldn't want to leave you with the impression that I've gone in search of friends. On the contrary, they have just turned up and come to me along the path of my journey. I feel these are the best sorts of friends to have — they are genuine, they spend time around you because they want to, not from any sense of obligation. These mates have been good and true to me; I look forward to sharing the future with them.

Let me introduce you to a few of these special people in my life. The first one I will mention was more an acquaintance of mine at university, someone in the wide social circle I acquired at that time. I didn't yet comprehend how fine a human being she was: that appreciation has developed over time. What makes our relationship a bit difficult is the distance between our homes. Seeing each other requires a good bit of organisation, but the willingness, on both our parts, to make the necessary effort has enhanced our friendship and, yes, mateship is not too strong a description.

It was through her that I met her husband, somebody I would have been highly unlikely to meet otherwise. He, too, has an excellent character, and knowing him has greatly enriched my life. One trait he and I possess in common — an obsessive-compulsive personality. It is important to come to terms with such home truths so they can be used to advantage and, speaking for myself now, so I can ensure I limit the harm it wreaks in my life. Come to think of it, a good number of my mates have this trait: it might be why I get on with them so well. Being aware of this I allow them some leeway in their behaviour and understand why they do the things they do in the way they do them. As my friends have had children I have been part of the journey as they have raised them. Like everyone, they have come across certain bumps in the road, and I have done my very best to help them steer their way through them. Alas, one child developed a serious health problem. All things considered, she has handled her challenges well. My role has been to try giving her moral support and discussing issues with her. It has been a delight to watch her develop into a fine young lady. I enjoy being involved with all my friends' children, taking my role as 'uncle' seriously and, of course, I get a lot of reward back for the contributions I make. Another of these children has attained a high level of achievement that makes me as proud as if I were their father. Sometimes all a child needs is encouragement, a spurring of that essential ingredient, self-confidence. Even though at times my friends have told me off for overdoing it, I know that my practice of moderately urging their children on to be and do better is exactly what they need.

One day I was speaking to a friend from university who said, 'The guy I live with is making dinner tonight. Please come along.' I eagerly grabbed the chance to go out and socialise, and ended up having the most wonderful evening. I clicked with the guy who was making dinner: he was an excellent complement to who I am — cultured, educated, extremely interested in the arts and an all-round good human being. We became close friends and did many things together, going to the theatre and concerts, discussing ideas, enjoying coffees together. We just enjoyed the act of living and, as you'll have already guessed, he was another obsessive-compulsive, always fitting more into a day than most people consider possible. He also happened to be a techno-wiz and has helped me a lot on my forced march to modernity. I just missed out on the technological revolution as it came full thrust as I finished uni and had my accident. Having thus ended up without much of the knowledge and skills we need in modern life, I have gradually made up ground with his assistance, though I am still well short of where I should be. There is also the problem that I was not brought up to be techno-adept, but to be more an intellectual.

The people who have helped me get by are many and varied, but we have in common that we all like to help each other out if we can. One bloke who became a mate is the partner of an old friend. In fact he is living in Melbourne — to which he has no deep connection — entirely because of the desire to be with his partner. The two of them have been very kind to me, having donated their time (the most valuable of all gifts). Now he is not somebody I would have met in the normal course of events. Like me, he suffers from a debilitating illness that has stuffed up his life and restricted him from engaging with it as he would have wished. Many a time, as I have been sitting here wondering what to do next, the doorbell would ring and he would say, 'Let's go out for coffee.' Life has been cruel to him, with a series of serious health setbacks arriving one after the other. None of this has stinted his generosity of spirit where I am concerned. As I know he does not really feel at home in this city, I have made a special effort to give him attention. It has even become a bit of a joke on account of the regularity with which I ring. But I think he deserves my attention. It takes no great effort on my part but is something I must do. Reciprocating mateship is how we feed the social being within, and he has had some serious health events one after another.

To have mates who live locally is important: this makes it easier to get out to see them and be in the social swim – to the extent that one can in these Covid times. In such times you don't want to be in cars with people, where it is hard to keep your social distance. I have a very good mate whom I met because he was often working on a house opposite my mother's. He has turned out to be a useful mate to have as he is a handyman and willingly comes to the rescue with all the little problems that arise from home ownership. We have a certain commonality in that we are both avid supporters of the same footy team. He also has a serious gardening interest and, luckily for me, lives only a kilometre and a half from here. It's an easy walk there and back for me but, as it is with all other people, you have to catch him at the opportune time – not always the easiest thing to do. For a time my little sister lived in the same street as him. This was great: when I had my fill of time at my sister's I could simply cross the road, visit him and refresh my spirits. Over time I became good friends with both him and his wife. What is the point of living, I ask myself, if I don't engage fully with its possibilities?

The next couple of blokes that have helped build my friendship nest are brothers of a woman who was a 'sort of' girlfriend at university. Both have enriched my quality of life, and one of them is younger than me (though that doesn't matter). He actually bought a home in St Kilda only half an hour's walk from here, making it very easy for me to visit. He likes to attend the theatre, and in summer the twilight market, a real delight, so we often accompany each other on these outings. We walk to the market with his kids and have a great time; afterwards we head off and enjoy an ice cream. These are about the only ice creams with which I indulge myself: my rationalisation is that it's an essential part of what is always a great evening out. Then every month, along with his big brother, we go the local farmers' market, then out for breakfast. This a great occasion: we all love it.

This mate will often ring up and say, 'Let's go do a coffee.' So we do that and have a good chat. And he helps me out in various practical ways, such as finding someone to install solar on my roof. But the main thing is that we enjoy each other's company. His kids regard me as a real uncle so I try to behave like one, always remembering their birthdays and congratulating them on their achievements. They are lovely children and I very much enjoy their company. (Kids are great when I can hand them back and don't have to take them home!) His big brother, also a close friend, is a gentle person, one who treads lightly through life but, like all of us, he has had his ups and downs, and I have been there to share the journey. Over time we have kept up a substantial email correspondence. It helps that we have similar interests: sport, gardening, the theatre. We, too, have created our own rituals. Every Easter Tuesday we go out and enjoy dinner somewhere. Habits that turn into traditions are the cornerstone of life's structure, in my opinion. For a few years he was living in Tokyo and I flew up to visit him: such a vast city would have been a bit much to take on by myself.) I am reassured we will continue to do good things together, support and encourage each other to live as well as we can for years to come. To me, this is the core of mateship.

One very good mate, based in London ,spends his life travelling around the world lecturing and teaching, which I feel makes for a very pressured lifestyle. About once a year he makes it to Melbourne for a very crowded couple of days. Apart from his heavy workload he has a host of people to see, including an elderly mother, but no matter how busy he is he remains a good mate and always makes an effort to see how I am going and reassure himself I am getting by. We always have a good time. I do wish he could spend more time in Melbourne when he does get down here, but console myself with the knowledge that we have been mates for over forty years and so it shall continue. His long-term commitment is just the opposite of the attitude exhibited by fair-weather friends.

Another mate I have known for over forty years also lives a half-hour's walk away. Our mateship has matured over time and we watch each other's back. He often gives me a lift to places. Like everyone, he's experienced various hiccups along the way and I have tried to be there for him and advise him as best I can if that is called for. There are limits though, I mean, what can you say when a sibling dies? All you can do, I think, is extend some brotherly love.

Now mates come in all shapes and sizes, so it's up to us to open our hands and greet them with genuine acceptance and warmth. I maintain a wonderful email conversation with a cousin in America whom I've never met and probably never will. I understand all her problems and offer my best advice where it is needed. She gives me a keyhole insight into the way things are over there — and I try to explain Australia to her, such a foreign place in her conception of things. Our views all differ according to where we sit, so I must tailor the type of mate I can be to the type of mate I am speaking or listening to. The last thing I would want anyone to think is that I am up myself so if someone extends the hand of mateship I shall grasp it and explore it – but always with the expectation that they have washed it in soapy water.

Shared Journeys

People often speak of being 'on a journey', and life has been seen as a journey by many philosophers down the ages. During this voyage there are many ports of call to destinations sometimes unknown. But to get where you're going you absolutely have to make the trip. The best you can expect is that all the digressions, meanderings and detours add up to a good journey — even if not an epic adventure like *War of the Worlds* or *Around the World in Eighty Days.*

When I was young my parents would take us to the homes of various friends to celebrate the second night of Jewish festivals. This is a thing Jews are supposed to do. One of these couples had a son about my age. Good for me, I thought. So we became friends, and did what friends do: we played with each other, slept over at each other's place and generally enjoyed one another's company. Little did I realise then, as I do now, that this was just the start of a long journey together that would be good for both of us.

Well, time pushed us apart. Religiously inclined, he joined a Jewish religious youth movement; I was anything but religious and instead joined a Marxist-Leninist youth movement. For many years our paths did not coincide and we would bump into each other only occasionally, greeting each other warmly whenever we did. Our academic trajectories were also very different: he came from a medical family and ended up a doctor. My background, as you know, led me to a study of the arts and history.

The jolt in my life was my accident and ensuing health issues; the jolt in his was coming to the realisation that exerting himself to be religious was not the right thing for him. With impressive strength of character, he discarded the observant lifestyle and embarked on a secular existence, while maintaining a deep connection to the moral and ethical basis of Judaism. He even became involved with a humanist group that regularly meets in a hall — something like a godless synagogue — where he practises Jewish life and philosophy in that form.

After this shift in his outlook, we drew closer again. He does many things that my health doesn't permit and I envy his engagement with his life (which I imagine would be like the life I would lead if only things were different). But instead we exchanged visits to each other's home — he and his wife to mine, I to theirs; and pleasant occasions they were. But I realised that as they were very busy people it would be ridiculous to place any demands on them or to expect anything. From time to time I would visit them and they would always include me in their social social events which is more than most people, who wouldn't bother. I would say that over the course of my life he has been a true friend: this has gone on for at least fifty years now. Yet I feel as if our trip has just begun. Long into the future we shall enjoy each other's company and, if Fortune smiles on us, continue to learn from each other.

Many of us have friends who go back a long time. They pop in and out of our lives at different points. I feel the thing that counts, and cements our friendships the most, is shared experience, building up a solid body of memories. With some people, the memories just vanish — they are not participants in your life, really — but when the memories are rekindled it is a warm sensation, like the sun coming out from behind a bank of clouds.

I have a very close friend from primary-school days with whom I spent many hours and did many things. Decades elapsed and I had no idea where he was or what life had done to him. Thanks to the magic of Facebook (which is something I neither understand nor want to understand), my mother found him and I got back in contact with him. So after these many years we have renewed our friendship as if no time at all had passed. He got a bit of a shock when I told him all that had happened to me. Like most people from those days, he had no idea what had become of me. His own road had been bumpy so there was plenty to catch up on when we gathered in a bar on what was a lovely evening. We see each other every now and again. Unlike when we were kids, it's not so easy to see each other these days as he now lives at a distance. But we learn some things in odd ways: he has told me how my dad helped him along his path in life. Must admit, it sounded typical of my dad — and of course it warms my heart to hear such stories. With parents like mine, I have a lot to live up to.

As the distance between us and our sometime companions in life broadens and then narrows over time, the important thing is to share the act of living as this enriches our being. May I continue to encounter diverse travelling companions on my path forward and bask in their warmth. Those who take a different approach exist in what I call the graveyard of life.

The Coeliac

I have a friend with whom over many years I have enjoyed dining out. This is our chosen mode of social intercourse. We have derived great joy and satisfaction from these occasions. We imagined and expected that they would go on long into the future as we learned and discovered the deepest recesses of each other's personality.

Satisfied as we were during our conversation-laden meals, my friend would afterwards suffer some discomfort and be quite unwell. It had nothing to do with the quality of the food we ate — I never felt the slightest discomfort — but her quest to discover the source of the problem took her to a wide array of doctors. Medicine is an imprecise science and, all the while, poor dear, she suffered. Ultimately, after undergoing a test, she was found to be a coeliac, meaning she suffered an immune reaction to any food containing gluten. To accommodate this required a total re-evaluation and reconstruction of her eating habits. As with any health condition she had to learn to live with it so our regular dining arrangements went from being a straightforward pleasure to a strategic headache, much to our cost.

To make matters even worse, her daughter had inherited this disease, which made planning to go out of an evening a real conundrum. There are various eateries that say they offer food for people with their condition, but often this is nothing but a bold lie. They are not careful to keep things separate so food gets contaminated and later my friend suffers the consequences. So if we want to go feasting we need to be very careful where we choose to eat and what my friend orders. Even with the risks involved we are not willing to forgo the right to live well.

We're not always successful but sometimes we are — and that's because we are both willing to confront adversity. If we need to devise workarounds, we do.

She is just one of various people I know who have problems — and solutions — unique to them. One mate is crippled with rheumatoid arthritis. Every now and again he would rock up in a car and say, 'Hey, let's go for a coffee, so long as I don't have to walk there.' Poor sod, he developed diabetes and that magnified his walking difficulties to the extent that he is now housebound. The solution I found was a telephonic one. I ring him and talk things through. He can enjoy a coffee in his place, and I in mine, but the social aspect of sitting in a café is what he was missing out on. In this way I improve his quality of life and mine at the same time. The examples go on and on.

The lesson is always the same: if we put enough thought into it, a good quality of life is attainable. It calls for endless creativity, but that is seldom in short supply. Take the bloke who can't get out because his wheelchair limits his mobility. Instead his mates come round to his place and have a night out in each other's company.

In short, disability is no fun. Often, a satisfactory response to its challenges requires a variety of actors — personal supports, if you will. If these supports fall away, for whatever reason, that makes life for the disabled person so much the harder. Where I can, I keep a lookout for ways I can help people. I go back to the friend you met at the outset. We help each other along — we are travelling in the same direction, after all — and by doing this we lead what we are presumptuous enough to call the good life.

A Sad Story

What I am about to tell I consider a very sad story, one in which I do not exactly cover myself in glory, because I failed to behave as well as I expect myself to.

When I was a young teenager, a lovely sweet dark-skinned girl captured my attention. I became good friends with her but in the years since then I have let the course of life stop me from building on that foundation as I should have. I have not lived up to the obligation I have of being a true friend. I feel a lesser person for this. As we grew and developed, my friend found it difficult to come to terms with the world around her. This kind of problem is loosely, but perhaps best, described as mental health issues.

Being in the world is not an easy thing for everyone. As time went on she developed schizophrenia, a cruel disease that robs people of their peace and sense of place in the world. To start with, it was not so extreme, and on plenty of occasions she was able to live a normal life, whatever that is.

Over time I kept up contact with her; every now and again, I would check to see how she was going and found her to be nice company. I admit I was still attracted to her. At that age I wasn't fully aware of the complexity of her illness. During one of her lucid periods I was seeing her quite a bit. For some reason she threw a party, which was a bit of fun in my quiet life, and I introduced her to a bloke I was mucking around with at the time. I took him aside and explained to him the fragility of her mental state but was crushed when he took no notice of what I'd told him. Since then I have not seen this bloke. Why would I? Under the impact of his attentions, her condition went from being manageable into a downward spiral that lasted for many years. She has suffered horribly, been locked up and made to take various powerful drugs with severe side effects. Her quality of life is greatly diminished. All this was withheld from those who had known her in earlier years, as she was incarcerated in places far from home. My heart goes out to her.

I hate being locked up in any way, even for a short time. Having often been a prisoner in hospitals, I feel for her. Occasionally I would bump into her mother, who would report her lack of progress and sub-optimal life. I had a genuine desire to visit her, to be supportive and there as a friend for her. *The least I can do*, I told myself. But her being kept at remote locations reachable only by car thwarted my good intentions since I don't drive. The system kept her out of sight and, for long periods, out of mind. It was custom-made to let her rot.

Frustrated at my inability to behave as I should, I inquired about other possibilities of visitation. Speaking to an old friend of hers I suggested we make a day trip, to bring some joy into her life. To my dismay this person said, 'Sorry, much as I'm fond of her, I can't handle seeing her in the state she's in, it's beyond me.' This woman proclaimed socially progressive views: so much for that! So I approached another woman, who was more of an acquaintance than a friend but still knew this woman I had first met in adolescence — and made the same suggestion of a day trip. She replied, 'I was never very close to her so it's not up to me, not my responsibility.'

Weakly, I threw my hands up in the air at this point. I gave up. Looking back, I should unquestionably have looked for other ways of visiting her. From everything I heard, there was no doubt her condition was getting worse and worse. The way I was reacting forced me to confront my own situation, and recognise the reality that if a degree of effort was required, then many people wouldn't bother with me. People are naturally self-focused: they get wrapped up in their own lives.

So, to circle back, I feel very badly at having allowed my health challenges to determine who I am. For me, not to act in a way I should is unacceptable. I owe it to myself to defeat my restraints and live life as it should be. As I write, I still have not followed up with this girl — I still think of her as a girl — but I can see that when I condemn people's behaviour it is not always because of their inadequacy or personal failing. Circumstances sometimes conspire to make it difficult to live our lives as we know we ought to do. Nevertheless...

Discord In The Workplace

I have a mate who had it all together, who possessed what you might call a stable equilibrium. Peace of mind was in his keeping; he looked out upon the world with a calm demeanour. Then along came Covid and his relaxed mode of being vanished, as if his personality had imploded. His former evenness of temper now gave way to extremes of joy and exaltation followed by a plunge into the depths of depression and despair. I call this bipolar: not being a trained doctor, I don't use the word in its classic sense — but it does describe the mood swings that take him from one emotion to its polar opposite . This, I think, is a very unsettling place to be so, yes, I have great concern for my mate.

At the start of the Covid crisis, offices and businesses shut down and people were told go and work from home. This is where my mate's conundrum sprang from. It is all well and good to say, 'Go home and work from there' but no one was told how to do it. This is what upset my mate's previously placid disposition and sent him oscillating from dizzying highs to unfathomable lows.

There he sat at his kitchen table. This was no holiday. No longer was his home a haven of relaxation and pleasure. The tyranny of life had now converted it into his workplace. At this point he threw his hands in the air and implored the heavens above for some revelation that would tell him how to deal with this drastic change in his circumstances. It was up to him now to find a way of restoring his peace of mind.

So he poured himself a strong cup of tea and sighed, 'Now what? Here is the seat of my freedom and relaxation, but also my place of work and effort and stress. How do I reconcile the two?'

Work must take priority, he reasoned. *I'd better act the way I do when preparing to go out to work*. So each day he got up at the same time, showered, put on his suit and tie, and then he was ready to commence his daily shift. This is where the problem began: no longer did his routine involve a morning commute. What was he to do? He was at a loss — and then a brainwave struck. He would simulate the commute and get himself into the right frame of mind. So it was out to the car, followed by some sedate motoring, a few times up and down the driveway in first gear — but this took only a few minutes. A block of time stretched out before him and how was he going to fill it? At that point his pet dog bounded into view, prompting the thought: *I can make the dog happy and do myself some good: let's go for a walk*. He must have spoken the thought out loud, because suddenly the dog yelped with delight. Instead of the hound's regular evening walk, which he decided not to change, there were now two walks a day: lucky dog! While the pet seemed to thrive under this new regime, however, its master did not. He soon became exhausted. Having tried a longer-than-usual route, he would arrive home exhausted, put the lead away and stare blankly at the prospect of a long day ahead.

Unused to doing work at home, my mate now forced himself to sit in front of the computer and focus. No idle chit-chat, no morning tea. Work could not be put off any longer. Rapidly he whisked through the various tasks that demanded his attention, so that by the middle of the day he could look forward to having a couple of magical hours to himself. Filled with a sense of accomplishment, he began climbing the ladder of exaltation. In a couple of hours he would have to be around — fully focused again — for some teleconferencing, but he told himself: *Hey, this isn't as bad as I thought it would be.*

How to spend his two hours of self-reward? A moment's consideration made it obvious. He could go for a swim or a ride on his bike. This was the activity that did it for him. All his life, riding had brought him bliss — when he could find the time for it. (Work commitments had taken up too much of his time in recent years.) Now he had the opportunity to indulge, to be young again, to stretch his long legs in harmony with the rhythm of the wheels. Each day from this point on he hit the road, feeling the rush of the breeze on his face. Gradually the endorphins kicked in and he got drunk on the buzz. 'Euphoria' is not too strong a word. This is the good side of the bipolar experience, and he hadn't just climbed the stairway to heaven, as the song says: he was taking the elevator.

Every day, after his ride, he would open the door, walk in — and immediately feel his spirits sink. There was no one with whom he could share his joy. He was missing that space where he would communicate with his workmates. Cudgelling his brains in a vacuum was not just isolating, but soul-destroying. He no longer felt part of the world as he slid from that giddy open-air high into the deep abyss of despair. He needed the office — but he didn't want to return there even if it had been possible, because then he would miss out on the pumping high of his daily bike excursion. This was a very real bind. His mental health was now at the tipping point but, as fortune would have it, life itself came to his rescue.

The lockdown finally ended and he had to return to the office. Happily, he was able to adjust to his old, now new, reality, without ill effect. What unsettled him now was that the office itself had become a different place, a new world. Colleagues now behaved and reacted differently. He had to navigate the new office dynamics like an entry-level rookie. He soon realised what had caused the difference, and concluded that social distancing fosters discord in the workplace.

The aftermath of this Coronavirus will be substantial and long-lasting. What they call long Covid is not just a physical effect. It has seeped into our daily lives, scarring the lungs of our economy. We must learn to recognise this and deal with it, each in our own way.

Skyhooks

When I was eight I went to my first camp. The big joke they pulled on us there was to ask each of us, 'Did you bring your skyhook?', knowing you would have no idea what a skyhook was. So right from the get-go you would feel a bit stupid not having one. This was dragged out by explaining that a skyhook was a multipurpose camping aid with which you could do everything: erect tents, dig holes, make furniture … there was no end to its all-round utility.

It always took newcomers a few days to realise those in charge were having them on, but it worked as a way of building friendship circles so, for years after that first awkward encounter, going off to camp became an annual fixture.

Talk of skyhooks faded until one year in my early teens the band Skyhooks burst onto the music scene. The giggle that name gave us!

For us, who knew the value of a single skyhook through bitter experience, it involved no great stretch to see what a positive influence Skyhooks (plural) could prove to be. The band and its music forged even tighter bonds among us. As the cool kids we were, we thought this camaraderie would go on forever. We would be looking out for each other at twenty, thirty, forty … friends for life. Time has sadly taught me — and I suppose the rest of our group — otherwise. The invasion of my life taught me the harsh reality of how shallow and unreliable some people turn out to be.

I bear no malice towards these people but have no time for them. It's like the dishonour that falls on a 'blood brother' in a secret society when one of the so-called brothers turns out not to give a damn about the others — the difference being I don't order violent action against them (I just *cut* them dead). The finger cut by the knife to mix the blood runs deep and stings. When people prove shallow and untrue to their word, well, the knife twists and turns. The worst of it all is that such people have no idea … To quote the immortal words of a famous Skyhooks song, ego is not a dirty word — and I won't let mine be soiled by people who I consider have proved themselves lesser beings than me.

Neighbours

You can choose your friends but you can't choose your family — the saying goes. I would add a variant: you might not get the neighbour you choose but, like family, you have to live with them. Our home maybe the fortress that shields us from the rest of the world and our personal space. But "No man is an island" (John Donne) and neighbours are closest to our domestic sanctuary and directly influence what we feel and how we relate to the world.

Everyone wants neighbours to their liking so that they can live well — but likes and dislikes vary. The street or block of flats you live in is your community, and we all want that to be a good thing. I was taught at a young age to look out for your neighbours and treat them well. We had elderly ladies living on either side. I was taught to speak to them with respect. Mum would send me in to them with plates of food for dinner. I admit to being unhappy that I didn't have other kids to play with next door but in later years I had a dalliance with a girl who lived around the corner (a sort of neighbour, you could say). I had a mate nearby and he had lots of other kids around him: they all played together and were a part of each other's lives. All I had was two sisters to play with so I felt limited.

Eventually, I moved into my own house in a small side street. This was when I learnt the importance of neighbours in all their diversity. My little street is well off the beaten track — which means it functions like a kind of village — and I am very happy about that. We 'villagers' are interconnected but still maintain our privacy. Once people move in here, a life sentence it is — except that no one is busy planning a breakout. As a result, the street has a number of elderly people, which is nice. Through them you can receive the wisdom of the ages, and the neighbourhood is friendly: as you move up and down the street, you are greeted warmly by people who ask how you are and genuinely care.

Yet they don't pry into your private life. When a community member is in need, the neighbours are glad to help each other out. I am most fortunate to have an elderly gentleman living next to me who over the years has been of great assistance. I am not a very practical fellow and he has helped me numerous times. Due to his age he does have a few limitations but the spirit is ever willing. Having got to know him, I have found I like the man as well as respecting and admiring how he goes about things. Whenever we see each other we say hello and stop for a chat, but there's no open-door policy. Each of us understands that the other likes to be left in peace in his own home. Instead of disturbing each other by knocking on the door all the time, we keep up a vibrant conversation through email. Because he's advanced in years I do what I can for him, bringing in the bins and checking to see if he is OK during a heatwave or when his partner goes away.

On warm days we take great delight in sharing a couple of beers. The street has a sort of barter system whereby we share our produce with each other. Every year I look forward to receiving a bag of Jerusalem artichokes from a Greek neighbour but, harmonious as that sounds, community relations haven't always been ideal. In any shared space there will be people who are unwilling to share. This you have to learn to live with: it is the way of the world. Of course it cuts both ways: I have to share the area where I live with others whom I would prefer had not come to be in our part of the world. Well, you can't expect people to move just because the way they live disturbs you. Unless you want to create a greater ruckus than the one you're putting up with, you have no choice but to sit it out.

A case in point: a while back there was a boy who lived across the road — he was not well in my view. He kept a menagerie of animals that disturbed the peace day and night — loud barking dogs, and a long-suffering bird with a spine-chilling squawk, but what took the cake was a rooster that robbed me of my all-important sleep. In the daytime, visitors saw the lighter side of his petting zoo, displaying great amusement at rabbits running up and down the street. But matters soon developed past the point of mere annoyance. Whenever he ventured out, he would take things from my front yard. Deciding there was nothing I could really do about this (garden boxes aren't worth tying up police resources), I sat it out..for thirty years — until finally I was rewarded. He sold the house and left the neighbourhood, leaving me to the peace and quiet I have always desired.

But there are different kinds of bad neighbours, just as there is variety among the good ones. On one side I have people who don't communicate or chat to anyone apart from themselves. Their boundary fence might as well be a castle wall: this doesn't promote the sense of community I value. A few doors up are some very loud neighbours who enjoy clubbing and being noisy at all hours of the night. They don't really bother me because I am fast asleep when they're carousing but again they contribute nothing to the notion of community.

I like living where I do because of the various amenities available to me: the beach, the lake, cafés and bars among others. Time has taught me that these things are not my own but shared with others, not just neighbours but folk who come from all over Melbourne to enjoy what's here. And their visits add to what's on offer, so that makes me even happier to live where I do. But a few of these visitors — who intrude into my home locality — make me wish they had stayed away. Why do they need to bash people or get drunk in the streets, use drugs (dropping syringes in an oft-frequented local park)? My message to them is a basic one: if you visited someone, you wouldn't trash their house — so please don't trash mine.

One mate of mine lives about a kilometre and a half away but I still consider him a neighbour. We just enjoy each other's company so we do go out and have a good time whenever we can. I am like an uncle to his children. During lockdown we have 'Covid coffee' together to preserve our sanity. Another mate with whom I have a lot in common — we support the same footy team, for example — is not so easy to catch up with. Yet another friend, who lives not so far away, has become something of a recluse. His unwillingness to meet anybody does no favours for my mental health — or his, come to that. His behaviour is what I consider downright un-neighbourly. Lastly I will mention a mate who gets himself into all sorts of fixes. I have tried to help him navigate his way through them, especially since his brother — who was a real guiding force in his life – died. The way I look at it, being a neighbour is not purely about where one resides, but amounts to a philosophy of life, a moral duty of care. When being a neighbour is done well, we are all better people. Surely being a good neighbour is not so hard.

Taxi Driver

Since I don't drive, from time to time I am forced to catch taxis to get around. There are both pros and cons to this. Although I am not keen about catching too many cabs, the occasional ride in one turns out to be a valuable experience. I have heard it said that taxi travel can work out cheaper than running a car. But in Melbourne my experience is that getting around in cabs is an expensive undertaking, even though I enjoy the use of a half-price card because of my health condition. For this and many other reasons, I take pains not to overindulge.

I enjoy getting in a cab driven by an older, long-time professional driver. With them I feel safer. As a bonus, they often have interesting tales, and wonderful observations about life. As many a journalist knows, their views are a good way of canvassing public opinion. Regrettably, there are fewer and fewer of these older drivers around as their type is gradually disappearing, for reasons I shall shortly examine. I consider this a great loss as the drivers replacing them are far too often not up to scratch.

I respect taxi drivers, who have a difficult and dangerous job, so I try to treat them well. Being on the road so many hours a day can be tiring, which increases the danger to driver and passenger alike. Besides that, it's impossible to know what some idiot behind the wheel of another car will do. If they smash into the taxi you're driving, you lose your livelihood. Scarier than that is that you never know who you're picking up. Sitting in the front passenger seat, I do my best to follow the conversation and see things from the driver's point of view. In this situation, some cherished moments can occur.

From many places in Melbourne it can be difficult to get a cab. Happily, my house and my street are not among them. Usually, if I call a cab to take me a decent distance, there's plenty of opportunity to strike up a conversation with the driver. This can turn out well, and even lead to moments of high humour. I recall once having a pleasant drive with a friendly cabbie but when I got to my destination and paid by card suddenly he went nuts. On seeing my surname he suddenly grew very agitated, asking: 'Is so and-so your father?' Yes, I replied, at which he loudly exclaimed: 'He taught me and he was a wonderful teacher. I very much want to see him.' Only later did I learn that Dad had saved his life. So I gave him Dad's phone number. He turned out to be an ex-student whom Dad remembered. So he organised with a couple of mates to take Dad out for dinner to discuss old times. They all enjoyed these outings and repeated them a number of times. Truth can be stranger than fiction.

On another occasion a taxi driver picked me up for a long-distance trip. Before the car was in second gear, he had started ranting about 'Keating this' and 'Keating that' and how he had destroyed the country because of 'the recession we had to have'. I could see this was a common rant for this particular character. Quick on my feet, I said, 'Hey, wait a minute, do you realise how important and significant Paul Keating was? He was so advanced that the things he did for the national economy they study in business courses overseas. A friend of mine doing a Master's had to learn about him and his achievements.' This was no flight of fancy on my part but a true story. By the time we reached our destination the driver had calmed down. Very pleased with the power of my speech, he had accepted my sincerity and ceased ranting about the former prime minister. I could see him musing and chewing over what I had said. This illustrates how, when it is well controlled and well used, language can make people rethink long-held views in the course of half an hour. But you have to observe your driver closely beforehand. You need to be on your game when you enter a cab — and especially careful not to upset the person behind the wheel if you want to arrive at your destination safely.

Reasons behind the exodus of older drivers range from age to safety to the impact of Uber on their viability. This is not good for people like me; it means I don't get the service I desire. Often, the people who have replaced these drivers don't know Melbourne nearly as well. Too many times they are unsure where they're going and in general are reliant on the GPS, which will get you from A to B but, more often than not, won't manage it by the quickest route. Hands-on knowledge is hard to replace. Many of these drivers speak limited English, so it is hard to communicate with them and they do not look upon taxi driving as a long-term profession.

Often I feel very uncomfortable. Not naturally good drivers, they often fail to pay due attention to the road. That doesn't mean they can never make me smile. A few times I have seen taxis parked in my street and beside them their drivers prostrate on prayer mats. This will bring a smile to my lips: this is modern Australia and all power to them. I like living in an integrated society and it brightens my day whenever I see a taxi driver heading in the right direction.

Closeness

Everyone lives at a distance from everyone else, be it great or small. In whatever way we can, we try to narrow the gaps. Instead of distance, it is closeness that contributes to our quality of life. We can be at a physical distance yet still be close: it depends how we approach the problem. It can be one of the most stimulating and rewarding activities in our lives to explore the distance between ourselves and others, if only to understand who *we* are. Consequently, distance is no bad thing as it forces us into navigating our way across 'alien territory' to create a respectful intimacy with those living on the other side.

I have an older sister who has lived overseas in various places for all her adult life. The barrier of distance is one we have overcome. In recent years technology has aided us in that quest, making snail mail redundant and enabling us to have a far more interactive relationship. Nevertheless, understanding each other's lives has been difficult. But there are upsides, too: for me it has had the advantage of visiting her in her various domiciles and getting a peep into the life she leads, which is very different from my own. Through these visits we have built a closeness, so much so that on hearing of my accident she left her job and got on the first plane to Perth to be with me – though she claims she just wanted to see me silent for once. But once was not a limitation: she has turned up out of the blue to see me after many of my subsequent health incidents.

Since living so far away brings great difficulties in its train, my deal with her has been to fill her in on what is happening here, especially as our parents have aged. In this way we have broken the space barrier, so to speak. I have a similar type of relationship with my dad's niece, who lives in Israel, and with many of my good friends who live abroad. With them, keeping up the relationship is difficult. Contact is, at best, fleeting. It was a challenge earlier generations sustained through letter writing. In those days an overseas phone call was a luxury. It had to be booked and people spoke quickly as it was very expensive. Today, Skype, WhatsApp and FaceTime not only push distance aside, we can see each other and how we are instantaneously. We want the people who we love and care for to be present and active in our lives. And, yes, planes have softened the crunch of distance but they cannot eliminate its effects altogether.

More intractable remains the distance between minds. This is a danger zone in which many landmines have been planted, so I will tread very carefully here. To start with, there are differences in the way people see the world and respond to it. I have my own expectations of how people should behave and act. Often to my distress, this leaves a large gap between me and other people: it is a harsh lesson I learnt that others' outlook on the world and notions of right and wrong behaviour often do not coincide with mine. According to my view of the world, there is little to be gained by being upset when people behave less than well. Where appropriate or possible, I will speak up if I hear someone being racist (that said, there is not just a distance but a gulf between people in this area). In the name of cohesion the best we can do is try to harmonise these differences so that they are not accentuated.

Sometimes it comes down to sheer personality. Some of us are introverted; others extroverted. Some are very confronting – I was that already before my brain damage exacerbated the tendency. In everyday life a difference of minds is inevitable, which should not surprise us as minds are bound to be at different levels of intellectual capacity or development. It's a simple fact that not everyone is as well educated as me. Accepting that, I cannot expect these people to approach things as I do. But what I resent is when someone assumes a difference in me because I speak differently. The way I look at it, there is nothing to be gained by putting people down because of the way they speak.

The Undead

I am talking about the undead. No I will not be referring to vampires but I am talking about another blood sucker that breathes and continues to do so by sucking the blood and life out of other people. They do not care — it is how they survive. They consider themselves upright, erect models of humanity but in reality they are the lowest of the low. They reside in the dirt and filth of the gutter and we do not want to be be like them in any regard. In fact, we strive to behave in the exact opposite way, with decency respect and loyalty.

Growing up, I spent time with people and created many lived experiences— what I considered the real basis of friendship. Some you consider will be life long friends — people with whom you will have a good rapport and will always continue to have good times with. When this did not come to pass, I was forced to reassess things. I discovered they had been possessed by the undead, their moral blood and decency had been sucked out of them.

I was brought up that if you see someone in need — you are to help out and assist as best you can. Don't just think about it, do it! I was taught this well by my parents through example. My parents are good people. This is what I call moral fibre and life blood. With this, people breathe, function and exist. It was to my amazement to discover through the act of life that too many people don't have this moral blood flowing through their veins. It has been sucked out of them and they have become the undead. I once thought, if i go out of my way, and help and assist somebody, one day in the future, when I need help, they would return my efforts. I believed in a reciprocity of good will, a common essence of life blood. But I have been disillusioned to learn that reciprocity is purely a nice literary idea. In real life, it doesn't happen. For the undead, I would say, it is beyond them to return a kindness. Unfortunately, I have a long memory. You could say, I have an ongoing knowledge of how both sides of the ledger stack up. Now big questions arise here, how do I respond to the actions of the undead? There are a variety of responses. The first is — don't get angry, get even. Due to empowerment, getting even is not always possible. There are other avenues that can be followed and done without draining the moral blood out of me and becoming the undead like them. i must always sustain my moral life blood and be aware of it.

At some point, when people have not been behaving as well as they should, I move them from undead status to that of dead and buried. I treat them as such should I come across them. One thing that gets up my nose — when I come across them in a public situation, they try and act as my best friend when in reality they are anything but. I have developed a policy of no free rides to deal with this. I will let nobody act as my best friend if they have had the moral lifeblood sucked out of them. The funny thing is these creatures get upset if i dont return their so-called warmth. I have concluded, instead of creating a public scene by being directly rude to them, I won't allow the moral blood taken out of me. It took time for me to find a solution but in time I did. I simply walk away and ignore them. This cuts to the chase. So as they are calling my name, I give them no recognition, I just walk off. Perhaps to drive the point hard, I will greet someone else. Over time, I have tried to give these people excuses for their poor behaviour — like they have poor attention span that is unable to carry through what they should be doing. Or I have allowed them the excuse — they have got caught up in the act of life and lost their way. This is not an excuse, it is an expression of adoration of self. I accept this is a feature of the society in which we live. But it is not valid, if we have blood pumping through our veins, it is possible to rise above this self-focus and do the right thing. There are a variety of other excuses but none of them wash with me.

To conclude — where does this leave me? I must sustain an idea of my own self worth and how I think I should be treated. I will not allow myself to be demeaned and try to get the undead behave in the way a person acts who has moral blood pumping through their veins. If they choose to be dead, they will be treated and referred to in that way. All this leaves me in the position that I must be well aware of my behaviour to and for people who are in some way in a difficult situation and it is my task to fulfil this need if I can. I must insure that through my veins pumps the best quality of ethics and behaviour. I have a very simple expression of this — I try and to make sure I remember people on their birthday and give them my best wishes. I think it is important to make people feel special, even if it is for just a brief moment.

Nine

Food

"The Nappy"

One of the great joys of life in Melbourne is going out to cafés and restaurants, sharing people's company over food and a drink. This is one of the keys to a good quality of life but how to behave in these places, and do this well, is a learnt thing, not something people are born with.

Eating-out behaviour differs from country to country, as I have learnt. One task I have taken upon myself is assisting people in passing these skills on to their children so that they become good healthy members of Melbourne society. The most valuable thing I can offer children is unconditional love: this form of love is a rare commodity, nowhere near as abundant as it should be. I feel it is critical for the development of any child: when sustained and maintained, it contributes to the healthy functioning of a good person.

I had a good mate with whom I would often go out to cafés and restaurants. He had a very young son, so young we might as well call him 'The Nappy'. So if we wanted to go out, well, of course, The Nappy had to be taken along. Once — it was Easter Tuesday, a public holiday in years past but no more — we decided to go out. I chose Victoria Street so we could get Vietnamese food. After a few minutes' search we found a parking spot. But as we were walking back to the main drag to find a restaurant it became obvious, The Nappy had to be changed. We stood there in a gutter — trying to look as private as you can in public — and did the needful deed. So we found a place, were seated with The Nappy in a high chair, and thought, *The day can only get better from here on in.*

Wrong. The Nappy somehow managed to knock over a bowl of rice. Hell, we didn't care about the hassles he was causing us because to him we were giving unconditional love. Over the years we took The Nappy to many places and — as you would expect after moving out of infancy — his behaviour improved. He learnt to be a good café dweller and every year since, as a ritual, we have go out for dinner on Easter Tuesday night as an expression of love for the child. He is a grown man now and eagerly joins us for dinner. Pleasure becomes tradition.

Adopting rituals adds meaning to our lives. The experience itself can be enriched too: unsurprisingly, The Nappy learnt to read so, before many years had passed, he could digest menus and order as he desired from them. Reading menus well and getting what you want is an art we endeavoured to teach The Nappy, along with restaurant etiquette. These are all important skills to learn, especially in Melbourne.

By the time he was thirteen The Nappy was already as tall as me and on his way to becoming a giant. Accompanying this growth spurt he turned into a human garbage disposal unit that would eat anything. We tried to teach him to discriminate. On each Easter Tuesday I would pull him aside and try to impart a pearl of wisdom. He was a curious boy so he would listen. One year, Easter Tuesday coincided with Anzac Day. So I asked him if he knew what the Anzac holiday was about. He replied it was about wars past and how we try to remember them. I said to him, 'Now the thing to remember is that war is not good. What we must remember is that when people go to war they don't all get to come home. War is senseless murder, for every act of bravery in it there are many more acts of savagery. So each year we take this moment to remember the horror and the sadness of losing those who don't return.' He looked at me, considered it and digested it. The Nappy was always open to new thoughts. I once asked him, 'What's your favourite subject?' He replied, 'Science.' 'Why?' 'Because it introduces me to new worlds.'

I was pleased The Nappy was coming to terms with who he was. For the most part this turned out to be an eating machine. To accentuate this he became a power lifter, and so turned his passion for eating into a thing of use. As he aged he continued to accompany his father and me out for meals. But he was dangerous. We would take him to the local farmer's market and before we had a chance to order breakfast he had already eaten two for himself. No longer did we have to change his nappy; now we just had to wipe his mouth.

Well, any food-related activity made The Nappy happy. When he would come here to visit, we would talk about things, he would give me badly needed assistance with new technology and you bet we would then go out to a café. I'm happy to report that our lifelong conversation continues. I will always be there to talk through aspects of life with him and help him navigate the world. Unconditional love demands no less.

Covid Coffee

Throughout my life, from a young age, I have been a serious *café* dweller.

Going out for coffee is not an act of indulgence for me but an important, indeed integral, aspect of life, one that confers a certain tenor and quality on the very act of being. Believing this, I am fortunate to live in a great café city such as Melbourne where I can obtain a satisfying cup of ambrosia with ease and at no very great expense. Over time I have enjoyed a range of good, even I would say special, coffees. The latest of these I call my Covid coffee .

As a child I would deliver short black coffees to my father for him to drink in bed. To me this was a joyous thing, an act of love and giving that gave me a warm sensation. Looking back on it now that my father has passed away, it remains one of the fondest memories of my life and of him. He would always leave me a little of the coffee to sip. For me this was the point of entry into the joys that coffee could bring. As a young teenager I learnt to know coffee drinking as a social ritual. Accompanied by a number of friends — many lovely girls among them — I would stop in to one of the small cafés on Swanston Street. There we would indulge in cappuccinos, not of the best quality but that didn't matter: we were there to share the vibe. These places had jukeboxes and we would reveal our personal tastes in music every time we chose a song from the narrow range on offer. But we had a great time, feeling adult to a degree, and ever since then coffee-based social intercourse has been a feature of my life.

The coffee lounge at Melbourne University was a favourite hunting ground of mine. With some friends I would go out at night and have revolutionary coffee, fuel for the political activity we were planning. It was on one such night, I recall, when we heard that Egypt's President Anwar Sadat had been murdered. That soured our mood and stopped any political activities for the night. During the recent lockdowns, when the cafés were closed, and the only brew we could get was takeaway, I discovered the latest incarnation of my lifelong obsession — Covid coffee. Strictly speaking, we are not supposed to have been seeing people and socialising. This is not very good for the mental health of someone living alone.

Together with a mate who lives well within the five-kilometre zone, I enjoy coffee time whenever we can. Since he is often away at his holiday house, this is not as frequently as either of us would wish, but with Covid restrictions he has been stuck in Melbourne. With a bit of creativity we came up with a solution. We meet, both wearing our masks, buy takeaway coffee and go for a stroll. This counts as exercise, one of the five permitted reasons to be out and about — and we talk as we drain our cups. Thanks to Covid coffee, once a week without fail we will have one nice memory from lockdown.

Breakfast

For something so delightful and socially useful, we should give breakfast more thought. Essentially it is what the word says: breaking the fast of the evening, grabbing a bite to eat in the morning to stave off hunger created overnight. It could well be our most important meal. Be it elaborate or simple, it is the act that sets us up for the day ahead.

Many just grab a quick bite on the run — perhaps a slice of toast and a cup of coffee: even this can be considered a meal. Pleasant enough taken alone, it can be an important act with whoever else has slept in your place. To breakfast with a lover is a delight, in many cases the first moment of social interaction for the day.

Given that it sets the tone for the day ahead, there are those who think you need sweetness to give you energy but others look with abhorrence on this idea and seek out something simple and nutritious, indeed something to tide them over till lunch. I first became seriously interested in breakfast when I lived in Israel during my gap year. There, breakfast is a big deal. All kinds of great dairy products are available and you can also get some cooked delights like *shakshouka* (a dish of eggs poached in a sauce of tomatoes, olive oil, peppers, onion and garlic). Working on a kibbutz I really got into it. There I woke up early and went straight out to work for a few hours, by which time I had worked up a good appetite. Working in the avocado orchard as I did, there would be avocado on French toast, with honey from the bees kept in the orchard plus various other accompaniments. It was always a very satisfying meal. Then straight after breakfast it was back to work. Commuting there and back was refreshing in itself.

For some people, breakfast can be ritualised: they must have the same thing every day. Some might be devotees of oatmeal; others must have yogurt and fruit. It doesn't really matter what a person's individual preference is when it comes right down to it. Personally I like variety, with baked beans on the menu one day, croissants another; or a mixture: whatever you choose, the important point is that it should give your day a kick-start. I used to think breakfast had to be something that was simple and quick. But experience has taught me otherwise. I also thought going out for breakfast was an expensive indulgence. Well, I was correct to a degree: it is not so cheap. And nothing compares to having it at home. But there are benefits in going out for breakfast. Some are calculable — breakfast patrons enable cafés to employ staff — and some are incalculable: to have a wonderful appetising meal delivered to your table is one of life's great delights, even if it can cost nearly as much as a restaurant dinner. Once a reluctant and rare face at anyone else's breakfast table, I now take whatever opportunity arises. To my good fortune there are a number of good breakfast venues near my home and they have great ease of access but because of the cost involved it is still wise not to overindulge. Having breakfast with someone is a very nice way to socialise, as is sharing any meal, and a great way to engage with people who are often too busy or tired to bother catching up at the end of the day. One friend of mine is a porridge addict and we have sampled that fare at various establishments, till finally we found one, a Turkish café, where the porridge is at a level above all others. It is so superior we call it super porridge. This friend is a very busy person (it would be fair to call him time-poor) but once a month we make a point of going to breakfast so we can see each other and enjoy each other's company. Whenever we do it we have a lovely time and walk away very relaxed. I feel that having breakfast out with someone you know is a stress-free activity. So there are a number of people I share such meals with. Through it I get to engage with the world in a fun way. So the beneficiaries are not only my taste buds but my integration with the wider world. It releases me, for a time, from the isolation that life has imposed on me.

Cake Shops

Genetics gifted me a sweet tooth, rendering me defenceless to tempting delicacies. Both my parents received the same gift and passed it on to me with a vengeance. I know where there are good cake shops all over the place, and with many of them I have developed a warm relationship, hard as I have tried not to frequent them.

My romance with cakes began when I was a little boy and my grandmother, who was a great cook, used to bake me a different cake everyday. I ended up calling her Nana Cook. She loved the title and kept on baking. Weekly, as a young boy, I was taken to Acland Street (described earlier) with my father's parents and spent a lot of time staring into shop windows. I was never encouraged to succumb to temptation in those days, with a single exception — a shop called Monarch, which sold *kugelhopf*, a kind of chocolate ripple cake. My parents used to get it sometimes. The shop is still there today. While I do my best not to indulge, I occasionally weaken and buy this cake — most lethal.

Some cake shops that I forged a relationship with over the years have sadly now closed. One was the famous Paterson's cake shop, an Australian-style patisserie that made the most amazing cakes from the occasion of my first birthday through to many years after that. I always chose the same cake: a chocolate curl (I haven't seen it anywhere else). When it finally shut its doors, I, and many others, shed copious tears. An institution like that cannot simply be replaced. Another shop of its ilk was Marjorie's, in Glen Huntly Road. By an amazing stroke of luck it was around the corner from my great-grandmother's so when it closed down it took faint memories of her with it. Still, I was privileged to have any memories of her, when most of my contemporaries didn't have a grandmother, let alone anyone from a generation further back, due to the Holocaust.

Over in Hartwell there is a patisserie where you can easily close your eyes and imagine yourself in Paris. Going there has always been an educational experience. And there are still any number of good Jewish cake shops around the place. At one shop I seem to put on a kilo every time I walk through the door. It has a most impressive range of goods, and even makes a decent Lamington. Most dangerous of all, it sells bags of broken cookies, but I have learnt that if they're broken they don't have half the calories — a fact of life. A good cake shop is always a joy to find. In my student days I discovered a wonderful Lebanese cake shop that stocked a great selection of baklava. One day while I was there, I bumped into the Palestinian representative in Melbourne who greeted me so warmly that the store owners thought I was a 'fellow traveller' and gave me a large discount. Being well brought up, I said 'Thank you very much' and had a good chuckle to myself afterwards. The world turns in very strange ways.

The Doughnut

More about my serious sweet tooth — I have always blamed my parents for this poor genetic inheritance. On reflection, however, I now view this verdict as harsh and unfair, and for this I apologise. Even if inheritance is a contributing factor, I see this sweet tooth of mine is a cultural acquisition. It is unavoidably genetic inasmuch as my culture is genetic. I am an Ashkenazi Jew and have been brought up not to resist the sweet blandishments that life has to offer. So I carry all the cultural baggage that entails — tooth, heart and cholesterol issues.

Culturally open to the ecumenical movement, I have no problems with Easter eggs, hot cross buns, mince pies and even Christmas pudding. It's not that I am averse to any of them but, as I was not brought up with them as part of my culture, I am happy to leave them to others.

The real danger to me comes from my own culture, Judaism. Its religious calendar is sprinkled with festivals all the way through the year, each coming with its own special treats. These can be lethal but over time they become an integral part of your being. In this regard, I am happy to embrace my culture and hold it close to me. All this is magnified each week with the Sabbath meal whose dangerous confections include a cake-like sweet bread called *challah*. As you might have expected, I am fond of the version with raisins in it. So culture is taught through the table symbolising life as a moveable feast. Of course Judaism is just one of the cultures in which I have been raised. There are plenty of temptations for the sweet tooth built into the fabric of the broad Australian culture, with its pavlova, lamingtons, Anzac biscuits and many other appealing delights. Considering myself part of our society, it becomes difficult not to indulge to some degree.

Australianness apart, I must confess a deep affection for the doughnut. Now one of the Jewish festivals, Chanukkah, is largely built around children. Participants are supposed to eat foods cooked in oil, as the role of oil is central to the festival's story. Eating doughnuts has become an accepted part of the celebrations.

Hooray! This sweet snack appears in many forms at Chanukkah, but the most common is the jam doughnut. Moving from place to place as a child, there were many differences to which I had to become accustomed but, amid all this change, jam doughnuts at Chanukkah remained a constant. I would wait all year to binge out — the crowning example of how my sweet tooth has been culturally determined, but far from the only one. Part of my childhood growing up in Melbourne was being taken to the footy. Even before entering the ground, we would lock eyes on the doughnut vans that sat in the shadow of the grandstand. The thing to do was buy half a dozen steaming hot jam doughnuts. Their consumption became an important part of sporting culture, which is the state religion here. So their enticing smell would make me think of footy, and vice versa. In this way one aspect of my cultural heritage reinforced another.

University inevitably broadened my education: there I developed a taste for chocolate-iced doughnuts. I would finish half an essay, reward myself by going to the convenience store for a choccy doughnut and then — all fuelled up — power on until the essay was finished. Constructing a personal culture on such sweet foundations is what you might expect from a reckless youth. Age can make us all a little more inhibited: today they have what are called Krispy Kreme doughnuts. So far, I haven't dared bite into one for fear of the consequences...

Until my accident I had my sweet tooth under control, indulging it only during festivals and the like. But my head injury from the accident unleashed my craving for the sweet stuff with an unbridled passion, to my great detriment. The problem is rooted deep in the way I have been socialised into this world, but since the accident it has required a superhuman effort to rein in.

As a result I am fighting a mighty battle that requires all the strength of character I can throw at it. Some days my nobler self is winning; on others I suffer all the pangs of ADD (Acute Doughnut Deprivation).

Ten

Home Grown

The Garden

I have always had an interest in gardens, since growing up in a house with a large and diverse Australian garden. It was something special. And, like most Melburnians of my generation, I was brought up on visits to botanic gardens all over the city and, in particular, The Royal Botanic Gardens. Later, I spent extensive periods on various kibbutzim — so my love of gardens runs deep.

I do believe gardens should be used to create produce, not just as aesthetic showpieces. When I studied town planning I learnt about the design ideas behind gardens. One of my regrets is that I did not pursue a graduate diploma in landscape architecture. I would have enjoyed this and suspect it would have provided me a good living. Where I live today, my garden is testament to a steady and satisfying journey. For years I sat looking out of my sunroom window all depressed. There was my backyard, not very large and, worse still, all bricked in. It had no garden to speak off, and there was nowhere to plant. It took me many years to think of how to transform it into the oasis it is today.

Over time I have learnt that a good garden requires deep thought combined with science and observation. Starting out with just a few pots containing different herbs I thought this was all I could do. From such humble beginnings I got a bit carried away. I collected a number of terracotta pots and put various trees in them. At the base of these trees I would place different items. Deciding I needed colour in the garden, I planted nasturtiums in some and marigolds in others — easy to grow, with a pleasing hue and partly edible to boot. So the trees grew and grew, the yard became covered in them and I ran out of room. Now I found myself in a state of perplexity.

Having envisaged a garden, I had delivered myself an orchard. I even had a tree bought at IKEA. For years I have nurtured it and finally it produced nice fruit. But even this left me far from satisfied. So after much pondering I came up with the idea of lining the side of my fence with garden boxes. I realised this could be done on only one side of the yard as the other was too dark to grow things in. And then it took me a couple of years to find someone who could and would do this for me: as with all things domestic, I discovered the greatest difficulty is to find someone willing to do the task. Then you have to hope that someone is the right person for the job.

The space for garden boxes being limited, I concentrated on using it wisely and with great selectivity. Generally, what I have put in these boxes has done well. I have tried all sorts of things but have found that every couple of years all the goodness gets sucked out of the soil, obliging me to replace and regenerate it. I have grown a large variety of vegetables which have satisfied and fed me. I developed the concept of the urban farm, where you grow what you eat, your dinner not sourced from hundreds of kilometres away but on hand and constantly in view. Not having to rack up 'food miles' is an important consideration in this day and age.

At one point I decided the trees in pots, although they looked attractive enough, were not doing so well. Forced to nut out a solution, in the end I decided to dig up a few of the bricks and plant some of the trees in the ground. The trees have done well. As it turns out there is a watercourse that runs underneath my property, so that whatever I plant gets well watered even during a drought. It is deeply satisfying when things work out: one thing that didn't was the passionfruit vine. I had tried it in a number of spots without success. Eventually I dug up a few bricks at the back and planted a vine and, much to my delight, it has flourished. I invested in a metal grate across the back fence and now the vine has covered it and looks great. The garden, as you can see, is my expression of creativity: it has become my paintbrush.

Each garden follows its own trajectory and builds over time. Much like people, it is a layered entity that forms and re-forms its own character and, also like each of us, it is a living, breathing thing with its unique intellect. I have tried to nurture and create my own by contributing things I have learnt along the way from university and life experience.

At one point, I was offered a good deal on a water tank so I took it. The tank's capacity was 2000 litres but I should have acquired a much larger one. At first I ran drip irrigation off it to water my garden and this worked well but it did have its limitations. The garden was issuing its demands, so to speak, insisting on something better. So I added a layer to its being with a pump on the tank and a sprinkler system running around the perimeter. This has been a great improvement, except that being so small it needs regular rain to refill it. During drought all I could do was to link a hose from the tap. I don't like using the tap but it is a lot better than watering by hand.

So as an organic creature my garden continues to grow. I enjoy it and get good use of it. There is nowhere better to sit with a friend, enjoying a cup of tea or sharing a beer. To do this I needed a table of some sort. Then luck came to my rescue. A Middle Eastern shop near here was closing, so I got a nice Moroccan table to put in the garden. It looks a natural. As to the use of my garden as a source of home-grown food, I always have something coming along to supplement my diet. This is the urban farm at its best. The hard part is to keep it going all year round. The garden is a pleasure centre that keeps on giving. Keeping it up does not really involve a lot of work — just consistent application, about half an hour a day. I never have to buy greens: I just pick them fresh as I need. And there is no point beating about the bush: it gives me a higher quality of life than many other people enjoy.

The Gardener

The way we interact with those who work for us is something that defines who we are. I have one abiding principle — I must treat people as I feel I would like to be treated myself. Nothing less than this lofty goal will do.

At various times in my life it has been necessary to call upon the services of a tradesman. I was not taught any practical skills — my father was not that way inclined — so to get anything done I need to get someone in. This is the point at which I feel it gets down to the nitty-gritty of human relations and what I call raw politics — how I interact with people. Now I love tradesmen: I regard them as the repository of great insight and knowledge, and know I have a lot to learn from them so I treat them with great respect. To me they are a lot more than paid servants, which is how many people treat them.

Although this attitude is deeply ingrained in my being — it is who I am — the accident has had an inevitable effect on how I come across. My self-expression is not as spontaneous or automatic and carefree as it once was. Today it is a lot more reasoned and considered, even calculated, and I have not decided if this is for the better or the worse.

We all learn from watching our parents, so the way mine have behaved has influenced who I am. I am glad to report that their behaviour has taught me to be a good decent person or, using the Yiddish term, to behave like a mensch. My father was brought up in an orphanage that my grandfather managed. Whenever a problem arose there, someone would come in and fix it. This is why my father was taught no practical skills and had none to pass on. He would also bring a tradesman in if a job needed doing. He would befriend them and treat them with great hospitality, in the conviction that these people are our equals and should be treated as such. Along with many other things I thank my father for teaching me this.

The first memorable example of this goes back to when I was a small child. Our house stood on a large block of land that was well beyond my father's ability to look after. It was obvious to him that he needed a gardener. Well, Dad, on finding this wonderful Italian gardener who lived not far away from us, hired him and gave him a free hand to do what he wanted. As this guy was the 'genuine article', he did a great job. Angelo became one of the family, and Dad became good friends with him. But one day he got sick (I think it was cancer). He had a wife and kids to look after, it was so sad. In time the illness progressed and eventually Angelo died, leaving his family destitute. Dad couldn't let Angelo's family suffer so he searched for a way to ensure they could survive. By a stroke of fortune he found a job as school caretaker for the wife. This meant they could move on with life. In doing this Dad taught me a valuable lesson: people must be looked after in their hour of need, even if it requires some effort. My grievance is with those people who have failed to do that for me. Through that example, Dad was teaching me good values and ethics. His whole life was built on treating people with decency. I have many more examples than space to relate them.

My parents would make a big deal of having coffee or tea with tradesmen, turning their visit into a nice social occasion. All this has seeped into the way I behave towards them, but I have added to that ritual. I like to discuss and inquire about matters with these people: I find they have an amazing wealth of wisdom and willingness to share it if approached rightly. It comes down to basic respect: if I expect people to listen to me I must listen to them.

One of Dad's great joys in life was taking on a new gardener. Real gardeners are hard to find; many so-called gardeners just rake the soil and clear away leaves: they lack vision. Dad was very lucky to find a woman who knew what she was doing. She took his large garden and turned it into an Australian wonderland featuring all sorts of native plants. It was such a success that birds not commonly seen in the city would come and visit. Not being a twitcher myself, I cannot add any detail about that but I have no doubt it was the case.

I personally dislike the idea of employing a gardener, it affronts my self-image. I like to think I am capable of doing things by myself but have learnt my limitations. When I was in hospital recovering from my fall and a minor stroke, a friend visited and told me I needed help cleaning up my garden. It needed to be made safe, he was most concerned. He then promised to set it all up, found a bloke and directed him what to do. Regrettably it turned out he wasn't up to scratch, wasn't reliable. I persisted with this guy for an extended period, though, because of the way I want to relate to people. I wanted to give him a good chance to show he could do it but after an extended trial I had to say enough.

Then I got lucky, finding another bloke who was very reasonable and had a passion for food cultivation. He had all sorts of ideas and did good things in the garden and then — family history repeating itself — his health deteriorated, it turned out to be cancer and he died.

But, as often happens in life, out of dark moments a light may shine; and before long I came across a wonderful Greek man who possessed the art and vision of gardening — a real talent with many bright ideas. He enables me to practise my beliefs: we work in tandem, one complementing the other. Yet again, worryingly, this gardener has health issues, but I do hope he has a good long life and over that time we continue to build something special. What else are we here for?

The Guru

I have a friend who is a grandmaster in the garden: once I even heard him referred to as the garden guru. So, I asked, if that's the case is his partner the high priestess? Sadly, they did not favour me with a reply. By profession the guru is a chef: he has an interest in all things food, and it is that interest which diverted him to the garden, where over time he has been known as the guru since I was a young man. He has been there every step of the way as I have traversed my tortuous path. I have learnt to value and try to digest all the wisdom and knowledge he tries to extend to me. Through the years he has become a valued and true friend. I don't see him often as he lives at a distance but when I do I always feel enhanced by the experience.

It was in my late teens, after my older sister had moved out of home, that I first laid eyes on him at her place. Only later in life would I become familiar with his many talents and be mesmerised by the skills he developed. I knew he was a talented chef and ran some good restaurants. As my sister would say, if you know enough chefs you will never go hungry (this sounded a fair comment to me). Then I discovered the guru was not just a chef but had a passion for food in all its forms — how it was created, prepared and delivered. A consuming passion in every sense of the word. To pursue his interest he purchased a farm: in short order amazing things began to happen there. One of them was a very special restaurant where the food you ate was grown on the farm itself so, while eating your meal you could walk around and see how it was growing. This was a singular opportunity to be in touch with the food that was being prepared for your palate.

It was out of his gardening skills that my friend ultimately gained the label of guru. He ended up with what was recognised as the best kitchen garden around, a thing of wonder and amazement. Often he would invite me up to have a look, but I didn't take him up on this for many years. It was not particularly hard to get to: a train passed near it three times a day. But one day my sister said she would take me there for a day trip and I could put it off no longer. On our arrival we found ourselves in the proverbial Magic Kingdom: the place was a real turn-on. I encountered so much that appealed to me on this visit that it motivated me to go up there again for a few days stay. This, too, was such a good time that I ended up going there yearly. I learnt so much from these visits, including what I would call his religious practice. His enthusiasm for all things that grow was boundless. Everything was structured and designed to get the most out of things.

He never stopped developing it. Every year I would see something new. He acquired a beehive and learnt all about that to pollinate his garden. Later on I learnt that one thing he had begun doing was to design kitchen gardens for restaurants — which involved a further extension of his religious perspective. Another year you would encounter the most amazing wood-fired oven, which he had designed and built. The pizza he made in that was mouth-watering.

Over the years he would drop into my house and try to give me advice on how I could improve my life. As a real guru he just loved to teach and express life's meaning. What I was doing in my garden tickled his fancy and interest, so he would try helping me to develop it. In fact, when I came out of hospital after my stroke, he was of great assistance in getting my garden and oasis together. He arranged for someone to clean it and make it safe, as well as bringing me plants. Each of his visits would deliver me a pearl of wisdom or two. Unlike many others whom I expected to behave well, the guru has been there for me without fail.

As time passed, the farm on which he lived and expressed his religiosity became a bit much for him so he made the rational decision to retire. He then moved to a lovely little country town, but once you have the spirit in you this is not something that can be easily extinguished. Maintaining his passion and joy in life, in his new abode he has created the most impressive of gardens, in which all sorts of wonders abound, but he found his vision gradually limited by practical capacity. His is a faith he has to explore, so in time he bought some of the land behind his block and expanded his garden into this adjoining terrain. By this point he had managed to attain a degree of contentment. With his knowledge and understanding he was now living in a nice place where whatever he needed was at hand and he could entertain with comfort and ease. Able to express his views and perspective on life, the guru had reached a good position and was able to live life well.

As the years rolled on, I would continue to return there, always learning more about the garden and how to meet life with tranquillity. A day visiting the guru is still the best of days and I return home with a warm glow: you could say his aura has descended on me. I am very glad to report that, yes, he is well settled and appears set to live out his days there in perfect serenity. The purpose and expression of his life unfolded. I have learnt so much from this man and will do my best to live up to the standards he has always expected of me.

Enjoy the Market

Markets attract us with their amazing variety. They add colour, texture and vibrancy to life and enhance our quality of being. Far more than mere hubs of commerce, they are meeting places for the community.

The first to imprint itself on me was Prahran Market. As a small child I often went there with my mother, and to me it was one of life's great delights. It was very different then to its modern-day incarnation. On your arrival at the market, a man seated in an overhead tower would direct you to a parking space. This was a unique thing in Melbourne: you always had to wait to get a spot and it was never easy. The smells together with the hustle and bustle from the stalls would entice us in, exciting us even before we'd found a park. Once we walked into the market court, there it was — the world in action. All over the place were fruit and vegetable vendors with all sorts of amazing stock, things I was often encountering for the first time. Mum and I would have a walk around just to see what was on offer, lapping up the bright, lively aesthetic.

One part of the market I relished visiting was the delicatessen aisle, home to a special cake shop. It was run by a lady of the extra large persuasion: she associated my arrival with my special treat there — her vanilla slices — and she ran to get them, her running being for me part of the treat. No matter how hard I search now it is a near impossibility to find a vanilla slice to compare.

When I turned eighteen and went to Israel for a year, my horizons broadened in many directions, and one of these was market culture. Each one I visited added to the breadth and depth of my understanding of life and its magnificent diversity. What captivated me then and still does is the Arab market, the souk, not just for the amazing things to be found in it but because of its lively and lived-in village vibe. People passed the time shopkeeping, talking, ambling and gambling. If you felt peckish, there were many places to eat, something like our takeaways and restaurants. The whole souk experience is a sensory feast for the eyes, nose and ears.

On the other side of Jerusalem is another kind of market, also an interesting lived-in space, called Mahane Yehuda. Primarily it is a sprawling fruit and vegetable market with amazing produce in a confined space but much of the interest lies in the streets around it. These are the *shuks* that cater for Jerusalem's ultra-Orthodox population. If you are lucky, you can find some gems, including the most appetising eateries, with a street of dips restaurants leading off to one side. All its noise and colour suddenly stop for Shabbat and Jewish holidays, a microcosm of the total transformation that comes over Israel on these important days.

Another little gem I found was a *shuk* in a place called Tira, which is an Arab neighbourhood on the edge of Tel Aviv. They guard their privacy intensely there. Once, when I turned up with a camera they forbade me entry. It was worth putting the camera back in the car just to be granted admittance to shops specialising in baklava and pita bread. Women go there for the best selection of dresses. But Israel was just the entrée: more attractions awaited me when I arrived in Europe. These days I can't pass a market without walking in and checking it out.

In Paris I was charmed by the neighbourhood fruit-and-veg markets lining the streets and in business just to supply the needs of that locality. This seems to me to go to the heart of what makes a good market. Also in Paris I discovered book markets that would be of real interest to me if only my French were good enough. From there it was off to Italy and Amsterdam where I found more and different markets again. The clothing markets in Italy were great — not only cheap but fashionable items all on display together — and I did take a liking to the food market in Florence. My mouth still waters at the memory of a few wonderful meals I enjoyed there.

Now let's bring it on home: one of the great delights that Melbourne has to offer is the Queen Victoria Market, not only worth visiting on your own account but a must-see destination for international visitors. One of the best things about the Queen Vic is having everything under one corrugated-iron roof. Its location in the heart of Melbourne, and the availability of same-day-fresh fruit and vegetables, fish, meat and poultry — combined with the riot of colour with which it greets you as you stroll down its many aisles — make a visit there something to remember for many months afterwards. If it's a tourist souvenir or a gift you're looking for, Sunday morning at the Queen Vic Market is especially good. When I was a student living away from home, every Friday we would go there to stock up on food provisions for the week ahead. Those were fun times. In the nearby streets are a number of good cafés and restaurants. One that was special in my mind was run by Buddhist monks and boasted an impressive menu of fake meat dishes. Very tasty. It was so vegetarian my parents used to go there with friends who considered it kosher enough to eat at but it always upset my mum when they ordered pork. She couldn't handle seeing her observant friends doing that but personally I looked on it as a bit of fun.

Markets can teach us all how to engage with other people, none more so than the popular farmer's markets you can find spread all over suburban Melbourne. Their special feature is that you can get fresh food and chat with the producer responsible for its being there. This is worlds apart from the impersonal space of a supermarket. The huge variety of stores caters for all tastes.

Several years ago I was walking into my local farmer's market, accompanied by a friend, when we bumped into his brother and family. Each month now for ten years we have developed a ritual of strolling round the market, browsing and occasionally making a purchase, then going out for breakfast and a chat. Quality time, relaxing time, and in this way raising our standard of living. We enjoy it so much that often we also go to the local night market.

Ice Cream

A number of years ago I took an extended trip to Israel. During that visit I spent a lot of time with some friends and their children who had visited Melbourne as a family and stayed with me. There were no barriers to overcome apart from language.

Now an Israeli summer is rather hot so, being a good indulgent uncle, I bought the kids lots of ice cream, which gave me the excuse to enjoy one myself. I think this can be fairly summarised as a win-win. Soon after I had departed for Australia, their grandmother took them out for the day and the kids asked her, 'Where's David?' She replied, 'He has gone home to Melbourne.' They pondered a moment, then looked up and asked, 'If David is gone, are we going to get any more ice cream?' To placate them, their grandmother had to go buy them one each.

I like being remembered in this positive way. It also bodes well for my future reputation: when these children grow up, the mention of my name will bring a smile to their faces and perpetuate their positive regard for me. I do like to bring positivity and happy times into people's lives where I can: it's one of those acts that have no downside.

Self-Entitlement

At my house I have, among many other things, a wonderful lemon tree and passionfruit vine. These bring me great joy. Every year I know that with the changing of the seasons there will be this tree laden with fruit in great abundance. But this doesn't happen by itself: for the tree and vine to produce as they do requires a lot of effort.

I do believe that I literally deserve the fruits of my labour, but certain others apparently take a different view. These self-adoring types ignore the availability of supermarkets nearby to satisfy their hunger. I find it unsettling that it is not just strangers who come and pinch this fruit, or demand I give them it as of right, but people I know. Someone close to me once grabbed a lemon and walked off with it. I demanded he hand it back. It was actually about the last lemon on the tree, and he was not entitled to it. Since then I have been reluctant to give anyone with such an attitude lemons from this tree I have cultivated. I refuse to reward bad behaviour. Just because I have something you want, that does not mean you have the right to take it. And among the things of mine you may not take is my dignity.

I even have a neighbour who comes and asks for a lemon but when I say no they ignore me and grab one anyway. I don't see the point in their asking if all along they have a thief's sense of entitlement.

This notion that gets up my nose when it concerns the fruit grown in my garden extends to the way people live their lives. I feel you don't deserve something just because you *are*. No, you deserve those things that you have earned a right to. Take democracy, for example: we don't just deserve it because someone else paid a price to preserve it; to keep deserving it we have to participate in it. In our country this is even enshrined in the laws of the land with compulsory voting.

I feel it is up to me how I hand out my abundance, my role to spread the joy as evenly as I can so people I know get their fair share. Even there I face various problems since everybody has a different idea of what their fair share is. I had a mate who was grabbing a few lemons so I said. 'Are you baking a cake or something special?' Calmly, without the blink of an eye, he replied: 'I am just picking them for where I am visiting next.' I was outraged, thinking (I may even have said it out loud): 'This is not your fair share.'

It amazes me, the greed that lemons induce. I disagree with the movie: to me, greed is not good. It leads to the downfall of people and society. The greed with which we have plundered the world we live in has led directly to the environmental perils with which we are now faced. Enough of lemon larceny: It's soured my tone. Better swing straight over to the vine, sweet delight that produces lust, joy and passion in abundance. My back fence is covered in it and it spills over into the lane behind my property where hundreds of large sweet fruit grow. I get none of these: they all get stolen, not just one or two. These pilferers are not just pigs but idiots: they pinch the fruit before it is even ripe. I guess there's no point in my belly-aching when *their* bellies could well be. Call it karma.

I would not want you to get the impression I am a miserable gardener. In fact I have a number of citrus trees that people can't see or reach, and this allows me to make many people happy as opposed to a few gluttons. Still, as I spread the bounty, I cannot understand why there are people out to deprive me of this joy when they have no need to.

Climate-Change Warrior

I have travelled the world and seen many places and many thousands of folk, rich and poor, haves and have-nots. Upon my return by plane I am struck — kicked in the jaw — by the plenty that surrounds us in all its guises. As a good traveller, I cannot avoid recognising the great disparity, though it takes time to sink in while I attempt to comprehend it. This is one of the great virtues of the Australian lust for travel: it expands our minds and changes our relationship to the world around us. In the taxi on the way home from the airport, I see kilometres of comfortable, well-maintained homes — not slums or shacks on the cusp of collapse. It is obvious that this is a land of comfort and plenty, and that people's day-to-day struggles here are of a different order to those of people in less affluent places.

Once home, I need to stock up on food. So I go to The Queen Victoria Market. There I find abundance with few limits. The available choice overwhelms me. I have lived on farms — kibbutzim — and seen how generous quantities of produce are created. Before long I am back in my garden re-acquainting myself with the joyful business of cultivating new growth, creating my own abundance. Then ethical issues arise: how to distribute my plenty? It is in great demand. All I produce is organic and tasty. From what I have seen in the world I have become a keen environmentalist — no chemicals here. And I aspire to do things Nature's way. All this will result in thriving output from my patch. Since I don't drive, my production of carbon is minimal.

I use little energy and, as I have mentioned elsewhere, I put in a small solar system. Where possible, I take pride in being a twenty-first century climate-change warrior. I am far from perfect but I put in a good effort. It is a revolutionary act to reconstruct your day-to-day life: True conservatives understand this instinctively.

Our relationship with Nature not only reveals who we are: it also determines what we are. I feel the need for respect and equitable distribution. It's not terribly hard to create abundance in the garden, a surplus left over after the producer has eaten their fill. But the joy needs to be spread around, with each person receiving an equitable share. (It astounds me how some people think they should get more than others even if they don't need it. This is sheer gluttony!) Over-consumption has been the curse of our world for centuries, and it stems from a simple vice — greed. If we could moderate our behaviour and just take our fair share, we would all be far better off.

The lesson applies to other areas of the economy apart from food production. For a current example, we could produce much more of the Covid vaccine than we need. So rather than hoard it for no good reason, it is up to us to share the excess with our neighbours in the region. Do that, and not only would we feel better: we would *be* better.

Eleven

Humour

Parent Teacher Night

Both my parents were teachers so they thought they knew a bit about education but the reality of life taught them a lesson that changed their attitudes dramatically. They never went to a parent-teacher night for me, they were always too busy and decided it was a waste of time. They used to say, 'There is nothing those teachers can tell us that we don't already know about our son, so why bother?' Luckily for them, I was a well-behaved child; I didn't get in trouble so the school didn't have to contact them about disciplining me. I was also academically adept so there was no reason to call them on account of problems with my grades. So, according to my parents, I was travelling smoothly but they had forgotten one important thing: school goes way beyond academic performance. In the educational process there is a significant social factor at play.

One day my parents were rung up by the school authorities and asked if they could come and speak to them. They were in shock, unable to figure out what this could be all about. So they went along, having never done this before. They sat down and were told the school had serious concerns about my learning. It turned out that there was a girl in my class who was totally besotted with me, driving me crazy and totally distracting me from doing any work. So the school wanted to know if it would be OK with my parents to take this girl out of my class. Being the young boy I was, I was oblivious to the implications of all this attention (it takes years to become aware of that sort of thing).

The upshot was, the girl was taken out of my class. I didn't really question what was going on, her departing the class was treated as something unremarkable, and as she was still in the school I did remain friends with her. In fact I never knew anything about this until years after I left school. I do wish I knew where she was today.

Co-ed schools do have benefits but there is a lot you must be aware of with early teens. Funnily enough, as grandparents, my mum and dad came to think parent-teacher nights were *very* important but in reality it is all about giving parents an ego boost about their child. What can a teacher say beyond massaging their ego on the subject of their child's performance and behaviour? Or not! If they can't manage, then you get them a tutor. My young nephew has all sorts of girl friends — innocently — but I doubt he will come across anything like the experience I have described here. I still don't think it was any big deal, just part of growing up, I think.

Hebrew

This is a touch of Australian Jewish humour. Before I tell it, an explanatory note. Largely speaking, Australian Jews come from two sources: there are Polish Jews, the largest group of all. Then there are Hungarian Jews, who are very different in many ways to Poles — the way they speak, behave and think are at odds with each other; there is not a natural mix between the two. There are many other Jews from all sorts of places but you could say these are the main two factions within the community.

Well, the story goes like this: One day a little old lady hobbles up to a respected local rabbi and says:

'Rav, rav, I need to ask you a favour.'

The rabbi looks down at her, scratches his beard and, after a moment, replies:

'Little old lady, I will do my best to grant your request, whatever it is.'

The old lady smiles, sinks to her knees, kisses the rabbi's robes and thanks him effusively.

The rabbi is overawed. He asks in a melodious voice, 'What is it that you desire, little old lady?'

'Rav, I want to learn Hebrew.'

'This is a noble task,' he replies, 'but why at this great age of yours have you decided it is time to learn Hebrew?'

Immediately she replies: 'I am a little old lady and I don't think I have much time left on this earth, but when I die and go to heaven I would like to be able to speak to people there. So, I feel I need to understand Hebrew.'

So, the wise rabbi, still playing with his beard, looks down at the little old lady and says:

'So what will you do if you go to hell?'

In the blink of an eyelid she replies:

'No problem, I already speak Hungarian.'

And there you have a simple story that neatly sums up Australian Jewry.

A Footy Tale

A father and his son were standing in court before a judge who was trying to determine the fate of the child — specifically, who would have custody of him. There had been a bitter fight between the parents about where the child should live. Now, after listening to everyone else, it was time for the judge to ask a few questions to help him determine the issue. This is a very difficult task: it takes a judge many years to learn the skills to do this wisely. He must ask the correct questions to obtain the answers needed to enable him to make the required decision.

In court were His Honour, the father, his son and a stenographer. A critical moment had arrived and so the questioning began. The judge needed to determine where the boy would be happiest. With the wisdom of the ages, he began by posing a few questions to ascertain if life with the father was OK. He asked how the lad was fed. All seemed satisfactory there: the boy was getting properly cooked meals with the occasional bit of junk food thrown in, no harm in that. The child had his own room, was happy at school, played for a footy team — so far, so good. As the inquiry was drawing to a close, the judge peered over his bench and asked the youngster in a very gentle voice: 'Do you have any problems living with your dad?' In an unexpectedly cavalier manner, he replied: 'Living with Dad is OK, but I'm fed up with getting beaten all the time.' Suddenly the judge came to life. Very concerned, he asked: 'What do you mean by "getting beaten"? Does your dad hurt you? Are you worried he will injure you?' At this the young fellow took umbrage: 'Hell no!' The judge persisted: 'So what do you mean by saying you hate being beaten? 'It's very simple,' came the answer. 'My dad is a fanatical Carlton supporter. The Blues are his whole life. But each and every week they're being beaten. It is terrible; I can't handle it.'

So the judge had to collect himself and deliver his verdict. He issued a simple directive. The boy could stay with the father as long as he wasn't taken to Carlton footy games. The child must not be brought up a loser.

The Jab

Way back in the Dreamtime when I was a young child beginning to form a picture of who I was and get a grip on this world, my parents sent me to the doctor. They wanted me to get a vaccination — tetanus I think it was, but I'm not sure. Well, the doctor pulled out a long pointy needle, at which I took one glance and said whatever my boyhood equivalent was of 'No way, Jose.' I immediately took to my heels.

The poor doctor, an amiable soul in a big room, had to chase me around his surgery for what seemed like ten or fifteen minutes before he could get a chance to give me the jab. In the end it wasn't as bad as I had feared. But before leaving the clinic I gave my parents hell for putting me through that. When the doctor told my parents what had happened they just smiled. What they were thinking seemed to be written all over their faces: *Our boy has a lot of spunk.*

After that experience I avoided needles and tried to avoid going to the doctor for any reason. Being a reasonably healthy child, there was little cause for me to darken another medical doorstep until I stuffed everything up in one shot with my accident. From that point onwards I have been pricked, pocked, poked and delivered into the hands of vampires (blood nurses) who all seem possessed of a relentless drive to suck me dry. All those procedures hold no great fear for me now. Spending enough days, weeks and months in hospital has turned them into almost everyday events.

It's reached the point where I derive considerable mirth from seeing strong, macho athletic guys who faint whenever it comes time for a blood test. I joke with them that they have to toughen up. So well adapted to the routine am I by now that the vampire and I are on good terms. There are no further worries with the needle: I just stick my arm out, say 'Go for it', flinch and look away.

Reconciliation with the inescapable realities of my life has been achieved by coming to terms with the situation I am in. I want the needle for the Covid vaccine even though I understand it can occasionally have some bad consequences. As I advance along the path of life, I would love to reach a stage where I am no longer pricked and poked because I have become a fully empowered being — but I fear this may never happen.

Hanging in There

A friend of mine has a lovely little sister who is fun to tease and play with. She has always found my turn of phrase a bit hard to digest but over time we have maintained a good relationship.

She would react badly to things I would say. For example, once while at her parents' I asked whether I could make a phone call and she said, 'Fine.' I sighed gently and then revealed that I needed to ring Washington. She heard and freaked out, but then I explained to her my friend was called Washington.

To a degree she had led a sheltered life and I liked to play with that. As she matured into an adult I would see her infrequently but, whenever I did, she was kind to me and we enjoyed each other's company immensely. I delighted in her outrage at the things I would say. After I had been out of circulation with various illnesses, she was kind enough to pay a visit to see how I was. More than with many other people, I used to have fun phone conversations with her. When she had become a mother, we were discussing the need to exercise so as to get her body in good shape, nothing unusual about that.

One day, determined to drive the point home, I rang up and asked, 'How're you hangin'?' (a common enough Australian vernacular usage). Then, after a pregnant pause, I added: 'All over the place?' and, to her credit, instead of yelling at me for my rudeness or sexism she totally cracked up, seeing the humour in it. I have made other comments to her along these lines over the years but, to be fair, she's not carrying many excess kilos. To me, she looks fine, attractive and appealing (not that I would ever say that to her). Yes, I hear other readers cry, 'What a sexist attitude you have!' But this is the world I live in — and her opinion is all that counts here.

The Singer

This is a very short story about good intentions that was told to me by a close friend.

My friend is an Argentinian who has a much older brother living in Buenos Aires whose passion and joy in life is to sing. Stretching his vocal chords is what he lives for. It transpired that the brother's local synagogue lost its cantor — that is, the person who sings during the service. It is an intimate role, one that binds the community together and gives it shape. So, out of the kindness of his heart, my friend's brother offered to fill in for the missing cantor.

This went really well. The community got what it needed and wanted; my friend's brother for his part was gaining great satisfaction. But then he hit a bump in the road. Somehow it got out that he was a communist, an atheist, and the community could not abide that. So he was sacked on the spot. The brother's joy turned to sorrow. What is to be learnt from this tale? For one thing, even with the best of intentions things don't always go as desired, or planned. But we still have to act with good intentions: it gives a lot to our lives and to others, and much is to be gained in the process.

Twelve

Guiding Lights

The Sage Plants

Over my life I have been blessed to come into the orbit of a number of wise, intelligent souls, and I do hope to meet more like them on my journey. Eagerly I have drunk in and tried to learn from what they have tried to teach me. I've tried to be a good student. The common thread to what I have learnt from these fine minds is not so complex: the virtue of generosity and humility. The benevolence in gifting me their learning has been boundless. I am indeed a lucky man.

There has been a steady progression of exemplars, starting with my beloved father, a spirit adored by all, and my mother, *The Angel of Odessa*, whose philosophy of active kindness is inspiring. Beside them was my special uncle, a true Renaissance man and a genius in his own right. Then I entered the realm of ideas, turbocharged by university, where I encountered some great teachers at lectures I attended. And not just attended in a passive sense: In the lecture halls I listened intently and sought to comprehend what it was they were telling us.

After uni, I embarked on a full life where, of course, I have come across many and varied people. They, too, have contributed to the breadth of my understanding of our cosmos. One of them was a truly great man, a teacher who became a great friend who I consulted often. He taught me to write and express myself better than I would have imagined possible. In fact, all these people who had blessed my life with their wisdom and knowledge to that point, bolstered my ability to describe the world.

And now I come to my latest adviser, the man I call *The Sage*. Busy as he is, he has generously given of his time and expertise in deep conversation about my writing, and I am greatly indebted to him. My writing skills were already adequate but he has fine-tuned them sometimes to sparkle and glow. I like this added edge he has delivered me. In his great wisdom *The Sage* has handed me lavish compliments. This has helped my self-esteem and emboldened me to be more adventurous. But, being the wise man he is, his praise also carries a solid and reasoned critique of my writing. With generosity he has tried to pass on some of the skills. Regrettably, I have not been able to master them as well as I would like, but our mighty *Sage* has not finished our conversation, and the most prized of gifts — his time — he keeps on giving. I thank him every so often and do so again here. I do hope our chat continues long into the future and that he lives for many years to come, watching the seed he planted grow until my work flourishes to its full potential.

You Can Be a Life Coach

My father became what could best be described as a life coach to a guy I grew up with: Dad kept him moving forward and showed him how to enjoy life. Theirs was a good, and mutually rewarding, relationship. When my father died a few years ago I inherited this title and the task that went with it. Personally, I am unsure how qualified I am to fulfil this role. In reality, this bloke teaches me quite a bit in how he lives his life so that a mutually beneficial relationship has been replicated one generation down. I am thankful for the time he allots me out of the very full life he leads. My motto is: Don't take people for granted; if they give of themselves, respond in kind.

When this guy turned thirteen he asked my father for some supervision and guidance, and this turned out to be the beginning of a durable bond between them. As he moved through each stage of his life, my father was there to lend his aid, like a favourite uncle, and he gained a lot from this. As the boy grew into manhood he understood that Dad had his back. When his mother suffered a most unpleasant death, Dad navigated him through the straits of grief; and was on hand to give his blessing when he married a very fine woman.

As I say, the coaching became mutual. I remember when Dad was already elderly, with his mobility much reduced, one day the lad rang him up and announced, 'We're going to the Grand Final parade today.' Dad went along. He was run all over town to see and do many things. At the end of the day he collapsed, exhausted, but with a broad smile on his face and eager to tell me all he had done and seen. The interaction between the two of them was lovely to observe. The big lesson they gave each other was a simple one: make the most of life. We must partake and engage in it. One day when Dad was in palliative care the young man turned up to bid him farewell. This pleased Dad greatly and gave me a warm glow as well. There was no need to encourage this bloke to be involved. He has many activities on the go at all times, especially in the more enlightened quarters of modern Judaism, contributing a lot to others with whom he deals, but Dad never felt neglected by him, I don't — and I cannot imagine any of them do either. Well, the torch was passed to me and I can do no less than gladly lift it and bear the flame aloft.

For many years I lost contact with this childhood friend: we had gone different ways. But the warmth between us never dimmed and recently we have renewed ties. To give him credit, he has treated me with care unlike many who have never bothered to lift a finger. The way I approached my role was to question and prod him, to proffer gentle advice on living his life well — until he accepted me as a kind of secular rabbi to him. His marriage is sound (he does the right things to look after it). He is involved in his children's lives but not so much as to interfere with their development. (And he is further blessed in that his own father is still around at the age of eighty-nine.) Professionally, he's at the top of his game. When Covid arrived I harassed him to embark on a fitness campaign, turning adversity into opportunity. In return, he gives me what I consider the most precious of gifts, his time. As we involve ourselves in the lives of people we know, we develop them and they us. In the process there is much to be enjoyed and gained.

Secular Rabbi

I am a total atheist. I have no belief in any god. In my eyes the edifice that is called religion stands condemned. My parents are partly to blame for this: they had me join a Marxist-Leninist youth movement. How could I come out thinking differently? I will only enter a synagogue to go to a wedding or a burial minyan — for no other reason. I see no point in the buildings per se: they could be better used for other purposes, such as a community centre or something similar. The same goes for churches.

Even though religion and all that goes with it are not for me, I do find value and utility in the culture that I was born into. Here religion is a lot more than simply a belief in God or a being that constructs and controls all there is. What has developed is a means, a type of tool, to help us live in the world we find ourselves in. This makes Judaism worth engaging with and discovering. With this goal in mind, we can investigate and participate in its cultural continuity. I find all its festivals, bar two, have relevance: those two are 100 per cent religious and their dates have no special significance for me. They are Yom Kippur and Simchat Torah.

Yom Kippur is the Day of Atonement, centred on a demand for personal repentance; on Simchat Torah, which marks the

New Year of Bible readings, the Hebrew Scriptures are removed from a cabinet known as the Ark of the Law and supporters celebrate their existence, often with dance.

In Jewish culture ways have evolved to deal with all the different aspects of the life cycle, such as death. Whether it's in expressing bereavement or channelling the impulse to charity, Jewish tradition has exalted one person above all others to help us come to grips with the life we lead. This person is called a rabbi; for Christians, a priest or a minister fulfils the same function. Now the rabbi is much more to his community than a Q-and-A search engine à la Google. A rabbi embodies and imparts the wisdom of the ages — and of the sages. His role is to help us function and behave better in the world around us. This is a vital role in the operation of society.

What a modern rabbi means to his people has developed over thousands of years. At its core he is the religious counsellor to his community, assisting its members to live in accordance with religious law and practice — to make the so-called word of God a lived and breathed reality. A further important role assigned to a rabbi is to engage in the study of religious texts. In this way many great rabbis have contributed to our comprehension of the world, Maimonides being the greatest of them. Other famous Jewish scholars, though not themselves rabbis, have made contributions in this vein, Spinoza being just one glorious example. The functions of a rabbi range widely, from explaining the significance of religious texts to dealing with the nitty-gritty of daily life.

The smooth functioning of the community hinges on his wisdom and advice. First there are the rituals of existence — birth, death, marriages and various less important episodes — to supervise. Then he is the go-to person called upon to assist in conflict resolution and philosophical inquiry. All this requires a high degree of learning as well as of wisdom. When someone is having a difficult moment in life the rabbi is there to consult. Topics cover the gamut of life's challenges so he needs to be flexible and adaptive. A wise rabbi may be an interventionist: he steps in where he sees it is needed, not merely waiting for people to come and seek his advice. You could say that the good rabbi leads from the front, and to acquire the suite of skills a good rabbi needs will take many years.

In our modern lives the close-knit small community has all but disappeared. So the need for a rabbi as the principal supportive pillar has mostly vanished. Even so, many of the issues that rabbis dealt with in days gone by persist. So now we are led to ask, 'How do we handle the conundrums of life without such a person as our guide?' The legal process is not a cut-and-dried solution: we still need people who can make its rough edges smooth. And, much as it would like to think it could, the Communist Party cannot fulfil this role. Could a shrink fill the void? I doubt it. I would suggest we need a variety of skilled people we can turn to. So it is by this route that I arrive at the notion of a secular rabbi

To tackle the many and varied issues that beset us all, in today's terminology we might call this person a life coach: someone who will keep us on the straight and narrow, pointing out the ethical implications of our intended behaviour. Step up, the secular rabbi — someone of recognised experience and wisdom who can dispense the needed advice without clothing it in the garb of religion. The secular rabbi won't run around advertising his status: that would be an act of conceit; he will just be there for people to consult in their difficult moments. The secular rabbi's reward will be the satisfaction of helping a fellow man or woman in their hour of crisis. Life experience would be the primary qualification for a secular rabbi, perhaps supplemented by a well-constructed degree in the area of social theory, not any formal rabbinical training. It helps that they should be familiar with the people they advise and themselves be part of the community.

It is very important that the secular rabbi try to behave at the highest moral level. The topics on which their counsel may be sought are too numerous to mention them all, but among them are relationships, sibling issues, financial problems and even parents developing Alzheimer's.

At university I studied how the mind works and the complexities of human relations. My subjects included politics and interdisciplinary studies, including a broad spectrum of social theory. To pull the lot together I delved into reflective theory, becoming adept at the art of human observation and listening to the real content of what people say. All this was compounded by certain life skills that I accumulated while working in a youth movement, and although I lost a large part of my cognitive acuity in my accident, these various skills stayed with me. My life experience in the decades since then has brought me to a point where, happily, I do perform the services of a secular rabbi. It may sound as if I'm a bit full of myself using the term self-referentially but the important thing is that I do try to care for people in the best way I can and to help them attain a better quality of life. Descended as I am from a line of rabbis and teachers, I see in myself a modern expression of that role. So, if you're in need of counsel, I am happy to oblige and give my two bits...

Thirteen

Reflections

Gazing Back

Please excuse my indulgence but it is time to cast a gaze back at what I have done with my first six decades. This is a moment for reflection. From all the stories and anecdotes I have written it might appear that I have lived a full, dynamic, action-packed life. Sadly, this is far from the lived reality that I recognise. There have been far too many moments spent alone, idle, wishing I had company, someone to join me in what I desired to do.

Sixty finds me philosophical, more accepting than before of this fact. To put it succinctly, I am not at the centre of other people's worlds; only at the centre of mine. Should people fit me into their busy schedules I consider myself fortunate. There is no point in harassing them to include me. I need to maintain my self-respect, my sense of self-worth, and will not allow others to demean me. This can be a very difficult position to sustain. It is a struggle I have seen most disabled people need to wage. The same struggle has led me to cherish people of worth. I take my moments with them and turn them into myth. This is my story-making, I do hope no ill will rises to the surface in my writing. As one person I communicate with says, it is my therapy. I look at myself on this milestone day and what do I see? The amalgam of my natural self, bound with the mortar of my studies and the harsh reality of lived experience. Of course I wish my accident had never happened. Life would have been very different. But life is not made up of 'would have' and 'what if'. I am the product of many events, that accident among them. It is up to me to deal with everything that went into the making of me, David at sixty.

Resilience

Extending the journey metaphor, mine has been a long one with many ports of call I have no wish to revisit. But after pausing at each location I have climbed back on board and continued on my way. This is how I have navigated the course of my life with its ups and downs. The ability to recover from setbacks — in a word, resilience — has served me well, without too great a strain. But, to be honest, there are some aspects of my former self that will never recover, leaving me to accommodate to this unalterable reality — and there is no point in denying just how annoying this has been at times. Broken bones heal — they repair themselves — but brain and nerve damage, never. I have had to learn to live with epilepsy and the left side of my body being very weak.

Nerve damage in one of my feet has not stopped me walking long distances but it does make putting on a shoe difficult. I very much enjoy the act of eating and sharing a meal with someone but this has been compromised. As mentioned earlier, the inability to use a knife and fork makes this a hassle. I have a nerve missing in my lip that causes me to dribble and make a mess. If I am careful and pay attention I can control the consequences of the missing nerve. This is only one of several simultaneous battles I am waging but I am always willing to have a decent go at things and, as long as people are tolerant, I keep front of mind the fact that I could be in a lot worse state.

My position has allowed me to be a good uncle to various children: I try to play my part well. I remember their birthdays and engage with them as people. Through me they learn that people are different and that this is OK. I have had many joyful times with all these nephews and nieces as children are not judgmental – unlike adults. Over the years I have had the privilege to meet and expand my circle of friends, people who value me for who I am and bother to care for me, so very unlike those who once called me friend and whose silence has been deafening. I have learnt about people both bad and good, and carry this knowledge as a cherished item in my baggage. The big thing I have learnt is who we are and how we behave. My experience has gifted me a philosophy and an attitude to life that sit well with me.

Partner Ship

Life is a voyage, with frequent departures to various destinations. I've visited so many that it would be unfair to say I missed the boat. Yet one important vessel sailed without me: call it the Partner Ship.

I missed out on finding myself someone with whom I can engage and enjoy the act of living. Without this person I miss a lot of life's joy, and my quality of life is greatly diminished. Put simply, I am lonely. At the very least I need someone I can talk to(and sometimes at). Being without this all-important other leaves me verbally backed up. So when I get a chance to talk I am like a machine gun. Regrettably, this does nothing for my social integration.

Prior to my accident there was a vast array of available single women for me to interact with. I did enjoy moving between them — before that fateful day. Afterwards I could no longer get out and hail them on the vast open ocean of society: instead of sailing or cruising on the high seas it was as if the waters had dried up. My life had run aground. As a young man with a young man's drives and ambitions, I now found myself powerless and that was hard to digest. While my peers were forming themselves into couples and establishing their future life together, I had all the appeal of damaged goods. It came to the point where I had to ask acquaintances if they would introduce me to someone that might take to me. It was one of those occasions that sort true friends from pretenders. Those who had deserted me couldn't be bothered helping — a pox on them.

I tried one or two singles nights: revolting. How could I succumb to that? I kept my eyes open and inquired but got nowhere. Eventually I found something called the Jewish Friendship Group but had no luck there. The latest thing is a speed dating night, which I'm a bit apprehensive about. Well-wishers say, what about cyber-dating? But that doesn't appeal. (I've seen a few disasters.) My voyage is not over and here I am in the crow's nest keeping a regular lookout. You never know who you'll encounter between here and the farthest shore.

Point of View

In my experience, living with a disability is as much about how you think of and approach the world as about physical limitations. To progress from day to day as a disabled person it is critical to comprehend what is happening in the world around you. An immensely complex and multifaceted endeavour, this requires great mental effort and is anything but obvious to the naked eye.

Looking deeply into many aspects of my disability would have been mission impossible without the use of my intellectual skills. I am lucky not to have been robbed of these along with other faculties due to my brain damage. If anything, they have been enhanced by my life experience. This has happened in two domains: one, the way my mind has had to tap into reserves of previously unused ingenuity to interact with the world around me (which, the way I see it, has undergone abrupt change — though of course I know that the change has been in my perceptions). Secondly, there is the question of how my disability functions in the social space.

To shift from being fully abled one day to being disabled the next is not a process but a quantum leap. There is no manual you can consult to know if you're taking the right steps. Being disabled is a lifelong battle fought day to day and hour to hour. Without the active participation of your mind, it is a losing battle; with it you can win. This is what victory looks like: here am I, in my own home, describing my inner and outer worlds to you. Here I sit in peace with what I was, with who I am, and I am content. This is exactly where I like to be.

Choice

I did not choose to become disabled. Since the day of my accident, all of my life has been perceived through the prism of my disability. What choices I have are structured by it. But I have discovered that the exercise of this limited choice has given me insights into who and what I am. When my glass was knocked over, not everything spilt out: a vital residue was saved.

Yes, life can be sweet and good; and it comes down to the choices one makes — the best of them made not on the spur of the moment but after due consideration.

From the instant of my accident all expectations I had for the life that lay ahead of me evaporated. My changed future still left me with choices to make. *How will I make the correct choice*? I asked myself. *Just have faith in myself*, was the answer that came back to me. But then the doubt: *Can I alter a choice if it proves not to be ideal?* I have found that with each choice I make I have learnt a bit more about myself, so that the answer is: *Nearly always, yes*. As I grow acquainted with the person I have become, I find myself better equipped to make wise choices. Where possible, I try to take my disability out of the equation. I also aim to behave well in all social settings. This is a very deliberate choice I have made yet, to be honest, I don't always succeed.

When it came time for my compensation case, which, from what had been explained to me, was going to be a tricky matter, several choices about my future life had to be confronted. First, I realised I could never be properly compensated for the things I had lost. How can financial recompense be fairly determined? So the choice for me boiled down to: Do I just take the money and run and blow it all on a good time, or should I be prudent and use it to create a better future. Tough choices, I think.

I concluded I needed money for a home as I would always need somewhere to live. I was able to do this easily enough but even this decision was framed by my disability. The home I chose needed to be within easy walking distance of the amenities and goods I would rely on for my survival. Given that my compensation would pay for this home, I realised I would get only one choice to find a good home, it being too difficult to keep moving. Through all this I gained some healthy insight into my surviving capacities. Money managed well contributes to my wellbeing: this I feel I have mastered reasonably well. There was even enough money left over for me to blow a bit on a good time (which I did). Another lesson I learnt here: if I think through things and implement well-considered choices they will have tangible consequences, so the better I understand the circumstances surrounding any choice I make, the better for my future welfare.

Let me now address the vitally important social sphere. The challenge was to engage with people I could trust were real friends, people who cared for me and wanted to be involved with me. It takes time to build a social network of this quality. And, to support it, once again I had to be a high-quality friend myself, someone of genuine value, consistent, caring and keen to assist others in need wherever possible. Good behaviour grows and is self-reinforcing over time.

Perhaps foolishly, I do believe that if I treat people as they should be treated I would be treated that way in turn. Experience on that score has tempered my earlier naïvety. Still, the choice of how I treat people is mine and mine alone, and I guard it fiercely, not holding others to blame for how I act towards them.

Help

More often than not, the disabled need some degree of assistance. Just how much comes down to the person's level of disability — and their willingness to accept this intervention.

Yes, first of all the disabled person has to accept that they need help. Only once this is understood can the issue of how much help they need be ascertained. When it was suggested to me that I should go down this path, I can tell you I was not happy. I didn't want to do it — end of story. I found the idea of paying someone to come and do what I should be doing an affront. I like to think of myself as capable and no way was I going to permit myself an indulgence as if I were someone of the *bourgeoisie* pampering myself by hiring a cleaner.

But arguments wear thin when you find that it's impossible to hide from reality all that long. I looked around and realised I wasn't doing a great job and, as that wasn't going to change, well, a bit of help would not be so hard to take. Some activities are beyond me and I don't want to be getting sick from living surrounded by my own mess. So what to do about it was the next challenge. I began by engaging a local cleaning lady. She came once a fortnight for a couple hours and did the basic tasks that go with good housekeeping. That worked out well: I liked her. She was a nice lady with ethics and a helpful attitude. She not only did those things I couldn't but also maintenance chores that I wasn't so good at. However, after some time age caught up with her and she gave up cleaning, leaving me with the serious problem of how to replace her.

At first I turned to council home help but, regrettably, found that a long way below perfect. The intentions behind the system are good but implementation falls well short of what's needed. Initially they gave me an hour-and-a-half a week but later this was cut back to an hour despite an assurance from council that it wouldn't do that. So far as cleaning went, this meant it wasn't possible to do the necessary work in the time allotted — more than a bit futile, I feel. It's impossible to do half a job. Yes, they are very cheap but that doesn't cut it for me: I was brought up to believe that if a job's worth doing it's worth doing well. Further, there were numerous tasks they were forbidden to do because of council rules — such as sweeping my front porch, dusting or mopping. So these things were left undone.

Worst of all, they sent me a bloke who stole a lot of money from me. To steal from the poorest people there are, let alone anyone who's disabled, is a low act. When this came to light, I received no apology. Apart from this, council home help suffered from inconsistency of service: I never knew who would turn up and sometimes no one did. While I doubt that anyone at council considered the impact this might have on me, the fact is that to counteract the effect of brain damage on my life, living even moderately stress-free requires that there be consistency in my routine. Upsetting that routine is physically and emotionally destabilising. So you can imagine the difficulties I was put under when they started providing the help on a different day week after week. I never knew where I was. Sometimes I actually received some good help. This would last a while, then something would happen, it would change, and again I was left with reasonable expectations of reliable service dashed. I don't mind letting someone I like into my house to do things for me but if for some reason we don't click I find it a real imposition. For instance, I had to have one person stopped after discovering that they were anti-Semitic.

Happily, not too much time passed before I found a decent bloke whom I had been told of. He came over, said, 'I understand this is important and everything must be sorted out to your liking.' He went straight to work, found me a Chinese cleaner who turned out to be just perfect and sent him to my home for two hours a week. This guy did what needed to be done without my asking — which was just great, as I don't always see what is needed. I was happy to have him in my house, and over time we became friends of sorts. For years I would look forward to the two hours we would spend together every week but, alas, just as Covid hit, he went to China for New Year celebrations and I never saw him again. It took a while but eventually I found a decent replacement.

The guy from Jewish Care was great. He looked after all my therapies and expanded them in due course. His helpful interventions were passed on to the NDIS, which as I have mentioned elsewhere has been wonderful to me, so I have ended up in a place I had never imagined when I began this journey.

In one sense I have been robbed of my life and have little time to myself. But I have been very fortunate that finally accepting I could not fully care for myself has added so much value to my life, with the benefits my speech therapist and personal trainer have bestowed on me — things I had not dreamed of. I would say if you're willing to ride the bumps, and lean in to all the twists and turns, this is a journey worth pursuing, one best regarded as an adventure.

Responsibility

Let me begin by busting a myth. Being disabled is not *carte blanche* to do whatever you like: it comes with responsibilities, just as being a mature adult comes with responsibilities. In some areas, these responsibilities are one and the same. The two parcels of responsibility add up to a heavy load at times but no one gets a choice to shrug off the burden. The only choice — if that's the word you want to use — is to work out how you carry out the tasks you must.

In my view the first responsibility of the disabled is to understand their condition and investigate all the ramifications this entails. The onus is on disabled people to understand and accept that over time their responsibilities will develop and change. An example: I know very well as a consequence of right frontal-lobe brain damage that my behaviour can sometimes become very confronting. Now self-awareness and honesty compel me to admit my natural personality was fairly confronting already, so my brain damage only accentuates this. But in the social sphere I must remind myself there are real limits to tolerance for such behaviour: if I don't, others will remind me instead. To control and manage my actions is not always easy — but it must be done.

When I first escaped hospital after my accident, I reasoned that since I had survived it was my responsibility to live as well as I could, so I must grab any opportunity that presented itself. So I took great pains to ensure I got my medication just right so that I could live in safety. As doctors are not always sure what the 'right dose' will be, this is not the easiest of tasks. To guarantee I could survive financially, I was put on the disability support pension. This is my wage, so in a sense living well with a disability is my job. In other words, the government pays me to look after myself. To earn my keep, I must regard staying healthy as my primary goal. In more recent years, my ability to carry out this responsibility has been boosted by the introduction of the NDIS, which has been a godsend. The pension comes with obligations; so does the NDIS. I need to live within their limits, and it is up to me to use its benefits to cover my costs of living, not to pamper myself with luxuries. What is given me is not for the purpose of living 'the good life', but to ensure I get by.

I have no need to rush out for food vouchers or to line up at food banks. I manage my money sensibly: no smoking or drinking. I find people leap to do things for me but this is upsetting when it becomes *disabling*. I want to control my own finances, to dress myself, to have my personal space respected: for someone to come up and touch me undermines my self-esteem and takes away the responsibility I have to present well. If these strike you as the responsibilities any adult would claim over themselves then this is a good place to stop, for you have understood my point exactly.

If Only ...

If only I knew then what I know now ... this is a very perplexing premise. Knowing then what we have learnt since could have changed our lives in so many ways. But to a large degree it is also a futile question. It is not possible to re-run the past any more than it is to predict the future. Simply put, the past is the past. We don't have the power to change it; the future, we do.

If only I had acted differently ... This is what we mean by hindsight: reverse 20-20 vision. We conduct our lives in ignorance of the future consequence our actions will have. The best we can do is ponder the alternative potentials of these choices and consider what we would do next time if a similar situation arose.

Wisdom is the fruit of experience, but to dwell too much on the past is not wise. If only I knew then what I knew now I would not have been driving where I was on the day of my accident. Too late to dwell on that; absolutely futile to ask, What if? I *was* driving and the accident happened. The futility of What if? can be extrapolated into many facets of day-to-day life. I tell friends with ailing or dying parents, Be sure to make your peace with them, or say what you deeply feel about them, *right now* because after the fact you don't get a second chance. You must live with the actions you take now.

Now we are acting empowered with knowledge, we are capable of shaping our future. In a way this puts an act of divinity into our hands. It all comes down to luck and self-belief. I am fortunate in knowing what I can do to construct my future. I must have faith in myself to make wise, well-informed decisions and, yes, to anticipate and be prepared to live with the consequences of my choices, whatever they may be.

Faith

Various people of my acquaintance have great conviction — what they call faith. Being the atheist I am, I pour scorn on this. In my view there is no God and so there is no valid religious belief. Of course my thoughts on this apply as well to many more people of faith beyond my acquaintance, be they observant Catholics or Jews. What I ask of all these people who hold faith in some form or another is that they be consistent — in other words, that what they preach or say they believe be carried out in their day-to-day life.

What I called lived hypocrisy disgusts me — take people who claim to be green and even preach the need to be green, yet still burn massive amounts of carbon in the course of their lives. In my view you can't have it both ways. It is impossible to be part religious; I cannot accept people half-doing Shabbat and sitting on this moral pedestal. It is impossible to be part religious.

I think it is time I looked at myself first and reflected on how my own words and deeds stack up. I have heartfelt convictions and admit I am opinionated. So do I reconcile these with the bulk of my actions day to day? I feel I do. Some of these convictions have been my saving grace, as a matter of fact. Being a child of the Moon landing I have deep inside me a great conviction and belief in the power of modern science to do things. I even feel that at some point a solution to global warming will be found. But I do feel sour when our government tries to use science as an excuse to do nothing.

I have especially strong faith in the power and capacity of modern medical science, so when I have been in life-threatening situations — alas, too many times — I have placed myself in the hands of doctors and in the belief that their knowledge will save me. This faith has been rewarded as I have survived each crisis, launched into my rehab and gone on to recover. So you can see why I take the view that a little well-placed faith can be beneficial. But you need to be aware of what is going on and not confuse well-founded faith with blind trust.

Enough

During the course of our lives we confront incidents that provoke a deep sigh, perhaps even a grunt, and then we say *enough*! I consider this a genuine and valid response to certain aspects of life. When this is recognised and acted upon our general being is enhanced. Conducted with due and considered decency, this brings our lives to a higher level, so I would propose recognising *enough* as an important part of the armour in which we combat life.

Enough comes about when we reach an impasse. To progress, this needs to be resolved. This may happen in the work place, maybe the type of work being done, the people we deal with, the office itself. In the home *enough* arises frequently, especially when bringing up children or perhaps trying to reconcile issues with a partner. Suddenly the penny drops — *enough!* At each point, deep from within the cry arises, I can't cope with this. The trick is to recognise these occasions and say *enough!* This will help peace of mind and quality of life. It is not a complex thing, it just requires some reflection. An area *enough* has arisen in the public domain is voluntary assisted dying. Here the discussion has been — if a person says *enough* is that good enough? I shall resist the temptation to be explicit as it is something we are all familiar with and it has brought tears to my eyes a number of times. In general, I have concluded when a person says *enough* about anything I just have to accept it.

Child's Play

I like to watch children at play. I feel a lot can be learnt from how they act when they're not following a strict adult routine. I like to watch girls with dolls and boys with cars. One thing I have noticed is that they are not all homogeneous; each child has a unique style of play. Some are very focused, others far more relaxed; and some, I find, are very organised. I have concluded that the way kids play reflects a lot about their inner personality. But it is those children who can amuse and occupy themselves that I find most wondrous to behold. They inhabit a world constructed by themselves and are content in it. They don't need the extras — and the external stimulus — that others demand. To pass time with no idea of time passing is a skill many, probably most, adults have lost — and that is a great loss.

You hear many a child exclaim, 'I am bored!' This sends chills up the spines of adults. Keeping a child constantly entertained is seriously hard and exhausting work. Whenever I used to say this, my parents would reply, 'David, go read a book.' I never found this a satisfactory answer but over time I have learnt the value and joy that reading a book can contribute to passing the time of day.

Boredom is a curse. It twists and turns like a dagger in the flesh. Sitting up in a hospital bed waiting for a visitor, this boredom can be soul-destroying but, happily, it can be confronted. I have a very active mind, even in its current depleted incarnation. It is always working and rarely takes a rest. If I don't occupy it, its constant motion seems to reverberate in my head. Compared to that, tinnitus would be a blessing. Disability can result in physical inactivity, but nothing stops the mind, even if it becomes numb with boredom for lack of an outlet. I had to learn this truth and the necessity of combating boredom if I was to preserve my sanity.

While forced inactivity may lead to boredom in some disabled people, I would expect it produces depression in many others. While the average person is commuting to and from work and then engaged in the job activity all day, their disabled counterpart is often at home alone with nothing but TV for company. Rather than sitting in a chair wondering how you are going to spend the empty hours that stretch ahead to the evening horizon, a life of your own needs to be created. It needs to include some purpose.

To a degree, how able-bodied you are counts. Luckily I can move around and do things: I am not restricted to a wheelchair. My mind still rages. It needs to be fed and exercised or I am in serious trouble.

People speak of killing time, or having time to kill. I want nothing to do with that idea. Instead my aim is to make the most of time, to use it to produce something of value. I still find reading is a first-class exercise for keeping my active mind occupied. During my university studies I read a lot as part of my study obligations, but now I derive great joy from reading for pleasure or based on my interests. Thus I have perused and enjoyed great literature, and to occupy and satisfy my mind I have read widely, everything from biographies to astrophysics. Already well educated, I have become better educated. To express myself physically and artistically, I work in my garden. Now, with all that I do, I am, if anything, short of time. Having dealt with the sharp edge of my disability — my alienation from the course of everyday life — I have reached a sweet spot and given boredom its marching orders. Along came 2020 and, bang, in parachuted Covid and, before long, Covid-normal. Without warning, the challenge I've made all these years to use time well, rather than just kill it, became an existential problem with a universality of application. What to do with their time has greatly disturbed multitudes of people since they were thrown into my boat — and many have struggled to cope.

Sent home from work without a manual on how to get through a day on their own, they soon found themselves adrift. Many returned to being a child — no doubt the one they had once been — unable to amuse themselves and with no clue what to do with this useless gift of unfilled time. I observed these people with a mixture of mirth and compassion. Through the same trauma I had not had anyone to assist me; many of these people had others within reach who could give them a helping hand if only they would take it. Far too many were overcome by the task, but I was pleased to see many more survived. In the end it is up to each of us to construct and fill time in our own way. While I passed many Covid-era hours observing adults being reduced to children, I found the spectacle nowhere near as enjoyable as I do watching children at play.

Covid Not All Bad

'A blessing on your head – *Mazel tov!*' That's how the fiddler goes. I love this song as it gets to the crux of life. We must be thankful for all the blessings that life delivers and not focus on the misfortunes that occur to us along the way. This sums up my approach to living: positive outcomes flow from positive thinking. While I have sat and observed Covid through our extended lockdowns I've been warmed, even uplifted, by the all the blessings this unsolicited situation has delivered. It has been far from all bad. For some, this time has been life-changing. My personal blessings have been simple: a fresh appreciation of life's value born out of the struggle that I — but also others in a similar plight to myself — have waged; a rebirth of honesty, with many people opening up and giving voice to both their connection with the outside world and the fact that life's path is not strewn with roses. Finally, Covid has only heightened my respect for the services provided by those people who keep my life on track.

For me, these gains have been worth the privations. May my life now move forward in a smooth trajectory, and I wish the same for all those whose lives have been touched by blessings in these times.

Chit Chat Email

Ever since I was old enough to talk, my mouth has been in constant motion. In the past I had a few girlfriends who worked out that the only way to shut me up was to kiss me. This I was able to tolerate. But for the rest of my waking hours oral and written communications are as dear to me as air and water.

I talk in such a fluent stream that 'babble' is probably a better word for it. Even in a dentist's chair or a lecture hall, or while watching a film, the impulse is almost irresistible. Long discussions with myself are a surefire way of clearing my mind. They help me clarify and sharpen my thoughts. I know it's only a figure of speech but I do feel that if I couldn't talk my head would explode.

Given my constant need to give utterance, I am a very social creature, so any obstacle to the flow of language is acutely felt. There has been no shortage of such obstacles since my road accident back in the mid-1980s. First of all, when I came out of my coma, I discovered that my speech sounded slow and slurred. This was very off-putting to others, but no more than it was to me. Whatever I said was difficult for the listener to comprehend. Foremost among the consequences this distorted speech created was to force upon me a social isolation I had never before known.

This isolation has been compounded by my limited freedom of movement. I cannot get about as I once did, and the fact I no longer drive contributes to that. Now dependent on people's willingness to give me a lift, I have found that if you can get them it is seldom at the time you desire. Also, the hours I keep are not very social: I am no longer the creature of the night that I once was. Being outside the social mainstream has further inhibited my ability to speak — and this setback just grows more serious with every passing year. The content of my desired communication gets backed up so, when I get the chance to express myself, I go hell for leather. This torrent of self-expression, while understandable from my point of view, can turn people off.

Not being in the workforce and being socially inactive, opportunities for self-expression come down to three small circles — family, neighbours and people I meet while out shopping. On second thoughts, there is one other outlet: my daily coffee — taken at a local café — is an excellent chance to meet and greet; and of course I leap at it. Mixing as a local, you soon get treated as a local. The phone, I have discovered, is not quite the 'magic bullet' you might have imagined it to be. You can't chat to people during the day: they are caught up in their work. Then at night, even if you can catch them, they don't have time to talk. For years, this was a factor of frustration in my so-called social life. Then modernity provided a form of salvation with something I could handle, though I would never describe myself as techno-adept. Email.

In a way it has been a lifeline. It may not make for conversation in the normal sense of the word and is devoid of the satisfaction you get from face-to-face talk. Nonetheless, it is a useful two-way mode of communication between me and other people, whether they live in the same street or on the other side of the world. Much of what is conveyed in normal speech governed by regular grammar applies to email as well and, in the end, it is only of any use if the person you are addressing responds, enabling a two-way conversation to develop. As in normal conversation you need to be understood, so spelling and typos become important; you have to pay attention to what you have written and correct it so your cyberspace recipient can follow you. With email and now smartphones you can chat with people where previously you were unable to do so. And these devices make it much easier to organise get-togethers.

Because of time differences I get emails at all times of the day, which reduces my sense of social isolation while keeping me involved in people's lives. Even more than in face-to-face conversation, you have to be careful what you say online as it may be held against you in future. Face-to-face it's deemed inconsiderate to fire off thoughts in a scattergun approach, leaving people confused and unable to keep up with the pace my mind works at. With email, you lack facial or visual cues to help you discern how well you are speaking. The tonality and modality of oral speech are lacking on the computer screen(emojis being a pale substitute), and the list goes on. Today, thanks to WhatsApp,Skype and FaceTime etc., you can speak face-to-face with people separated by distance but I don't find these systems totally satisfying — and you both have to arrange to be in front of a device simultaneously despite often vastly different time zones, which can prove quite difficult to manage.

Good manners count. For some reason, email users can become easily affronted when they would have been less likely to do so in person. With the written word they have time to ponder the deeper meaning of what you are saying and it often requires guesswork that often miscarries. This means you need to be careful what you write, not overly flippant. I have found this medium can often be hectic, lending itself to easily heated emotions. This tends to happen when I am conversing with a number of people at the same time, firing away emails that appear to demand urgent responses.

Once I was in conversation with London, Tel Aviv and America all at the same time and by the end I felt as exhausted as you do at the end of a long intense chat. But email can be a lot of fun, too. A kind of uncle figure in my life lived in San Francisco, which didn't make it easy to chat. So once a week we would write each other a good-sized email message, and in this way I got to know and understand him better. His emails were a delight to read. He was a very intelligent man and they were laced with great wit. It has long been recognised that the art of conversation can create a close bond between people, and this remains true in the world of emails.

Home Maintenance

Only once I had bought my house did I really discover what's involved in looking after it. And this discovery is not a one-off lesson but an ongoing education that lasts for many years. It is also a battle. Things go wrong at the drop of a trowel; strategies misfire; something always needs fixing. It is a deeply satisfying activity to adapt the house to suit my living requirements. Quickly I came to the conclusion that doing all this is like paying rent: it amounts to a financial impost you have no chance of dodging. Then another realisation dawned on me that has guided me along my path: simply put, my house *is* my standard of living and quality of life. So what I put into it raises the level of both. All money spent is well invested, seeing I receive a tangible return for it in the form of a better life. I soon learnt the lesson that awaits all householders: if you don't keep doing what needs to be done, your home will deteriorate beyond your control and become a heavy weight on your shoulders. Since it is too large for all the challenges to be met at once, the wisest policy is to keep chipping away at it.

So, bit by bit, I have tended to every demand placed on me by my house and now I am on top of it. This is the case because I have been diligent when major tasks come up, which they will do from time to time. A couple of these have arisen lately. First, I had to re-stump the foundations and then I discovered a new kitchen needed to be installed. Happily, I've been able to do both. I was interested to find that the house stumps were made not of wood but of brick, which had worn away with time. No longer do I have that sinking feeling that I'm going to fall through the floor, plus the floor no longer creaks and squeaks as it once did. One unforseen benefit is that the windows no longer rattle. But one task leads to another: as a result of the re-stumping I brought in a cabinetmaker to solve a minor issue. It was he who took one look at the job and declared: 'The whole kitchen needs doing.' I bit the bullet and had scarcely completed the work on that when I had to move on to redoing the laundry. Yes, a householder's work is never done. One last task flowing from the re-stumping: I now need to re-lay the carpet after the old stumps imprinted the existing one with marks that ruined it. I will be exceedingly glad once all this is done. But to complicate matters I have been doing these works during the days of the great virus. In my own way, I have often got the impression that I'm driving the national economy forward all on my own (perhaps a slight exaggeration).

I see doing things for my house as doing them for myself. Investing in myself is very important because it motivates me and lends purpose to my days. Over time I developed my Victorian homestead into a very nice villa without doing major renovations. I am very pleased with how it looks now: comfortable, but not pristine — if anything, slightly dishevelled. I don't want to live in something out of *Vogue* magazine. There must always be some room for improvement (if it's not the laundry, the kitchen; if not the kitchen, the sunroom). My house is a reflection of me.

Not all the problems that need fixing in a house can be attended to straightaway. There can be great difficulty in getting a plumber or electrician to visit at short notice. In this day and age it is hard to survive for long without electricity. At one point I became paranoid about my house burning down, so I was anxious to install a safety switch. But for this to happen the house needed rewiring as what was there was very old. It took years to find a tradesman who could and would do this job, which ended up costing me a lot of money I could ill afford. The long wait itself added to the expense. The lesson I learnt from this was the imperative to get things done as soon as possible.

A Victorian villa built by tradesmen in an age when the quality artisan reigned supreme is a very solid structure. I am spared the problems that other people incur. But there is a flip side to my good fortune: when something goes wrong, it is very hard to correct. The tradesmen and material that built houses this sturdy no longer exist, so substitutes have to be found. Let me give you an example: once, thieves broke into my house by smashing the leadlight on the front door. They cleaned the place out (apparently they had a van parked out the front and filled it with my goods). It was hard enough to replace all that had been stolen, but then replacing the leadlight became an issue. No one, it seems, made it to this quality anymore, which came as a great disappointment: I'd very much wanted to replace the stolen panes because they cast a lovely light through the house. The quest to find someone who could produce such an item to an adequate standard was long and difficult. Once I had tracked down a possible supplier, I had to take my place at the end of a queue of people waiting for something in the same line. The wait was worth it, though, as once again leadlight is a most attractive feature of my home, bestowing on it a great feeling of warmth.

Sometimes the old craftsmanship throws up wonderful surprises. At one point I decided to rip up the carpet in my hallway and have the floorboards polished. To my delight, when this was done I discovered I possess the most magnificent Baltic pine floorboards, something very special. It is almost impossible to buy wood like that today, and it is so striking as anyone who enters by the front door can see. The leadlight glow fairly bounces along it. I feel that with a house such as this it is important, as far as possible, to execute any refurbishment in accordance with the original style. Provided it can be done at all, this is costly, but I feel it is worth the investment — which leads on to a belief of mine. Surrounding myself with as aesthetically pleasing an environment as can be produced means I will be living in the nicest possible world. This is a lesson I learnt from my colourful grandmother, Nana Cook (The Dame), who would always say the best is the cheapest in the end.

How people approach improving their built environment often reflects their upbringing, I feel. I have mates who want to do everything themselves, no matter how big or small the task. They will even take it as a personal insult if you suggest bringing someone in to effect the improvement. These friends have usually been taught by their dads how to be handymen. They fixed things around the home while growing up, and this may be because they had the skills or simply that they lacked the money to pay a tradie. But undeniably they would have obtained satisfaction from the creative task of how to approach practical problems and resolve things. My father was many things but one thing he wasn't was technically adept. He didn't have a clue and didn't care about it. If a job needed doing, he believed, you paid someone to do it and would expect it to be done well. I was taught by his example to be an intellectual, which requires a different frame of mind. Technical skills are simply not part of my vocabulary: I accept and understand that. This makes it all the more important to be able to find people able to do the tasks that cannot be shirked. There are times when I wish that I had the skills my friends possess to do things around the house, so much do I hate being dependent on others. This gripe extends to my disability. Far too often I need to call in someone to assist and do things for me that I would be much happier doing for myself. So I do try first before capitulating to necessity. Disability is not my only opponent in this regard, though. To the ageing, technology can be a bugbear: it certainly is to me. Show a malfunctioning tech gadget to a kid and they get it straightaway; adults unfamiliar with this stuff must be shown at least a few times how to fix it. So I would argue that acquiring computer skills in a way mirrors the inculcation of home maintenance skills.

When everything indoors has exhausted my capacity for improvement, I have only to step outside the sunroom to experience great delight and joy. I am now in my garden, a sort of second home within my first one. Like my house, the garden that sits behind it demands ongoing and constant attention. In lavishing attention and care on them, I am creating a better me.

Clean Heels

Restlessness is a syndrome that affects a number of people I know. It is a hallmark of the lifestyle these people enjoy but I think I would find it stressful. People who show a clean pair of heels are always on the move, never stopping in one spot long enough for dirt to accumulate under their feet.

I have often observed that once someone adopts this lifestyle it is hard to escape from and becomes a self-perpetuating thing. It typically reflects in their repeated commission of carbon sins. It is easy for all of us to lapse into this lifestyle to some degree: it appears to be a by-product of modern life. The idea that every holiday we have to be jetting off overseas or driving interstate instead of getting our feet dirty at home creates carbon emissions.

But this is just one minor way in which the syndrome — to which we are all subject — manifests itself.

As I say, for some people this malady is a lifestyle choice, not something imposed on them. But there is a touch of the chicken-and-egg argument as to which is which. Some people choose jobs that require them to be perpetually moving about. Keeping your heels clean forces you to follow a rather inflexible lifestyle. Their entries and exits from airports are governed by plane schedules. Other routines — from when meetings are held to what day they get their washing done — rule their lives, with insufficient time set aside for physical exercise and looking after their health. In fact, they don't rule their lives: timetables or other people's expectations do.

Keeping a clean pair of heels sounds glamorous — always heading off to enviable destinations that may be meeting places for them but are holiday resorts for other people. Sounds great, doesn't it. But, for those living in this 'dream reality', it sounds far better than it actually is. Being constantly on the move –— with your clean heels but itchy feet — means visiting great places but getting to see very little of them. Imagine being in New York every other month but never getting to see a show on Broadway or going to the Met. Moving on can be a healthy thing but never pausing for breath is decidedly unhealthy.

Every few days our clean-heeled friends wake up in a different city. Sooner or later, they blame all this work-related travel for their frenetic lifestyles. So when the weekend comes, or it's time to take a holiday, do they stay still, let the grass grow under their feet? No way. Those who are constantly on the move, whether for work or pleasure, seldom reflect on the damage they do to themselves and the world. While they're trapped in an endless spiral of carbon pollution, woe unto the rest of us who lead sedentary and mundane lives.

The Freezer

Concern about global warming has contributed to turning me into an environmentalist. It is important to care for our Earth and the way we interact with it. One of my big bugbears is the way energy is used. A core problem for most people is how to live — but not wastefully — in comfortable climatic conditions, not being too hot in summer or too cold in winter. When it comes to efficient cooling and heating, I guess being single makes it easier for me to control the relevant inputs and outputs. I feel bad if I overuse energy that is solely for my benefit. This feeling probably stems from observing the ways other people are profligate in their own use of it.

Nowhere is misuse more flagrant than in the matter of air conditioning. People put it on and leave it on, even if in doing so there is no real effect. Why leave it going for half an hour in an empty room? I personally like the heat and have no great need for air conditioning. Anyhow, I live in a cool house made of double brick and bluestone: it is always a few degrees cooler in here than outside, plus it doesn't bake easily. This results in an energy problem in winter, though. It is like living in a freezer, with me cast as the ice cube. To warm the house requires an amount of energy I am not willing to consume. Believe me, I have thought my way around the problem. There is no need to heat most of the house, only the room I sit in, so I turn the heating on for a while and then turn it off, using the warmth I've created. I find it hard to turn the heating on during the day: that doesn't sit right with me. But don't get me wrong, there are limits to austerity. Heating goes on morning and night. Getting warm is the priority.

When Tony Abbott was in power, I listened to the public discussion about global warming and ways to deal with it. In the end I came to the conclusion that either you are with him and other fools or you take a stance opposing them. And it cannot be a question of mere words: action must be taken affecting your personal lifestyle or your principles count for naught. As I saw it, there was only one thing to do: install solar panelling on my roof. This involves a lot of money for someone on my income. Eventually, I reasoned the cost of doing this was not excessive: it was equivalent to the price of a holiday I wasn't having anyway. So to be on the right side of the argument I had a small solar unit placed on my house. Economically, it was not a sensible thing to do. With the size of my bills — and some of them are so low — it will never pay itself off. But what I care about more is the amount of pollution I am *not* putting into the air.

I feel good about doing my bit towards carbon reduction — and the fact I don't drive adds to the value of my contribution. Instead of throwing things out, I like to recycle them, give them a new lease of life. I cannot abide waste: using everything to its full potential means that, through adopting this principle in my garden, following the cycle of nature, I have learnt to live within the harmony of my place. With a little thought and effort, we can all create domestic harmony through our energy choices — even those of us who live in a freezer.

The Author — Why I Write

I was born 5 January 1961 in the middle of a heatwave. I'm the second in the family. I have a sister who is older by a few years, then along came a younger one. I thought that was a mistake, she should have been a brother. No matter, she has been a wonderful sibling, the kind you would let draw you on the cover of your book. I went to Camberwell South Primary, otherwise known as Peate Avenue. When I had grown up (somewhat)I went to Camberwell High from Years 7 onward and did my final year at Kew High, finishing school in 1978. I spent the next year mostly in Israel, followed by a brief European tour. On return, I did a Bachelor of Arts at Melbourne University with a double major in history and politics. Life was in a nice groove. But in 1984, while travelling from Perth to Darwin, I had a serious car accident and suffered severe life-transforming injuries. Later, in 2002, I had a heart attack and bypass surgery. It was then discovered that I have genetic problems with my colon. This needs to be watched but is no cause for alarm. Following that, on a trip to Israel in 2015, I fell, hitting my head and having a minor stroke. In 2020 Covid struck and in 2022 I was diagnosed with stomach cancer and spent months in hospital which included extensive surgery and chemotherapy. I had an all-too brief spell back home smelling the roses but another fall and further complications put me back in hospital. To finance my ongoing care, I have now sold my beautiful St Kilda Victorian house of the past nearly forty years. But life for me is far more than the catalogue of disasters recounted here. Being thrown from life's expected course has given me an off-angle view, some would say unique take, on what might otherwise have passed unwitnessed or been taken-for-granted.

Over the years many people have said to me: 'David, you should write your story.' My instinctive response has been — 'Why bother?' I am nothing special. But, hearing this, people still press me to put my story on paper. 'This is a lot easier said than done,' I reply.

Well, I am not a blunt stone. I do listen to people and take in what they say to me. So, over a period of many years now, I have considered ways I might put my story down, on paper or an iPad. As if to prepare myself, I have kept my writing skills up to speed with voluminous email correspondence with many people. At times I have got myself into trouble with my blunt and colourful writing.

But my emailing as a form of written conversation has helped me develop many of my ideas. I do have an active mind — what is left of it. I must spew things out, cannot help myself. This has posed a detriment to my speech and interaction with people. I feel people have to accept me for what I am. But I have always been like this, a very confronting person. It is not part of my brain damage, but I will admit my brain damage does accentuate it to some degree. My interactions with people have always been turbulent but, as I said, I bear no malice nor do I wish any harm. I do hope people recognise this, but also that I like to tease and niggle people in what can be a mischievous way. I have learnt, however, that I must be careful and modify this. I do not wish to offend or upset anyone — even though at times certain things raise my usually low blood pressure. Sorry, I tell a lie. I do hope some people consider that their actions towards me and other disabled people have been less than virtuous and that, over time, their attitudes may change.

Again, in preparation for writing my story, I have read many memoirs and biographies and tried to digest the different ways people recount their lives. I have also questioned people about this. One day, after he had produced his own intellectual memoir, I quietly asked a man whom I regarded highly as a mentor, 'How do you write a biography?'

Knowing me well, he tailored his answer for my benefit, replying in hushed tones: 'David, biography is to be written with humility.' He obviously understood the full weight of his words, as well as the degree of difficulty in living up to them. It was one of the most precious observations he made to me. Sadly, he passed away but what he taught lives on in me. I am very thankful for everything I learnt from him: he set my feet on the road on which I am still travelling.

I have found putting my thoughts down in writing gives me a better perspective on the way I am conducting my life. Until I did so, you could not say they formed a coherent whole. Now, with every story I complete, something more holistic emerges.

I have developed a two-pronged approach to writing. Through the storytelling, I produce what you might call faction, a combination of fact and fiction. To produce faction I need to muse aloud and let my mind wander where it will. While doing this, I feel my ego straining at the leash. It is very difficult to restrain myself and maintain my humility. Over my shoulder, as it were, I hear the advice of my mentor as if he were still in the room with me.

When writing I think of myself as opening windows on to my mind. Through the windows you may see a mirrored wall, reflecting compartments of my mind with their overlay of images and realities. Through this process I feel it is possible to get glimpses of me and the person driving the life I lead. I hope to reveal a coherent philosophy of life derived from a rich brew of learning and the harsh realities of lived experience.

My aim is to build a picture that enables people to get inside my mind and see how it functions. I have grouped my stories according to several themes, even though I wrote about what struck my fancy on a given day, not caring to 'complete' each chapter before turning to the next. Further, I have tried to do this through the magnifying prism of disability, which both inhibits and inhabits — and in any case governs — my life. It is this aspect that gives me something different to say and makes my perspective worth investigating. As I open the door and welcome readers into my mind, I hope that they find it contributes value to the way in which they confront the complexities of their own life. I am fervently hoping that those still reading have feasted on my stories along the way.

They will know that what I have written is not ideological piece of work or statement. That I will leave to the greats. My book is rather simple — the perspective of an educated man modified by his lived experience in all its dimensions. I do hope it is modified by a core value of ethics and decency and framed with my own unique humour. I do hope the reader can see that this perspective is a coherent way to live and conduct life. It is a philosophy and perspective viewed through disability. I accept there must be flaws in it as I am far from perfect. But I feel that in my storytelling I have something of value to offer. I thank my dear parents for endowing me with such a way of approaching the world. What I offer is a composite of many things including the wonderful spaghetti westerns of the epic theatre. My wish is that people live up to the standards that I bring them and take them to a higher level. I praise the elders of this land on which I sit past, present and future.

David Bereson

Acknowledgments

For the most part, those I wish to thank in the writing of this book and the authoring of the life that produced it are embedded in the stories I tell. There you will meet my dearest parents — who could forget to thank and acknowledge them, my inspirational mother *The Angel of Odessa* or my late *Peter Pan* of a father whose charming innocence and wonder at the world so lit up my life. You'll find also in these pages my larger-than-life grandmother *The Dame* and my wonderful sisters Ruth and Miriam who have bookended my life and lovingly kept me going. It was nothing for Ruth to drop everything and jump on a plane to be with me during periods of extremity and for Miriam to look out for me in so many ways. She sees me purely and has drawn me to a tee in her wonderful portrait that is on the cover of *Dig Deep*. Indeed, I thank all — according to their dues — who have enriched my life and who have in one way or another drawn me to write about them or episodes involving them. I thank my mentor the late Greg Denning and his wonderful wife Donna Merwick for the guidance they gave me and the way they stood by me and held true in times of adversity. I hope you can see in the pages of this book the imprint of the many lessons Greg taught me. My speech therapist Sarat was a great encourager —

she got me to write and to keep it up and I am so glad that I did. *Dig Deep* was driven by my experience of the world as a disabled man. I am deeply humbled and forever thankful for a life, while dramatically changed by accident and ill-health, was nonetheless there to be lived. None of it would have occurred without my medical rescuers at the time of my car crash and the interventions by health professionals along the way who have many times saved my life and kept me surprisingly able and alive. There are many of them and I won't single them out but please know that I am forever grateful for their knowledge, care and dedication to keeping me and so many others as healthy as we can be and marching on. I go forward as ably as I can but wish to do so as part of a fully abled nation — one that owns up to its past, recognises its privilege and gives everyone a voice.

www.ingramcontent.com/pod-product-compliance
Lightning Source LLC
Chambersburg PA
CBHW020314010526
44107CB00054B/1832